A CHILDHOOD DERAILED

I0519171

A Neurodivergent Journey
from Resilience to Joy

JEANNE POUSSIÉRE

Paperback ISBN 978-1-960007-42-1
eBook ISBN 978-1-960007-43-8

Published by
Orison Publishers, Inc.
PO Box 188
Grantham, PA 17027
www.OrisonPublishers.com

Please note that this book, in its candidness and honesty, includes explicit swear words and possible triggering depictions.

Names have been changed to protect individuals' privacy.

Contents

Prologue: The Encounter vii

Chapter 1: On the Run 1

Chapter 2: The Mother's Story...5

Chapter 3: The Mother's Family...7

Chapter 4: First Signs of Awakening.....................................11

Chapter 5: Her Death Day...17

Chapter 6: The Father's Family 19

Chapter 7: Words...23

Chapter 8: Nana's House...27

Chapter 9: The Voice 31

Chapter 10: The Nuns...33

Chapter 11: More Instructions 35

Chapter 12: The Brother 37

Chapter 13: The Move 41

Chapter 14: My Rules 45

Chapter 15: Another Death 49

Chapter 16: Big Changes...53

Chapter 17: Illness and Injury 57

Chapter 18: The Island...61

Chapter 19: After the Island..63

Chapter 20: Margo...67

Chapter 21: Abuses—Physical and Sexual—
and Trauma..71

Chapter 22: Ages 10 to 12 75

Chapter 23: My "Get Out of Jail Free" Card 81

Chapter 24: Teeth...85

Chapter 25: Male Friends 89

Chapter 26: Searching for the Truth............................93

Chapter 27: High School...97

Chapter 28: Sophomore Year 101

Chapter 29: The Father Goes Away...........................107

Chapter 30: Junior Year 113

Chapter 31: Work..117

Chapter 32: Being Real...121

Chapter 33: High School's End..................................129

Chapter 34: Clothing...131

Chapter 35: Post High School 135

Chapter 36: Drew..139

Chapter 37: Its Name Was Grief 143

Chapter 38: Getting Married 147

Chapter 39: Post-Wedding 151

Chapter 40: My Sally...155

Chapter 41: New Cousins..159

Chapter 42: Endings and Beginnings 161

Chapter 43: Desolation Arrives 165

Chapter 44: And Next 169

Chapter 45: On the Edge 173

Chapter 46: Kait and Jeff..177

Chapter 47: My Marriage 179

Chapter 48: Counseling 183

Chapter 49: Walking Through 187

Chapter 50: CW Again 191

Chapter 51: New Beginnings 195

Chapter 52: The Abyss 199

Chapter 53: A New Life.....................................203

Chapter 54: College and the Medical Center 205

Chapter 55: New Friends 209

Chapter 56: Another Death, More Incidents
and Another Move...213

Chapter 57: Substances 217

Chapter 58: New Skills and Another Death 221

Chapter 59: Dr. H 225

Chapter 60: 1979 to 1980 227

Chapter 61: Going Downhill..............................233

Chapter 62: Back to Reality 239

Chapter 63: The Mother's House.....................243

Chapter 64: Transition Again............................249

Chapter 65: Don, In and Out and Another Again..............253

Chapter 66: More Changes..............................259

Chapter 67: Roger, Carol and Bill 265

Chapter 68: Ari...269

Chapter 69: Becoming Who God Created Me to Be.........271

Epilogue: Just a Dream....................................275

References...277

Prologue
The Encounter

1988

It was an ordinary Friday night at my condo. I was managing almost constant anxiety and depression, going deep within my metaphysical and philosophy books and pondering the possible existence of an actual god and researching belief systems. Disgusted with most of what I read and tired and frustrated with the endless searching and questioning, I pushed them all to the floor, stood up and said out loud, "I don't want to be tricked. God, if you are REAL, You'll have to show me." I then went to bed, not giving what I said another thought.

The next Friday, coming home from work a bit late, I went to the bedroom to change into pj's and experienced an unknown fragrance as I climbed the stairs—a fragrance that just became stronger as I entered the bedroom. The fragrance itself was like no other perfume I had ever smelled, and I searched the bedroom and entire second floor trying to discover the source. I opened every bottle of perfume and cologne in my room; none of their fragrances came even close. The fragrance was enthralling and all-encompassing, as if someone had literally spilled an entire container in every corner.

And then…I wasn't in my bedroom anymore. I was standing within a scene out of a science fiction movie. The scale was as if I was transported to a reverse world of the Brothers Grimm. It was immense. The light was different. It was something like sunlight, but this light was without shadows and with the hue from a perfect summer's day. There were groupings like hills of rock to my right, but they were made of amethyst and quartz-like stone. Blended in between the rocks was green but not jade or emerald; more of maybe a combination of both. The shapes were unusual; they were more like my first experience viewing the red rock formations of the Badlands, or Hoodoos in Bryce Canyon, or the Toadstools of the Grand Staircase-Escalante National Monument that I had seen from an airplane some 15 years later.

On my left was a path that I was encouraged to follow that led towards an utterly diaphanous building. The structure was huge. Its color was like a translucent moonstone or off-white opal, with a depth of many layers. Its architecture resembled an Acropolis-type of building, but it was much larger with multiple rooms upon rooms and many levels that spread out in four directions like the points on a compass. Again I was encouraged to enter this building. "Encouraged" is the only suitable word as I was never ordered or told. It always felt like I had a choice. There was a presence experienced close by but not actually seen. It shimmered when it encouraged or informed.

The inside was colossal, open and with many, many rooms but no walls. The light was the same inside as out, with no shadows. I wasn't afraid, overwhelmed or cold. I'm always cold. The room I was encouraged into was round and comprised of three levels with stairs and walkways that encircled the second and third levels. I was stopped at the middle level. From below rose an image that reminded me of the roots and branches of a tree, except I was informed it was my image, my story, my life. ("Informed" is tricky to describe. It was more like "encouraged"; it was as if the thought or direction was communicated or placed in my mind, not actually from my mind. I didn't hear it or think it. I experienced it.) On this "tree/me" was recorded every choice I had ever made, as well as all the choices built on those choices. It looked like a hologram, as it was multi-dimensional. I could see the thousands of choices that birthed other choices as well as the ones that ended in dead ends. The choices were seemingly color-coded and emboldened and categorized by shading that led from positive to negative results, but only the positive ones were emboldened.

I was totally mesmerized and awed by this whole process and stood seemingly enveloped, following the trails and outcomes of every significant choice I had made since age three when I ran away. In this entire encounter, I was always aware of the differential in size. I was so very small to their everything so very big.

Eventually I was aware of being back in my bedroom. It was Monday morning. I was totally aware of this experience but didn't think about it other than I was amazed that I was not tired, but I was concerned that I soon would be. I showered and went to work; I had a full day of clients. I thought about it a little, tiny bit on the way home, zeroing in on the fragrance. It wasn't that I was afraid or reluctant to think about it; it was more that I didn't know what to think. I had no idea how to process this event. I knew of no known experience rack to hang this on. The time was pre-internet. I would have researched this out at the library, but I had no idea what to call it or even what had happened or even if anything had actually happened.

Later that night I started with what I did know. It wasn't a dream. There was a lapse in time passage. The only tangible things were the fragrance and my going to change into pj's. I came home on a Friday evening, smelled a fragrance, and entered my bedroom to change into pj's, and next it was Monday morning in my bedroom, I was awake on my bed, not in it, and I was not in pj's. Smells sometimes precipitate seizures, but I didn't think that was what happened as I had no headache or confusion. I had no loss of elimination functions. There were no negative indicators. Still, it was a possibility to be ruled out.

I worked out a plan to smell as many fragrances as possible and to tell no one as not only did I not know who one would tell something like this to, but I also didn't even know what something like this was. And I wasn't volunteering for crazy.

I came home from work somewhat cautiously every night for a week, but there were no smells or events. I started smelling my way through Jordan Marsh's (now Macy's) perfume counter at the local mall. . Two visits of smelling proved uninformative. I did discover that one could smell only so many bottles of perfume before they all smelled alike. I knew then that this was going to be a much longer search than I had realized.

The next Friday coming home I was a bit more on guard and very slowly climbed the stairs, but the condo just smelled like my condo. Other things that happened kept it all out of mind. Then I woke up Saturday morning to the smell.

And I was back looking at my tree/me, my story and all my choices. As I continued following the branches and threads, I was informed (as in directed) to see that what stood out this time was the emboldened choices—and they by far outnumbered the dimmer ones, the poorer choices. I was confused and positively overwhelmed. I experienced the knowledge that I wasn't what all those people said I was as a child. Someone important had seen ME. I was known. I wasn't invisible. I had never been invisible. I wasn't the No Thing, the Nothing. I was never the No Thing, the Nothing. I was intentional and had always been intentional. I wasn't a throwaway. I had value. I was important. I was loved. I had always had value. I had always been important. I had always been loved. I had never been alone. The Voice had always been with me. And I experienced all this from the inside out. It was so real.

The Encourager directed me to follow the shimmer, and we went down another path to an even larger building of similar architecture. This was the largest, most majestic structure I'd ever been in. It reminded me of the pictures of the ancient Greek or Roman architecture of the Parthenon or the Colosseum. Again, the light, like a sun, was the same inside as outside and there were no shadows here. There were no walls, either. The room was vast, like two football fields, but double the width, and I'm directed to an elevated stage-like platform with a huge podium.

There was a large stool there and I was encouraged to use this stool, but it was so big and tall that I had to climb up its rungs as if they were on a ladder. At the top of the stool, I could see a mammoth-sized book, and I was encouraged to read this book as it has the answer to every life and being question I've ever thought as well as those I would ask in the future.

I had to stand on the stool to read this book and I had to use two hands to turn the pages, and I read until I was aware again that it was Monday morning. I was not tired but lay very still as what I read was so amazing. I tried hard to hold onto it in my mind. But all I ended up with was this amazing sense of peace, of feeling loved and a knowing certainty that I was and will be okay.

I had another usual work week with further excursions to the mall for smell tests, but nothing was even similar. I was somewhat discouraged but determined. I went over every detail I could remember and was amazed at how vivid both encounters were and how unlike anything even close to a dream or anything imagined in my life previously they were.

The next Friday night was uneventful. No smells. But again, I woke up to this fragrance the next morning and was instantly back reading, standing on the stool, turning these huge pages with every question being answered with details I could never imagine. With each page I became more excited, and I so wanted to shout all this amazing knowledge to everyone who would listen. Shout it out, write it out…but I couldn't, I'm informed, as it was not mine to share and I would only remember it in my bones. I would know that I know what I know and would recognize TRUTH when it appeared. I wouldn't have any God or life questions ever again.

I was back in my bedroom and it was Monday again. I intentionally focused to salvage any pieces of the book in my mind. I could recall the building, the stage, the podium, the stool, the climbing up the stool, and the enormous book itself, but the pages were blurred.

This encounter became the most significant episode of my life and, step by step, choice by choice, influenced and changed almost everything in my life. For about two years I continued to smell women's perfume and some men's cologne without success. I then researched and sent away for samples of exotic fragrances from the Middle East and the Orient. The last purchase arrived in 1990. I never opened them. I stopped questioning if the encounter was real as I knew it no longer mattered. I realized all such encounters were ineffable and unique to the individuals they happened to as all new information is processed through a sieve of all one's previously accepted information, and this was my Encounter, unique to me and for me.

— 1 —

On the Run

I ran away at three years old. I remember it because it was the first memory I can recall clearly that wasn't just a picture alone or in a grouping or a tape-like replay of a voice or scene. This memory had a bunch of thoughts attached to a series of pictures and then an end action, a choice. It was a three-year-old's choice from a three-year-old's reasoning of sorts. It also was fueled by an inside voice to run. I was scared. I was looking for someone to protect me. I went to find someone who would love me. I really did experience the word "love." At three, I couldn't have defined what love was with words. But even at that age, I recognized that love was a behavior that grew a feeling experience. Anyway, off I went running through the backyard to the end of the cul-de-sac and to the fence, following the fence to a hole, going through the hole in the fence to the woods, and running through the woods to a new world filled with other children playing. It felt safe.

Play. Playing was safe. Children were safe. I remember the streets and the houses on those streets and the children who lived in those houses. One house had a swing set. This swing set had a trapeze bar and gym rings. The girl who lived at this house could hang upside down from her knees and by her ankles and do tricks with the rings. She could do cartwheels, flips and back arches too. I wanted to stay. "Big deal," you might say. But it was a big deal to me. That girl triggered an interest that became an obsession, a

1

foundation that saw me through my childhood and most of my adolescence before eventually morphing into a lifetime action plan. I became hooked on gymnastics until age 16. All the hours of practice over and over towards perfection, the discovery of the joy of trying, and the gift of endorphins laid the groundwork of structures and disciplines that I unconsciously drew on at every crossroad in my life.

As a very small child, repetition to control one's mind and thoughts; latency's child, perseverance through pain; as a pre-teen, to know I was not for sale to anyone for any reason and the strength to fight; as an adolescent, that I would never be a member of a hive and would forever remain "far from the madding crowd"; as a young adult in despair of life, that all those tools were mine to use to dig myself out of the pit I was pushed into and reclaim my life and sanity; and as a post 30-year old, to find God in strange places—all these came from a choice at age three. Those children and that neighborhood became my playmates and play place five long years later.

Three is an age when the now can seem to encompass forever and play pushes against time, warding off the dark. On that night, it was likely some other child's parent called the police, as I got my first ride in a police car. The father was mad but oh so smoothly, smilingly polite to the police.

The police took me home to my nana's house. To the parents. At least, "parents" were what they repeatedly told me they were. I do not think the label made much sense to me at that time. My world became a place of Before and After. My Before world was my grandmother, Nana, and her house and maybe my friend Mary Alice up the street. The Before place was a world where no one ever yelled or hit or had hands that left one uncomfortable.

I have thought a great deal about my family over the years. The Before is much more difficult to describe in words than the After simply because of my age and because it was mostly devoid of distress and pain. In the absence of pain or unrelieved continual comfort, time in minutes, hours, days and weeks blend, indistinguishable unless marked by something suddenly different. No one identifies suffering from "Post I'm Comfortable, Safe and Happy Disorder"; although, one can have flashbacks of positive memories as well as negative ones. Humans are neurologically hardwired to remember the negative. Sadly, by age five, most of the safe Before memories, along with my Nana, were gone. By age eight, Nana's house and my being able to read music and play the piano and any sense of continuity, predictability or safety were gone as well.

There are actually two different kinds of memory. The first, "explicit" memory refers to your ability to recollect specific things, such as the names of your friends, or where you parked the car. The second kind, "implicit" or "emotional" memory, is less specific. It's visceral and powerful…. It creates the inner atmosphere of your mind, your felt sense of who you are and what living feels like; as well as your deepest assumptions and expectations about the world.

One of the ancient brain structures, the amygdala…is neurologically primed to label experiences as frightening and threatening… (Moon, 2009).

The amygdala almost instantly codes, compares and stores implicit memories for fight or flight. Positive memories, on the other hand, take longer to register. The good news is that the principle of neuroplasticity suggests that the more aware cognitive aspects of the brain may be able to modify the negative views of our mind's inner world.

~2~
The Mother's Story

Later, the family stories came in pieces that the mother doled out at whim. Mostly they had to do with her: all the amazing men she had dated, all the adventures she had, and the many wonderful stories of her childhood. She shared these tidbits at times in my childhood and preteen years when I was curled up in a ball, sobbing. They did not comfort me, but they did confuse me for years.

My nana's home was a modest New England-type on a main street in a small town in Massachusetts. I was born in 1945 close to the end of World War II in Europe. At the time of my birth, the father was in the Pacific and had been overseas in the Navy for almost the mother's entire pregnancy. By her narrative, we lived with her mother (my nana), my aunt and the brother. After my birth, the mother reported that she was extremely ill with an infection. I went home with my aunt and nana and the mother remained in the hospital for three more weeks.

The father returned to the United States from the war in the South Pacific in August 1945, four months after my birth. Reportedly, he was ill and was sent to a veterans' hospital several states away. . The mother took the brother and moved there to be with him. After his discharge from the hospital, he was assigned to some position there. I stayed with my aunt and nana. Mother reported that she came back to visit me every four to six weeks or so for a weekend.

Somewhere during this time, the mother's youngest brother and his second wife and their infant son moved into my nana's house. Exactly how old the brother and I were at this event was never shared. They slept in either the third-floor bedroom or the bedroom adjacent to mine. The sad part is I don't even know if all or any part of the mother's stories were true, but these were the only family history ever offered. Even then, the information was only gleaned because of one old photo with the mother and the brother sitting on steps in front of a house, waving to whomever took the photo, which caused me to ask. The brother looked to be about two or two and a half years old in the picture. I would have been about 7 to 12 months. The mother let slip that it was "their" out-of-state house. I have no idea how long they lived there; it was possibly a year. I tend to think that this piece of her shared history is true.

It took years of subtle questions to get a story, as the mother did not play direct. She did not really play or tell the truth, but neither did she lie. She would have been shocked if someone accused her of lying. Instead, she spoke "misreality." No, I did not misspell. Long ago I coined this word to describe the mother and the ways she touched my life, as I never could find any explanations that fit until I was a mother myself. And it wasn't as if she didn't recognize reality. She did. She just picked and chose her way through using her own rules. By the time I learned to frame the right questions, there was no one left alive to ask but the mother. The withholding game was a special game she played with the father and me. She was the first deconstructionist I ever knew, and she lived it as a lifestyle.

Despite all the wonderful stories of her childhood, her brothers and her father, I never believed much of it was real. Not only did her mother and sister seem to be less than competent compared to her, her brothers and her father in her renditions, but they also rarely were even in the stories. When they were, especially when my grandmother was in the stories, they needed to be rescued by her or were labeled as eccentric. It always left me wondering, if they were so incompetent, why one would leave one's newborn baby for possibly a year with them.

As a child, however, her family stories gave a surrealistic quality to my own reality and life with my family, as if I were somehow a third person narrator viewing it all from a great distance. Both parents and the brother needed an adoration that my young age didn't equip me to give. I didn't understand that I was meant to be just a mirror. I didn't understand back then that I wasn't real.

~ 3 ~
The Mother's Family

From the mother's accounts growing up, her family had been wealthy, living in a much grander house on the "right side" of the tracks. Her father made lots of money, and she and her two brothers and one sister went to private schools and grew up with the best of everything. Her dad never yelled or got mad at her or her siblings and showered them—her especially—with cars, jewelry and other gifts. She loved to talk about going to Europe every summer beginning in her teens and about all the famous people she met and played with there in her 20s and 30s. By her account, her dad lost most of his fortune in the stock market crash of 1928. The family did okay until his death in 1937, at age 50. By that time she and her brothers and sister were all adults. After his death, my grandmother was forced to sell a great deal of her belongings and move to the smaller house I called home. Reportedly, by the time of my grandmother's move, both of the mother's brothers were married and only the mother and her sister lived in this house with my grandmother.

The mother had gone to college and worked as a gym teacher in a working-class suburb of Boston. Her sister was an artist and reportedly worked for the telephone company as an illustrator. The father taught English in the same school as the mother. That is how they met. She told me that she didn't like him much, but they had a lot of the same friends who did activities together, so they were often in each other's company. She reported not liking his always being the center of attention, but that he was a good dancer. They did date. When I was a child she told me of the many, many men she had dated and who were wonderful; how awesome her life was before the father; and how he didn't compare favorably with any of them.

However, apparently something changed. She married him. The story line was that he enlisted after Pearl Harbor in 1941 and was commissioned in the Navy as an officer and was ordered to report. They got married at night on October 31, 1942, Halloween. The father was 38 and she was approximately the same age. Why approximately? She could never be pinned down. Even various documents, licenses, passports and even the national census reports stated differing years. Mother would adamantly defend these various dates were not lies on her part.

The mother had two brothers, the oldest (Mother's Brother #1, or MB#1) and the youngest (Mother's Brother #2, or MB#2). She had the one sister. My best guess is that the mother was second oldest and her sister was after her. I don't remember her sister at all, although she lived with my grandmother when the mother and the brother were there. I am guessing that she also lived with my grandmother and myself when I was a baby. However, she was gone by the time the father came back to the house.

Mother's sister married someone who worked in the diplomatic service, and, per the mother's story, he was stationed in Trinidad, British West Indies. She had no children. The story was that my mother's sister died before she could return to the United States. My best guess is this happened in 1950. I still have the memory of standing on the stairs of my grandmother's house when the mother received the phone call. I can still see the hall and the sun coming in the window. It's a picture frozen in time.

MB#1 became a lawyer and married a woman from Europe. I think he was in the service during World War II and met her there, but I am not sure. The mother's story was that he was supposed to go to medical school when he returned home, but being married and his wife being pregnant, he went to law school instead. For whatever reason, the family, or just the mother, were upset that he had married and didn't get to become a doctor. They had three children: a son, a daughter and then another son.

I remember going to visit them by bus at approximately age five or six. They lived two states away from us. I liked them both. Their eldest son and daughter were much older than the brother and me, and the other son was younger. I think we visited them a few times, and the visits were pleasant. I say "pleasant" because no memories but a few still pictures survive in my memory. They later moved two hours closer to us, but we rarely saw them.

8

Their oldest son, the family story reported, went to live in Florida and died there sometime during my teens. Their daughter got married, moved a half hour away, and had two sons, but we never saw her again or met her children. I never knew their names until a few years ago.

Their youngest son married a woman from Europe and had two children, both girls. They lived in many places. He tried to rally cousin contact several times but didn't have much success. Ironically, they had moved to the same state and lived in the city where I worked 20-plus years ago. I stumbled across his name listed in the phone book, wondered whether it was him, reached out, but never heard back. One of his daughters reached out to me through Facebook Personal Messenger several years ago and reconnected me with her father; however, it only lasted a short period of time. I may have offended him, but I have no clue. It's been my experience that asking questions of family members is like trying to interview members of the CIA, the KGB or the Mafia.

Mother's Brother #2 had the most contact with our family. He was the only sibling the mother spoke about in any depth. She and this brother were weirdly close and relational. Much later, when older, I realized they behaved more like an intimate couple than brother or sister. But then, I really had no idea how a brother and sister related. In behavior, the mother was only visibly close and relational with MB#2 and the brother.

The mother described MB#2 as extremely popular and charming in general. Everyone reportedly loved him. I think he was the only sibling to attend the town high school, most likely because their father had already died and my grandmother could not afford private schools. The mother was immensely proud of his being voted class president while he attended there. I believe he went to college.

He reportedly married a local woman from a wealthy family, and they moved to California where, the mother said, he was a great success and made lots of money. He had one child, a girl. According to the mother, he lost all his money and came back to Nana's house. For reasons not mentioned, his wife filed for divorce and full custody of the child. The mother was never able to speak to this wife or her family again. His wife was awarded the divorce and full custody of the child. He was legally denied any contact. The ex-wife and her family moved back to California.

This most likely was in the late 1930s or early 1940s. From casual research, a woman getting a divorce and winning full custody with no visitation hardly ever happened then. Fathers almost always won custody of the children unless it was proven that the child was in danger from the father.

Why the mother told me at all is a mystery. No other sibling or cousin knew this. We were going through some papers after the father died and a picture fell out that showed a woman holding a blond child, and I questioned who they were. My guess was the mother knew the real story.

It was still a surprise when I found out that the brother didn't know about any of these family members. An even bigger surprise was when the brother asked MB#2's subsequent children as adults about this, and they became quite upset as they never knew their father had been married previously. Obviously, they had no knowledge of their half-sister.

Somewhere between 1945 and 1947, MB#2 married a woman from the South. They had a new baby, a son, and they moved into the attic or the bedroom next to mine in my grandmother's house when I was a baby. I have no recollection of how long they stayed. Although, I'm somewhat certain that MB#2 was "the man in the attic" who was coming to get me as a small child.

He, his wife and baby boy would visit often after the father returned to the grandmother's home. A daughter also appeared at some point, but I have no memory of her as a baby. I do have many memories of their son as a toddler. The house was a livelier, cheerier place when MB#2 visited; the mother laughed and the father smiled more. But I didn't think it was a real smile. The father always acted happy and charming when around people who didn't live with us.

I have always had this one outstanding early video-like memory of MB#2. I am hiding behind one of my grandmother's big burgundy velvet wingback chairs in the living room and watching the parents and MB#2 interact. I don't know why I was hiding. I don't think I had to hide. It was more that I didn't want them to know I was watching them. It was like watching strangers acting in a movie; they didn't feel real. It's so hard to capture a three- to four-year-old's epiphany that this uncle's charm didn't really love. I remember choosing not to be tricked by him anymore. Just how he may have tricked me is not remembered. Right there, in that minute, I made a life choice. I would just love MB#1. He wasn't as much fun, but he was gentle, and he was real. No tricks.

— 4 —
First Signs of Awakening

Many narcissists are obsessed with money. They think about how much money they have, how to get more of it, how to keep it away from others, and whom to manipulate to get more—including how to take family members money/inheritance. Money is their substitution for love, warmth, and affection. Having as much money as possible, even stealing it away from family members, is the narcissist's unwavering goal. Thoughts about obtaining more money are always on the narcissist's mind. Having an abundance of money makes them feel more entitled and superior to others (Burgmeester).

1972

The average person does not give incest a great deal of thought. I know the mother never did. Not that she wasn't properly shocked when a friend or neighbor related a rumor—the mother was always proper. In fact, I don't remember ever hearing her use profanity or yell or fart. She was a lady. For that matter, so was the brother. I was never quite sure what being a lady embodied. I know ladies never raised their voices. It seemed to me that ladies never did much of anything. But I was wrong.

Sometimes, when watching the mother, I would be reminded of a picture I saw once when I was small: three little monkeys, one covering his ears, the other his eyes and the last his mouth. This was the mother. Now, the mother did not look anything like a monkey. In fact, she was very attractive then. She only resembled them metaphorically. This was the way she went through life, along with having fun and playing games.

The mother was a master at "seeing nothing," "hearing nothing" and "talking about nothing" and having fun and playing games. Although, I was never sure exactly how she defined "fun" or why it was only located in her life. She detested "playing games" of the bought variety, like the board game Monopoly. She only played her own, which were inversely proportional to the degree to which she refused to play anyone else's. The mother said she hated games. I believed her. But then, the mother never ate dessert. How could you trust someone who never ate dessert?

I never understood why she married the father, or any man, but he obviously had his uses. She seemed so placid and proper next to him. Or maybe it was only the contrast: the mother, the good, peaceful pond, against the father, the booming, crashing ocean. Actually, the mother was a swamp. The father had few subtleties; he didn't need them as the mother had them all.

Incest is the only universal taboo. Our family had only one, and it had nothing to do with incest. Anything and everything was okay if the mother did not see it, hear it or have to talk about it. It wasn't that she was easily offended; being offended was something you could see. She just didn't want to know. Not that the system did not occasionally break down; it must have, but it was hard to tell as nothing ever marked the event.

The mother was the sole perpetrator of misreality in our house; the father and the brother were the audience she played to. The father was frequently banished from never-never land. I never liked him much; we weren't supposed to. He never played by her rules. I don't think he ever knew there were any. The father thought black was black and white was white; mother was never black or white. Red could be blue on Monday and green could be blue on Tuesday and something could be gone by Wednesday; the mother was morally color blind. Not that she was either immoral or amoral; she simply ignored them as categories. Being fluid, they expanded or contracted

12

to her will. Oh, she was properly definitive when socializing and a great abstract adherent of right and wrong and loving one's neighbor; she was, after all, a lady and a pillar of her church.

The worst offense in our home was showing anything, especially anger, and love had something to do with money. I don't think the brother ever committed any offenses that showed; he was perfect, except for his asthma, which was the only recognized infirmity that had any credence in our house other than the mother's migraines. They both suffered admirably well and with a great deal of poise and class. The brother has always done everything with poise and class.

The mother never spoke about money; the father rarely spoke about anything else, except concupiscence, and the mother would never speak about that either. It wasn't that money was an important thing in the family; it seemed at times it was the only thing. Money, the concrete, was interchangeable with money, the abstract, provider of all things. We all collected and horded—each penny safely hidden away from each other—so we knew who we were. Money could alternately be god or dirt, good or bad, love or hate, full or empty, strength or weakness. You may wonder what concupiscence had to do with money. Absolutely nothing. Absurdities ran rampant in our house. Everything and everyone were for sale, from love to loyalty to your body; it was a barter system. Of course, no one ever talked about it, and I doubt the father ever knew he was acting out his part.

Amorphicity is best played out against a black and white background. The father, the withholder of money; the mother, the giver of nothing. No wonder he ran and hid on his boat, leaving us penniless.

The mother was never unkind. The father and the brother were. I don't think I ever heard her say an uncharitable word in public. The mother never visibly acted the snob; she was the lone member of her own class. However, the brother is. The brother is a tentacle of the mother as the father was the audience she fed off. Never a borrower or a tentacle be.

The mother was never visibly mean or cruel. The father and the brother were. She was simply absent. I never saw her hurt a thing; the father and the brother did, but no one ever talked about it. The mother never got angry, and neither did the brother; the father was always angry. The mother never touched me. The brother hung me. They mother rarely touched the father, and the father never touched the brother, but the father touched me. I never touched any of them.

The mother never gave incest a thought.

That essay was written spontaneously in 1972, six years after my marriage, five years after the birth of my first child, two years after the death of my second child, and one year after the birth of my third child. Many attempts were made to revise, add and/or alter it over the years. It has remained intact (except for a few changes by my editor). I don't know why I could never change it. Possibly it was because it was so spontaneous, as if another distant author claimed rights to being and heralded the journey about to begin. I think I've always been a little in awe of it. That's not because it was well written or especially clever, but more that at the time it was written and with the style it was written, it was totally alien to me. But it was a slice of truth.

Until the death of my second child from sudden infant death syndrome (SIDS) in 1970, I had never spent much time reviewing much about my childhood or my family. I had never looked back or dwelled too long on my choices. I seemingly just lived in the moment I found myself in. That's not to say that I didn't dip into the pain and sadness. I did, late at night. Alone. I visited the replay of the tapes of the day but not the tapes of yesterday, carefully peeking at any corresponding reaction in the safety of my room. Viewing each memory from a distance, like a video. Momentarily monitoring and aligning each emotional facet as the memory played out. Storing each picture, word, reactions and thoughts in their separate compartments. It was a place to visit to never forget who one was, where one knew ones was real.

I'd built a bubble of sorts, controlling what went in or out. Outwardly, I could seem friendly and fun; sometimes I'd look spontaneous and impulsive. Ironically, however, I was very, very careful and cautious. Watching, always watching. Constantly weighing what anyone close by said and did. Constantly weighing what was reasonably acceptable behaviors, dress, speech and attitudes displayed by peers. Trying them on for size; accepting some, discarding others. Analyzing everything. Always physically in motion, if possible, creating reasonably acceptable facsimiles (RAFs). When motion was not possible, I read. "Hyper-vigilant" is a more accurate depiction of how I experienced life. Safety was the goal. Fear was the motivator. It was not fear as in being afraid of spiders or anxious about a future event; this fear's real name was terror.

It wasn't that I "forgot" incidents and traumatic events that happened. I could, when alone and safe, recall and/or replay most incidents from ages three to seven, more through latency and all in adolescence. I didn't know there was a name for what I had. I'd never heard of an eidetic (photographic) and auditory memory until late adolescence/early adulthood, and I only recently heard the term "eidetic" used as well for the voice memory tapes I can play. I could freeze frame images and replay them back in slow motion, taking in people's facial expressions, gestures, tone of voice and body language as if it was a movie and I was an impartial bystander. I thought as a child that everyone could do this. I also never heard of hypermnesia, also known as hyperthymestic syndrome (enhanced memory). But the incident memories I could make flat, one-dimensional, like reading a history book: matter of fact, cold and lifeless. I had no emotional reaction to them. There was no PTSD designation then. That bubble burst the day my second daughter died.

~5~

Her Death Day

Images from my daughter's death day are forever etched in my memory as the day my world shattered. Friends and my husband's relatives came to our house from midmorning on, but not my family. The father did not come; nor did the brother. No aunts or uncles, no cousins. The mother taught school 20 minutes away. She came at 4:00 p.m., after school. She rang the bell. I answered the door, letting her in. Apparently I expected consolation and compassion from her. I was wrong. She pushed past me, heading to my oldest daughter's room, saying, "Thank God my Sally was okay." She never said a word otherwise. She never gave a hug. She stayed in my oldest daughter's room.

Devastated. Is there possibly another more horrific word representing greater destruction? Maybe annihilated. Even worse was the realization that I was Nothing, the No Thing, the No One and the No Body of my childhood. The one whose father only called her "you f--king, lousy, dirty little son of a bitch" for all of her childhood.

From that day on, over the next five years, I slowly slipped toward the edge of an abyss, venturing dangerously close at times to its center. I had not yet heard of PTSD. All those separated and stored tapes of my childhood and adolescence rewound, joined together and played out over and over and over, accompanied by the thoughts, pain, sorrow, fear, terror and every other emotion magically stored on their own, separate, previously one-dimensional tape. All of them crashing, pounding together like waves destined to go on forever. And tears—never-ending tears. I was defective. I couldn't even die of a broken heart. One's heart must be whole to be broken to death. Unfortunately for me, the pieces of my heart, both unrecognized and named, could endure agonizingly forever on the way to the abyss. What did I fear? Everything and anything. People. As a small child, I thought I was losing me. At ages seven to nine, I knew I was fighting for my mind. I ran, I jumped, I practiced and I read. I watched and waited. I never labelled the constant fear until the day the father died—and only then because 50 percent of the weight that fear had levied, lifted. That night of the day of his death I dreamed that I blew him up in his old car. In the dream I was arrested, but that was okay. I felt free. It was only after that dream that I realized how fear had ruled my life and my choices. It was only after that dream that the migraines stopped and the blind auras that preceded them stopped and the walking and roaming at night while I slept stopped. It was after that day that I understood the difference between fear and terror.

There is a chasm of difference between the feelings of fear and the emotion of terror. Fear and anxiety are often mixed together, as in the phobias. One can have anxiety about and a fear of something that never happened or might happen. This type of neurochemical experience originates in the neocortical regions of the brain and are mental associations and reactions to emotions (see below) and are subjective. They are influenced by personal experience and beliefs and memories; they are the conscious evaluations of what we are experiencing.

Emotions are lower level responses occurring in the subcortical regions of the brain, the amygdala. They are biological responses to stimuli that create biochemical reactions in one's body that alter your physical state which is why emotional memories can be so powerful and interruptive. Emotions come before feelings. They are primitive survival reaction responses to real events. They are physical and instinctual and can be objectively measured by instruments that can measure body reactions (McKay, 2015).

If one has experienced violent near-death experiences, the triggering and reliving of such an event neurochemically surpasses regular anxiety. It becomes annihilation anxiety.

— *6* —

The Father's Family

T he father rarely talked about anyone in his family. He sometimes referred to his mother as being a saint. He never elaborated. I know they were of French ancestry. A few times he mentioned his father had "taken his mother from a nunnery in France at age 14" and that she died when he was young. But that was a story he apparently told only to me. A few times he mentioned that all of his sisters died before reaching puberty, but I never knew their names or anything about them as people or his relationship with them. I thought he was the youngest, but he was the third youngest. His father was a skilled worker who owned his own small business. I found their names in the United States census of 1920. He did mention one brother dying horribly from a brain infection.

His father (Father's Father, or FF) came to live with us at Nana's house when I was four, for three to four months. I remember him vividly. He was very old and mean. His teeth clicked when he ate. He walked with a cane and would try to hit the brother and me with it. He stayed in the attic bedroom. The father sent him down to his oldest brother (Father's Brother #1, or FB#1) down South to live with him. FB#1, while backing the car out of his driveway, ran over FF, killing him.

While the father was hospitalized in 1976, he recounted stories about how wonderful his father had been and how many life lessons he had learned from him. One story stood out from the others, capturing, I thought, some of his father's essence. When the father had returned home from college and wanted a car, his father had found one and sold it to him. It didn't have an engine. Life lesson apparently was don't trust anyone. He sometimes mentioned that his parents came over from France together. But it wasn't true. According to the brother, the father's parents came from Nova Scotia. I was in my 40s when I found this out.

The father went to a Catholic college out of state and later attended law school but didn't finish. He reportedly worked as a theater director and had newspaper clippings that reported feats that landed him in the Guiness World Records. He told lots of stories; some proved true. At some point he became a teacher at a local junior high school where he met the mother.

Both he and the mother had major surgical events in their young adulthood and were told they would be unable to have children. The mother survived major surgery before antibiotics were used and the father survived a catastrophic accident that required a surgery never tried before. Now, I grew up in a very small town where everyone seemed to know everyone else's business, and if I had not met and spoken with the doctor and nurse who cared for each of the parents when their surgeries took place, I might have questioned these stories. The father was reportedly in the hospital for months, fighting infections after everything was reattached. This was in the 1930s just as sulfur drugs were being introduced. His weight, at one point, went down to 80 pounds.

At the father's wake, I met FB#4 and my much older cousins who had grown up in the same town and attended the same church of my childhood. Neither my brother nor I ever knew they were there. The children of FB#4 grew up knowing who we and who the other living brothers were. I don't know why the father never shared about his brothers or his family's history, but he must have felt it was necessary to keep the information a secret.

The father's three brothers ran away before age 15. The father was the only one to remain at home and graduate high school and then attend college. The second oldest, FB#2, would have been 14 when he disappeared, according to the father, for 30 years. Informed by my fraternal cousin RO, this brother, FB#2, joined the Navy at some point in his youth but stayed in contact off and on with the other two brothers, FB#1 and FB#3, until he, FB#2, retired and joined them down South. However, he was mostly out of the country for the better part of 30 years. I only discovered my cousin, RO, in the 2000s. He spent lots of time with this uncle, FB#2, growing up, and RO shared many amazing stories. He shared that this uncle, FB#2, apparently had married multiple times, simultaneously, to multiple women around the world. He, RO, was attempting to locate any of this uncle's many children, our "other" cousins, wherever they were in the world. My cousin also told me that when this uncle finally returned to the United States, he went down South with wife number ?? (I'm not sure which one) to FB#1's home and met up with FB#3 and his third wife. They went away together for a month to FB#3's home out west. At the end of this month, reportedly, the brothers switched wives. FB#1 had one daughter. FB#3 had one child by his first marriage, cousin RO. However, he gave RO away to FB#1 when RO was a baby, so he grew up with this uncle and his daughter at his home. FB#3 had a daughter with his second wife, who left him at some point. This daughter also grew up with cousin RO and FB#1's daughter. RO was 10 years younger than FB#1's daughter and 20 years older than FB#3's daughter. I was able to meet both of these cousins 20 years ago. FB#3's daughter did not want to have anything to do with any family member of her father.

I had met FB#1 once, the summer I was five years old. To a five-year-old, he just seemed to show up at the island where we were staying and visited a month or more. Obviously, the father must have known he was coming; there must have been contact. Apparently, I liked him a lot.

The family story, told repeatedly, was that I was inconsolable when he left, begging him to take me with him. I remember. But I've never understood how the parents and the brother repeatedly found this story so amusing to ridicule and mock me before other people. When I was older, I was embarrassed for the parents. I would have been shamed and mortified had a young child of mine begged another adult to take her home. Unfortunately, it was not the only incident.

~7~
Words

Words, both written and spoken, and their meanings have always been very important to me. My earliest memories of the father are of his reading stories to the brother and myself at bedtime. *Black Beauty* was the best. I loved horses. Family stories teased that my first words were not mama or dada but horse. If any of the family's stories about me were true, it was that one.

The other books he read most likely had a profound influence on not only how I viewed the outside world I found myself in, but also colored and mapped my inner world. I'm basically referring to the years I was three to maybe four and a half, as by the time I started school at five I could already read. I believe I somehow taught myself to read so the father would stop. I do not know if this is true. I have always thought so. I have strongly disliked anyone reading to me since I was small. It has always been an incredibly profound visceral feeling akin to someone grabbing one and holding one captive while trying to bury one alive in a small dark coffin and one has to kick, scream and claw to survive. It's a bit over the top as a reaction. After all, the reality is that the person is only reading to you.

Sometime after I was returned from running away, during my third year, my nana moved out of her own house into a rented room in a local home in the same town. My Before life was leaving. I don't have any picture memories of her other than from her knees down and her shoes. She liked dark-colored dresses. I can, however, play the memory pictures of her house in my mind, room by room. If I could draw, I could capture it all: the outside and inside of her house, my home, especially the wallpaper in her bedroom. I remember going with the mother to visit Nana in her rented room. I remember the funeral home nearby. I don't remember ever seeing her. She died when I was four. I think they made me touch her. That memory came back when I was married and pregnant with my first daughter and attempting to prepare and cook my first turkey. I touched the cold, dead bird with my bare hands and froze. A brief picture flashed with the thought that it was just like what it felt to touch my dead nana. Never, ever have I touched a chicken, turkey or any raw meat without gloves since that day. At age 35, the mother read me the letter that the father wrote to my nana, telling her that she had to leave her own home because he thought she was interfering with his marriage. It was very dramatic. The father was always dramatic.

After *Black Beauty*, he read Dickens and Shakespeare to me at bedtime: *Oliver Twist* and *A Tale of Two Cities* topped off with *Hamlet* and a touch of *Macbeth*. Once I could read by myself, the father stopped reading to me. I can't even imagine why he chose Dickens to read to a three and four-year-old. I wish he hadn't. By the time I was five, I really thought the world was as Dickens described it in his representative but horridly vivid classics. For those who have never read *Oliver Twist* or *A Tale of Two Cities*, they are novels that Dickens wrote in Victorian England to address the social and financial disparities between the classes of those times. The poor were represented as having to live by their wits. Women and children in general did not fare well. Poor women and children fared even worse. Punishments for minor thefts were barbaric. The stories left me terrified. This was the second epiphanistic moment of my life: I knew life was unfair and being a child or elderly was very dangerous and there was no one to help. I was alone and now almost constantly afraid. I was so sad too that there were so many throwaway people. Not too much later I grew to love all Dickens's stories. I taught myself to recognize real. Those books were a truth, a fictionalized history of how people treated other people.

There's very little I remember prior to running away. There are bits and pieces of memories of my grandmother's dresses, shoes and legs, her house, furniture, paint colors, the house itself and the yard. There are a few bits and pieces of memories of events. I remember the first dog, a Dalmatian named Daniel, and I have memories of watching the father train him. It was before we spent summers on the island. This dog never went there. He ran away after only a few months, or at least that's what we were told. This was after the father had returned to my grandmother's house and after the "running away" incident.

I do remember when I first slept in a regular-sized bed. I remember the mother "pinning" me in with safety pins and talking very seriously that I mustn't get out of the bed or the pins would stab me. This was before the father returned from upstate New York. The brother is nowhere in the memory as he and I shared this bedroom later. I'm guessing I was probably 14 to 18 months old. I include this memory as there was a family story that I was told of much later as well as a much, much later incident where I may have relived this story, or at least part of it. In any event, a friend of my grandmother's, who babysat for the brother and I, many years after my grandmother's death, told me stories about when my grandmother and aunt cared for me while the mother was out of state. This woman, Mrs. W, reported that suddenly, for no known reasons my grandmother could ascertain, I refused to stay in my crib.

Now, I remember exactly where that crib was. It was against the opposite wall from the room entrance, between the door that led to a small balcony and a window on the other side. Mrs. W. said that no matter what my grandmother did nor how many times she tried, I screamed, clung to her, was inconsolable and would climb out when she left the room. It's my guess that whatever triggered this reaction was the initial incident that started and led to a coping reaction of "running" from fear and danger that has lasted a lifetime.

What was I so afraid of? All I could ever do was guess that it had to do with the people who were living in the attic at my nana's house at the time. I don't think I was ever afraid of my grandmother, and I have very little memory of my aunt. The mother, the father and the brother weren't living there full time yet. However, my uncle, MB#2, his wife and their infant son may have been living at the house during this time.

The much, much later incident where I may have relived this crib memory or part of it happened in 1967. My daughter's birthdate. The obstetrician whom the mother recommended was cold and distant. It was several weeks past my due date, so I was induced. Labor was long and hard with labor pains under three minutes for 36 hours. The local hospital was a teaching hospital, and my obstetrician was department chief at this time and supervised what seemed like a hundred interns. The year 1967 was still way before non-medicated labor, and delivery and natural childbirth information was not available or allowed. It also was before written consent.

The mother didn't hang around. She went to play on the father's boat. The husband dropped me off at the hospital and went to a friend's party. And there I was, terrified and alone. Nurses gave me lots of shots that seemed to make the pain worse. They put me in a short "johnnie" that only covered my breasts and left my abdomen and lower parts completely exposed. They moved me to another room and transferred me to a much smaller, narrow gurney-type bed that turned into a crib when they pulled the metal sides up. These sides were at least 18 inches tall. There seemed to be a constant flow of people, all men, who stopped by this crib, each giving me a rectal exam every hour or so.

Sometimes a nurse would speak. She would say "Mrs. B." I didn't know who Mrs. B was. I didn't know who I was. I didn't know where I was or what was happening. What I did know was that I was terrified and in horrible pain. I was certain that people were hurting me, and I had to get away. So, I climbed out of the crib, found my way to an elevator, pushed the button for the lobby, and almost got out of the hospital. I was put back in the crib. They tied me to it. Later I found out that they did rectal exams to chart the progress of the baby's head. Since they were teaching a lot of interns, they did a lot of exams. I also found out that the drug they gave me was scopolamine, possibly coupled with morphine.

Briefly, what my research showed back then was that scopolamine in the 1960s was considered a "truth serum" drug and reportedly used by the CIA and other agencies in other countries for interrogation. It caused people to be cooperative. It also interfered with one's memory recall of events during and after said events. It was widely given to woman in labor in the 1950s and 1960s since it was thought to induce cooperation and compliance and block the memory of pain and labor events. It was later found to cause damage to babies in the womb as it crossed the placental barrier. It currently has many medical uses. It is a popular "date rape" drug. This drug didn't cause me to forget the pain or the memory of what occurred. Rather, it caused me to forget who I was and to possibly relive a memory of abuse as a toddler.

8

Nana's House

The Gift
They had eaten it all when she arrived;
Chewed and swallowed it.
A second thought they offered last place
And least.
She took a corner next to the wallpaper.

She knew for certain by then;
Knew deep in her toes
The size of things.

The proportions were large
And out of balance.
A dust kitten among cyclones.

They blew her all over the house.
She gathered nothing
But grew from habit.
Her gifts went unopened.
The flowers,
Pulled up by their roots,
She gave to herself.

—jp, 1972

The parents weren't poor. They weren't well off either. Nana's house was a comfortable, modest, seven-room house in a mostly well-to-do small town of 3,000 people. Ninety percent of the possessions the parents had had belonged to my nana and were from a time when the mother's family lived in a much grander house. The brother and I didn't have a lot of the same material possessions that our friends had, and the only things I can remember really wanting was a black Raleigh three-speed English bike, roller skates, a pogo stick and a swing set with a trapeze, rings and parallel bars. And, of course, a horse. I asked for one every birthday and Christmas. We both got Columbia bicycles when I was five. Mostly I liked trucks and Lincoln Logs and most of the brother's toys. I had some baby dolls, but they were boring. The dolls I wanted to play with I couldn't. But I could look at them every day. They were in a large, locked glass cabinet in my room. They were the mother's. I was only allowed to touch them once a year. I didn't sit and play much unless it was a card or board game. I liked doing things that required movement. If I was sedentary, I was reading.

I have memories of a pink coat and matching hat that the mother made for me for my third or fourth Easter. She liked to dress me up when I was little. I think she may have liked me as a doll. I liked the piano lessons, but I really wanted to take acrobatics. But the mother wanted me to take ballet. I wasn't very girly. I wasn't afraid of the usual things that scared girls. I collected frogs, salamanders and snakes. I loved to fish, dig for clams and sea worms and play ball. The brother and I would spend hours at this swamp behind what was then his school. I can still hear the mother's scream when she first found them in my underwear drawer.

I think I was a healthy child who got the usual colds and childhood illnesses of the late 1940s and 1950s. I had lots of genital and rectal irritations and abrasions that the mother would treat with Vaseline cloths stuffed in my butt. But that went away after age nine. Chickenpox was a rough time. I had to stay in bed with the shades pulled down in my room for three weeks from secondary complications. It was scary since I didn't understand why I couldn't get out of bed. Mostly it was lonely, and I couldn't see well enough to read. I don't tolerate being ill very well at all. Even small temperatures trigger flashbacks of being helpless, dependent, frightened and alone. The parents would pull the shades down and close the door. It seemed as if I was alone for days.

All children experience fears at some point in their early development from both real and imagined events. In "good enough" parenting situations, an adult can comfort and mediate a child's distress. Over time, the comforted child not only learns to distinguish real from imagined but also is able to access and use those comforting skills absorbed from the parent(s) to soothe him or herself. The neural chemicals and responding organs activated by such usual events lay down, in simple terms, input and output chemical-like roads, streets and highways in the brain that will develop into positive, adaptive responses to stressful and fearful events and stimuli. By the time they are young adults, non-traumatized (neurotypical) individuals will have mostly developed nontoxic neural superhighways to deal with life's positive and negative situations.

As one can imagine, repeated toxic stressors of neglect, physical and sexual abuse, viewing and experiencing violence, war, caretaker alcohol and drug addiction, and/or repeated life-threatening situations with no adult intervention or comfort, cause children to develop far different roads, streets and highways and can remap perceptions and change neurochemical responses in the brain (neurodivergence). Then add to that recent research that has demonstrated that trauma toxins can be registered genetically and passed on generationally (http://learn.genetics.utah.edu/content/epigenetics/inheritance). Such ongoing overdosing of toxic neurochemicals can adversely affect learning, emotional, cognitive and social development.

In late spring of 1949, I had just had a birthday. I was four. Two events occurred. The first, in May, had to do with a dress. It was a Sunday, and my family were going to early church. The mother picked a torn dress with buttons missing. I liked the dress. It was yellow with big brown butterflies on it. However, I didn't want to wear a damaged dress. I wanted another dress. It was getting late. Father said to put on the dress. I tried to show him why I couldn't wear it. He slapped me, and they all left for church without me. After I stopped crying, I walked up the street to my friend Margo's house to play. I rang the bell. Her mother opened the door wearing her bathrobe. She asked me if I knew what time it was. I didn't. She said it was 7:30 a.m. and that Margo was still asleep.

She asked me where my parents were. I told her they went to church. She told me to go home. So, I started for home. Margo's house had a long driveway, and by the end of it, the nice police people were there and took me home and stayed until my family came home for church. Father was ever so charming to the police people who basically told the parents that they couldn't just leave a four-year-old child alone. Once in the house, wow, was I in trouble. Father could really get into spanking. However, what I was punished for was confusing. I was not punished for stubbornness or not obeying. I was punished because I involved outside people. I talked.

The second event occurred about a month later in early June. The parents were going out to a big social political event. They wouldn't get home until the early hours of the next morning. We had a babysitter. Her name was Bonnie. She was the teenage daughter of the car mechanic who worked on the father's car. It had been a warm day. After dinner we had been sitting out in our pj's on the front porch. I fell asleep. When I woke up, the whole house was dark, and the front door was locked. I rang the bell and pounded on the door for what seemed like hours. I was terrified. It was so cold. I was still sobbing uncontrollably when the parents returned. They laughed. I thought they thought it was funny that the babysitter had forgotten me.

— 9 —

The Voice

On their own each of these events were minor. However, each event blended into others and began responsive behaviors that lasted a lifetime. The damaged dress event melded into hundreds of clothing incidents until I got my first job at 15 and could buy my own clothes. The door being locked was just the first time; it was followed by years of my brother throwing me outside and locking the doors when the parents went out. Once I could, I have *always* had an extra key to where I live, and later for my car, on my person or easily accessible.

On our way to our island that summer, at a rest stop, my dog, Nikki, would not get back in the car. He was afraid of the father. The father left him there. By the time we made it to the marina and our motorboat, it was dark and stormy. On the water was a raging nor'easter. The marina people advised the father not to try to get to the island with young children, that it was too rough. He didn't listen.

Riding in a small open boat in high winds, rough seas and torrential rain, even at the end of June, is just not pleasant. The summer months of June and especially July in the Northeast on the Atlantic coast have very high tides during and close to a full moon. Add a nor'easter to it and it becomes flood tides.

Due to the fear and my feeling powerless to protect myself, already a mainstay of my daily life, I remember this trip well. It was the third epiphanistic moment of my childhood. We had made it to the approximate entrance to the river that led to the island. However, it was impossible to tell. Everything was gray; nothing stood out for bearings. It was a high-water flood tide storm. Low visibility totally obscured any delineation of where the marsh banks should be. Looking into the wind-driven rain hurt. The father guessed and was wrong. We were over thick marsh grass, and it claimed our propeller. It was a reality moment, played out frozen frame by frame, like an old slide show, in slow motion. The father was yelling and then screaming at the mother. The brother and I were sitting, soaked and cold, in the wind-driven rain in the stern of the boat. I was so terrified that I felt frozen, numb. The father was still screaming and swearing at the mother, then he was choking her. I remember my body feeling so numb that it felt as if all that was left of me were eyes and thoughts. Terror can be either ice cold or red hot. I didn't know then that it was being recorded for future playback. Then the Voice on my thoughts very calmly said, "This has nothing to do with you. They are crazy. Do the best you can." And I did. Afterwards, the mother comforted the brother. No one ever talked about it.

At the beginning of this island summer of my fifth year the mother was also pregnant. Having no clue what that meant yet, I remember thinking she was just fat. We had several boats with motors and small dinghies with oars. Ideally, we went over to the mainland in a motorboat, but this time the motors didn't work. The father put the mother, the brother and I in one of the small dinghies to row to the mainland. The brother and I didn't understand then that she was miscarrying. All our dinghies leaked. The dinghy was filling with blood-colored water. I remember asking her where the blood was coming from. She responded that she sat on a pencil. It was a long row. Father and some man took her to the hospital. The brother and I were left with a couple on the mainland for about five days. They were kind. Father went back to the island until it was time for the mother to be discharged from the hospital, and then we all went back to the island. Later that summer the brother pushed me off a sand shelf into the river.

Drowning isn't too bad. It beats being hung and repeatedly smothered. It's pretty, looking up at the sunshine streaming through and bouncing off the sand particles in the water. The first time you breathe in water is very painful. The second time, not so much. By the third time, I could see that bright light people refer to when they recount a "near death experience." What was amazing, besides the light, was how quiet and peaceful it was once one stopped struggling. Then everything just slowly got dark. Being resuscitated is way, way not pleasant!

— 10 —

The Nuns

I started school: kindergarten. With the nuns. There were lots of children at the school, so it must be safe, I thought. I wanted to go to public school where my best friend, Margo, went. But the parents said no. Kindergarten was a long walk to reach, but it was fun. I made friends and had piano lessons with my teacher, played with Margo and her brother after school, and got a library card. I loved books. I knew I would find the truth in books.

Kindergarten was great until my first Lent, shortly before my sixth birthday. Being in parochial school, the whole class was marched over to the church across the street to do the Stations of the Cross every Friday. There on the wall in color were the 14 plaques accompanied by a vivid, detailed narration by the nuns. It was downhill by the second one. By the last few I was in total horror and crying silently. Silently, because by this age I had learned that my tears made adults angry. If people could hurt women, children and old people and throw them away and no one stood to stop them; if they could do that to God's Son and even God didn't stop them, then there was no hope. It was the fourth epiphanistic moment of my life and the most pervasive: God threw His only Son away. Poor Jesus. I was so on my own. "Father" was a nasty word.

My sixth year also was full of many minor epiphanistic events that melded into it being the year of the fifth epiphanistic one. That summer the brother pushed me off our dock into ten feet of water. It was just a repeat of the first almost-drowning. To this day, I have a love/fear relationship with water.

That fall I was in first grade and the brother in third grade. He was already a junior altar boy. The nuns loved him, but me, apparently not so much. I had been out of school ill for a few days. The mother had forgotten the brother's lunch and, not wanting to leave me home alone, brought me to the school, leaving me outside sitting on the stone steps while she brought his lunch to him. Apparently a nun looked out the window and saw me sitting on the steps. By the time I returned to school with a note, my nun teacher accused me of lying and said that I had been seen on the steps with the mother trying to pull me into the school, but I was refusing to go. It was like being blindsided by friendly fire. The more I tried to explain she was mistaken, the angrier and more adamant she became. She hung a "Liar" sign around my neck. The parents thought it was funny.

Not too many months later, I was playing "cowboys and Indians" (it was the 1950s) with the brother and our next-door neighbor, Mike. They captured me, tied my hands behind my back, stood me on an upside-down milk crate, put a rope around my neck, tied the rope to the crossbeam that supported a big clothesline, and kicked the carton out from under my feet. They hung me. Hanging is not as pleasant as drowning, but as an experience it's quicker than smothering. I lost consciousness much more quickly. I don't remember being rescued. Reportedly, the mother just happened to look out a second-floor window and saw me swinging and took me down. I was punished for letting them do that to me. I was very confused.

Off I went to school the next day with a bandage over the one-inch-wide rope burn circling my neck. My nun teacher asked me what happened. I told her. She chastised me for being a bad, horrid child for telling such obvious lies about the brother everyone knew was such a good, holy boy. She hung the "Liar" sign around my neck and took me to all eight grades to introduce me as a despicable little girl and sister. The gauntlet was thrown. They hadn't begun to see despicable. The nuns and the parents could keep the brother. I didn't bother to tell the parents what happened at school. I didn't need another punishment or need to give them any more laughs.

— 11 —

More Instructions

Time with the father was never dull and almost always scary. Even when nothing traumatic happened, one knew it was only a matter of time. Despite his being a teacher, I don't think he knew how to relate to children, so at home he either defaulted to rage or teaching. He spent months, after dinner, teaching the brother and me Morse code. We each had our own practicing units hooked up to a battery to produce the correct sound. We each had our own practice card, but at ages six and seven and a half, we both were failures.

During dinner and right after were the most dangerous times. We were captives. Dinner, again, was either rage time toward the mother or teach and quiz time for the brother and me. Whether we were required to chew our food and beverages 48 times after each bite or drink or be quizzed on the parts of speech, sitting down to dinner was tense.

But, as a child, I didn't spend any time really thinking about myself or feeling badly for long. Thinking about myself ended badly. I did sort and categorize the little and big events while alone at night and look at the feeling reactions those incidents produced, but not for long. Like Scarlett in *Gone with the Wind*, I'd think of them tomorrow. I did know not to talk about any of it. I knew no one would believe me. I know now I must have been angry, but that energy I probably funneled into practicing gymnastics for hours. I didn't feel angry. Just scared. And there were some parental inputs that defied categorizations of my young filing system. I wouldn't ask the nuns. So, they sort of free floated for years. Like concupiscence and the mother. How do people file their mothers not liking them? That piece of reality didn't strike me until my younger daughter's death. Later, as an adult, I knew there wasn't another six-year-old child in New England and maybe the entire United States who knew the definition of "concupiscence," let alone how to spell it. And, at age seven, I didn't have a clue what lust was. I read that it could be sex, as in desire, but that was mostly a dead end for my understanding. I did know that lust was considered a "deadly sin" by the Catholic church. I wasn't asking anybody.

I knew what that saying, "God helps those who help themselves," meant. It meant the throwaway people had to do it on their own. I knew God threw away Jesus. I knew people threw Jesus away too and said horrible things about Him and did horrific things to Him, and He really was good. I wasn't. His Father, God, didn't or wouldn't do anything to protect Him, and He was supposed to be wise and good. But I didn't throw Jesus away with His Father. I just had to help myself.

Somewhere between the ages of seven and ten, the Voice I experienced broadcasted many directions. I didn't dwell on comparing my life to my friends' lives; if I caught it happening in my mind, I'd turn it off as I knew I was just another "speck" among billions of other "specks," some throwaways and some not, saying to myself that my life was "worse than some but better than most."

One of the strongest directions I got from the Voice was when I was between the ages of eight and nine. It was after a bad beating by the father. The new house had ground level spaces under the porches. I was under there with my dog, Murphy, sort of crying on his shoulder. The dog did something I didn't like, and on impulse I lifted my hand to hit him. Before I could, the Voice instructed, "If you do that, you will be just like them." It was a frozen moment choice. My hand literally froze in the air. I was horrified. I never, never, ever wanted to be anything like any of them. And I wasn't. One didn't hit children or animals.

~ *12* ~
The Brother

It's always been difficult for me to describe my relationship with the brother. Being 18 months older than me, he was always mostly just there, like a structure. At Nana's house we would attempt to play together, but it was more of a side-by-side, parallel play. Playing together didn't end well for me. He always called me names, but then the parents did too. I was the "too" child: too loud, too quiet, too lazy, too restless, too stupid, too silly, too cry-babyish, too clumsy, too ugly, too fat, too messy, too selfish and just plain bad. He usually hurt me. He loved to chase and tackle me, sit on me and tickle me until it became painful. Once I no longer reacted to the tickling, he went to putting a pillow over my face and sitting on it until I passed out. Smothering isn't pleasant. It's on the list with hanging. This went on until I was about 11, when I inched away and hit him over the head with a heavy object, knocking him out.

I have no clue how I felt about him back then. He was just the brother. We walked to and from school together. Later I realized he had a role to play. He liked to scare me and tell me yucky stuff, but we also could be silly and laugh. He could be nicer sometimes when we were out and away from the parents, but he also could be cruel when they weren't around too. I always gave him the benefit of hope. He listened to me sometimes, and it was as if we almost connected. But then it would be gone.

By the time I was eight, I didn't bother to tell anyone about the things he did to me. Telling only got me punished and accused of lying and trying to get him into trouble. I can still see the smirk on his face when that happened. He was the good child. I was the bad child. I only remember feeling confused. He treated me most of the time as the parents did. I don't think I expected anything else. I don't remember being angry at him or feeling jealous or envious. It was just the way it was. He was the brother. His mother's child.

When I was in the second grade and he was in the fourth, his nun teacher told his class about the concentration camps the Nazis had set up and the tortures they had done to the Jews. She apparently went into specific details on the tortures used, and he seemed delighted to share every one of them with me. The stories made me sick and more terrified than ever before. I could not get the horror out of my head. I didn't want to believe him, but I wanted to know the truth. I found it. It was called the Holocaust. The lists of throwaway people were getting much larger. I added the Jews to the list of throwaway people, along with the Native Americans, the African Americans, women and children and Jesus. Wanting to know the truth was becoming a life quest.

The brother was seemingly perfect, born with the proverbial silver spoon, blessed by fate. It was fascinating to watch. We lived in the same house, but it was in two very different worlds. No matter what he did or didn't do, he seemingly received everything he wanted. Everything just seemed to flow to him as if it all was his due, not only as a child and adolescent, but also as an adult. I always thought my perceptions of this were colored by my upside-down, thrown away eyes of childhood. But it was not just my perception; it was his as well. Many, many years later he addressed feeling some anxiety, waiting for his luck bubble to burst. It hasn't.

There were only a few times I was aware of being angry with the brother, and each time had to do with my children. The first was after my daughter, Sally, at 14, weeks shy of her 15th birthday, had gone on vacation with the brother and his wife to help watch their son as a toddler. Unbeknownst to me, the brother's lawyer and the lawyer's then third wife had stayed with them for a week. This man represented successful organized criminals and set off every icky vibe I had. He had already made my daughter very uncomfortable at the brother's wedding reception 18 months earlier, which the brother found amusing. The lawyer this time went too far. My daughter told the brother, and he did nothing to protect her. She refused to ever work for the brother again.

The second was when my son, CW, came back from his stint at the beach house watching their son for three weeks. This was the first time CW had ever been away, and I gave exact instructions on what to do if he became ill and when to know to take him to the emergency room. I included our insurance card. CW did become ill, and they did have to take him to the hospital emergency room. What I didn't know until we picked him up at the end was that the brother deducted the cost of the ER visit and the antibiotics from CW's earnings, which was basically his entire earnings. This resulted in CW's reimbursing himself from a money stash at the brother's house. The brother was furious and wouldn't even discuss why he didn't use the insurance card or why he would do that to his only nephew. CW has never spoken to his uncle since that day. The brother has never apologized or owned how cruel his actions were.

The third, and the worst, was during my husband's 40th birthday party at our farm. The brother pulled me into a room to brag about having to "buy" himself out of his illegal business from organized crime, where MY children were being threatened if he didn't do what he was told to do. He laughed. He bragged. It was years before I could forgive him, before I understood that my forgiving him and the parents had nothing to do with them but everything to do with setting me free.

~ 13 ~
The Move

Sometime during the fall and winter of my seventh year, the town took my nana's house by eminent domain to build a new high school. We had to move. The parents selected what I thought at the time was a monstrosity of a house, but it had a big yard and was in the neighborhood I had run away to when I was three. If I cut through other people's backyards, I could still get to my friend Margo's house quickly.

We moved a few months after my eighth birthday. It was the strangest feeling, like falling into an endless dark hole, walking to and from school past my nana's empty house. Stranger still was watching, day by day, as the wrecking company demolished it until there was nothing left but ground and the entrance over the sidewalk, our former driveway. I can still picture the rooms stripped, exposing my nana's wallpaper to strangers, as I watched what little safety I had destroyed to rubble. I might not have had any picture memories of my nana, but I had so cathected every room of her house.

There was nothing warm about this new house. I probably would not have liked any new house, but this one was huge, cold and scary, as if nothing of warmth had ever lived there. The house creaked at night as if someone was walking around. I was terrified. The man in the attic had followed me. I was afraid to fall asleep. I slept mostly sitting up in a chair backed into a corner, with a knife nearby.

Everything was worse in this house. It took forever to fall asleep, and I was always cold. The nightmares were worse. The parents were worse. The brother was meaner. It was an old house, and something was always breaking. It took longer to walk to school.

I couldn't read music anymore or play the piano, and I'd wake up in the morning in bed completely dressed with my shoes on or find myself standing in the brother's room in the middle of the night in front of his curtains counting the holes in the lace. I counted things a lot then. I was sad most of the time and cried a lot. The father was angrier. The mother was somewhere, but rarely near me. I started spending a lot more time not behind my eyes, everywhere I went, even at school.

Everything felt different in the new house. I was different. In the house I tried to be very quiet in my room. I wrote a lot, like a journal, but mostly poems. I hid them. When the father found them, he would read them at the kitchen table, and they all would laugh. He would say things like, "Wow, the stupid little bitch thinks she can write," and the big dark hole would get bigger and darker, calling me to jump. If the brother got me and I yelled and cried, no one came. But if I closed my bedroom or bathroom door, a parent would appear instantly.

There was even less adult supervision. I mostly did what I wanted and went where I wanted, and no one ever asked where I was going. Just be home in time for dinner. When I wasn't at my friend Margo's house, I wandered. Sometimes I wandered in the seemingly huge expanse of woods about two miles from the house; sometimes I discovered whole new neighborhoods of children and made friends or went down to one of the ball fields. During school vacations in the spring, I'd get my fishing pole, make a peanut butter sandwich, go down to the river, climb under the bridge and fish for hours. A bit older, at age nine, I started taking buses to other towns, then cities.

School was not pleasant. By the second grade I had declared war on the nuns. They told me I was bad. I was closer to a mute, miniature Gandhi in the classroom than bad. Good girls were rewarded with wearing a child-sized nun's habits for a day. They often would tell me I was never going to have that happen. I was passively resistant. I had constructed a wall around me that only other children could penetrate. I was not passively resistant with other children. I wouldn't tolerate anyone bullying me anymore, nor would I let anyone bully someone near me. There were lots of fights. I became my own definition of Robin Hood. If no one else protected the weak and innocent, the throwaway people, then I would. I spent a great deal of time in the Mother Superior's office. She was decent.

After so many years of being accused of lying when I hadn't, I embraced it with 100 percent of myself. I was going to be a great liar. And I was, passively and totally straight-faced in time. All the books I had read with negative heroes, like Robin Hood, even Dickens' stories and multiple others, had plenty of liars, pickpockets and thieves to emulate. I didn't know then that it could become addictive. It was my own revolt against the world of others who chose to allow there to be throwaway people.

— *14* —
My Rules

Somewhere between the ages of eight and nine, I became determined not only to protect and rescue animals but throwaway kids as well. At this age, I wanted to become a physician. Once I discovered and read Freud, that goal changed to becoming a psychiatrist. I was sure I could find the truth in these fields as well as the tools and skills to help the throwaway people. Someone had to help them. They were everywhere I looked.

By ages seven and eight, I already had profound reactions to things around me. I didn't like clowns. I wasn't afraid of them, but I thought they were creepy. They weren't real. I didn't like magic or magicians. It wasn't real. And mimes made me angry. They could talk but pretended that they couldn't. What they did wasn't real. I wouldn't talk to adults, but I didn't pretend I couldn't. I thought adults, clowns, magicians and mimes were just tricksters. They, along with priests and nuns, were tricksters. I despised being tricked. I wanted to know what was the TRUTH and what was REAL, and I thought I could find it in books.

As a child, I only lied to adults. Obviously, in retrospect, it was an angry child's choice. But I didn't know I was angry. Angry was the father. I didn't know then that anger and rage were different and had many faces. Many of the novels I read as an eight-, nine- and ten-year-old emphasized how crime didn't pay and how people, especially children, lied and stole for attention and love and really wanted to get caught. They showed how older criminals lied to themselves and were arrogant and thought they would never be caught, so they made stupid mistakes.

I, however, had rules. My biggest rule was never, ever lie to me. Then there was, don't tell stupid lies and never, ever get caught. My rule was to always remember to keep a lie simple and always remember what I said, who I said it to, and why I said it because my knowing the truth mattered. I knew that if I lost the truth, I would lose myself. Since the biggest crimes I could commit in the parents' eyes was to want attention for myself or bring someone's attention to them, I needed to be positive that whatever I chose to do was something I wanted to do and I needed to do everything I could not to get caught. I needed to have a plan and be careful. I didn't need to worry about my loose lips sinking any ships as I never told anyone, anything. I never shared. Not even with Margo.

I don't remember exactly when I started to steal, but I think it was right after the Christmas before my ninth birthday. It had to do with a child's idea of fairness, the parents and the brother, and the carnival that came to the town every year in in the spring. Where I grew up was an affluent small town. Friends had all sorts of toys and wheeled vehicles, record players and records, pretty clothes, shoes and lots of underwear. They would have small change for gum, ice cream or candy. I remember wishing I could have undamaged clothes and lots of underwear. And phonograph records. But neither the brother nor I ever asked for much. He had more undamaged clothes and a lot more underwear. He may have asked his mother for them. I never thought the parents had as much as Margo's or most, but more than some.

The carnival was the best. The mother gave the brother a small allowance. Sometimes the mother would give me a quarter if I asked; mostly she'd just say, "Ask your father." Never a good idea. If I asked the father for anything, he would snarl and say, "I wouldn't give you a used postage stamp." I rarely asked. So, every week I took a quarter from each parent and saved most for the carnival. As far as I know, they never knew.

At the new house, spankings morphed into beatings. I avoided the father and fended him off as best I could. I always tried to be eight to ten feet away from him. Sitting at the dining room table or kitchen table, though, was way too close. My chair was always closest to the father. No one would talk. Then the games would begin. The brother's head would be in his plate. The mother would say something neutral. The father would disparage her, and the baiting game would begin. The mother would shut up. The brother never spoke. It was like watching the same scene over and over, every night. The father would work himself into a rage, and objects would start to fly in the mother's direction. She would try to placate him. He would start to push her around and get physical. I would say to myself, "shut up, shut up, shut up," but something inside would build until I couldn't hold it back. I would just react. I couldn't stand watching her be hurt, so I'd deflect him, and he'd turn with a smile and grab me and start pounding away. The mother would take the brother and leave. After it was over, I would usually be in my room sobbing when the mother would come in, sit on the edge of my bed, and tell me how wonderful her father had been to her and all these cute little stories of their times together. She'd say how she had a good father. Her saying this repeatedly caused my world to spin and the floor to move. It was surreal.

By the time I was nine, using his hands wasn't enough, so the father graduated to an old barber's leather razor strap and a whip. He also was drinking more and added a few new games to his list. I was also bigger, still afraid and cautious, but I didn't care that much one way or the other what happened to me. The worst game was I had to make and bring him his coffee after dinner every night while he sat in the family room. The coffee had to be hot, and nothing could spill. Over and over, he played this game while he called me every four-letter word, profanity and insults in his vocabulary, which even for a teacher was unusually broad. This game could go on for an hour or more. And even if, finally, nothing spilled, it would start all over again as the coffee would now be cold. To this day, I cannot carry a cup with liquid in my hand without shaking and spilling some. The game would usually end with my crying and running to my room. He always followed. It wasn't pretty.

～ 15 ～
Another Death

At this time my dog, Murphy, and I were inseparable, except when he went out to do his business. There were no leash laws back then, and dogs were everywhere in this neighborhood. I loved him so much. I loved horses and dogs—cats not so much. There had been an incident back when I was four or five when watching a handicapped neighbor's toddler in the cul-de-sac. We were walking by some thick bushes, and the little girl discovered some kittens. We picked them up, and this crazed mother cat attacked us. I picked the toddler up and held her high, but my legs got shredded. It was terrifying. Another neighbor came out with a broom and swatted the mother cat away. I gave cats a wide berth after that, but they were interesting to watch. Everything was totally about them. They were only loyal to themselves and their needs. Cats were the animal essence of my family.

Murphy didn't like the father, and the father didn't like him. Murphy always placed himself between the father and me, if he could, and would growl and bare his teeth if the father came at me. Father would kick at him any chance he could, so I kept the dog with me when the father was at home. When I was ten, Murphy became terribly ill. I begged and begged the father to let me take him to a veterinarian. He laughed. It took Murphy four days, vomiting blood in pain, to die. I just cried in a heap for days. I didn't eat, didn't go to school and didn't sleep. I just cried. It seemed as if everything that I loved, died.

Murphy's death left me inconsolable. And probably angry. Probably because I don't remember being angry. Being angry would have been like the rage-man. Anger was loss of control. Anyone who lost control was contemptible. Such an awareness then would have incited self-destruction. My dog's death was pivotal. I was tired of being a victim, tired of being someone who got slapped, hit, kicked, hung, smothered, laughed at, tricked and abused. I wanted to fight back. I wanted power. So, I went to the library and got books on power. There wasn't much, just witchcraft. I read everything the library had on witchcraft. I wanted to be a witch. I didn't think of it as being a bad witch or a good witch; I just wanted power. That summer I drew a pentagram in the dirt, stepped in it, read the magic words from a book, and poof, absolutely nothing happened. I was disgusted. To my child's mind, this was as big a trick as a God who cared.

I didn't want power to hurt or use people. I wanted power to protect myself and other kids and animals and to keep the bad people away from me. I knew hurting other people was being like the parents and the brother, and every ounce of my being rejected that kind of power. That kind of power birthed the conditions that caused throwaway people.

But my running away from the father upstairs to my room stopped. This ended sometime between my tenth and eleventh year. After a particularly brutal beating where he pounded away saying he was "going to break me if it killed him," I responded then that he'd "better kill himself or me and get it over with as he was never going to break me as I would rather die." And I really didn't care which choice he made, not only with him but in general. I was tired of being ridiculed, mocked, cursed, touched, hit, punched, tortured, tormented and laughed at by them all. Not caring anymore and saying that to him changed everything. Three new responses were introduced, changing my before and after reaction. The first was that I hid the whip and barber strap.

This was a major change in many ways. It evolved slowly. I was becoming less of a victim. At the new house, the father would berate the mother for never giving me any "female chores" or teaching me how to cook or clean. Never mind that the brother never did any of the "male chores" either. I did those: mowing the lawn, raking leaves, chopping wood, etc. I liked those chores. They were outside. I still do.

The father left the brother alone. It was an unwritten rule: The brother belonged to his mother. The father decided he would teach me "female chores." The first chore was washing the dishes. I liked this one. However, my playing with the soap bubbles and styling the dish mop's "hair" made him epileptically furious. He would have to demonstrate the right way to Wash the Dishes. He would stay watching for a few minutes and then leave. I would revert right back to fun. The second chore was vacuuming the entire 19-room house on a Saturday morning. I didn't love this one. I didn't get to do it for too long, though, as I wasn't vacuuming "the right way." So, every Saturday he was home, for maybe five months, he would barrage me with insults and swearing, take the vacuum away and demonstrate How to Vacuum the Right Way. I would watch, and he would really get into it. After ten minutes or so, I would quietly wander away and out the front door. I always loved that Mark Twain story.

Hiding the whip and razor strap was a pushback. It was amazingly empowering and emancipating in ways I only understood on the surface at the time. Watching the rage-man's reactions when he couldn't locate either implement of pain and power, watching (from a safe distance) him melt and dissolve into incapacitating frustration and helpless fury, was like watching a howling red-faced infant rage on. Ironically, he never asked if anyone had moved them. I would have been my first guess. Nothing was ever said about any of this. The mother and the brother would just disappear. This was my first awareness of a cognitive behavioral intervention with an adult, somewhere between my 10th and 11th year.

~ 16 ~
Big Changes

How did I feel about these new, emerging coping strategies? Very mixed. The survivor me felt empowered; maybe I could protect myself. The objective observer me knew this was not the way a parent/child relationship should play out. This me knew that I was living in an upside-down world, one where a child shouldn't have more ability to weigh out possible unintended consequences of one's choices and behaviors and have more self-control than the adults around her. The mind part of me was totally disgusted with the hypocrisy of the adult world that spoke out of both sides of their mouths, saying they cared and yet throwing anybody under the bus for money or power. I looked hard and long to see any goodness. The "damaged child upside-down eyes" were all I had. I didn't see any.

The second new response was, instead of running up to my room, I ran out the front door. This was an amazing thing to watch. Rage-man, the father, would come out of the house and, standing on the front porch, right before my eyes, would morph into wonderful-sweet-man for the neighbors. Instead of saying, "You dirty, f--king lousy little son of a bitch, get into the f--king house," he would say, sweetly and calmly, "Please come in now," over and over until wonderful-sweet-man would start to melt and morph back into who he really was. I, by this time, was at least 500 yards away and ready to run. But he never chased after me. Over time, I built myself a cave-like nest, a safe place under a neighbor's grape arbor. I buried water and snacks and hid warm stuff and a flashlight. I wouldn't go home until after 9:00 p.m. or 10:00 p.m. in the summer when it was dark and my father would have passed out. No one ever came looking for me. No one ever talked about it.

The third change was I stopped the "get me my coffee" game. My best guestimate is that this game stopped closer to age 11 as the first two had to be already in place and practiced or I probably wouldn't have lived. I'd had enough of rage-man terrorizing and tormenting me. It disgusted me to react like a pitiful victim. I had made the decision that I'd rather die than comply and play. The last time he told me that the "coffee was cold, take it back and make me more," I threw it in his face and walked out the front door. No words ever memorialized the event. This game was over.

There were other events that launched off of these three. During this transition from my 10th to 11th year, the brother stopped smothering me. Instead of just lying there like a helpless doormat waiting for anyone to intervene as he put the pillow or cushion over my face, I picked up my mother's heavy, leaded glass ashtray, hit him over the head, and knocked him out cold. There was never a thought about doing that. I don't think I would have lied to myself about it. It just seemed to be a reflex. It was a heart-dropping-to-the-floor moment; I thought I had killed him. Time stopped. He lived. I was glad he was not dead, but NO MORE PILLOWS!! I was my hero. I chose never to hurt the parents or the brother.

I have never wished anyone dead either, or for anyone to go to the hell place. Never as a child, and never as an adult, did I wish those. I thought most people suffered enough. I thought life was suffering. Why would anyone wish more suffering on people? However, I did wish for a lot of people to please go away and leave me alone. Only once did I ever wish harm to befall anyone, and that was an impulsive reaction in the ninth grade. It made a tremendous impression. The boy I was dating broke up with me to date a senior with a sports car. He was taking her to the big football victory dance instead of me. I wished she would break her leg, and she did. This event kickstarted a great deal of introspection and decisions. I never wanted to even wish hurt or harm on anyone as doing so would leave me as despicable as I thought the parents and the brother to be.

Never, except for once during this 10- to 11-year-old age span, do I remember the mother ever hitting or slapping me. Her abuses and torments were much more subtle: rejection, indifference, withholding and absentia. I had to be desperate to ask her for anything—desperate in the sense that I had to be prepared for the consequences to myself for asking, as in getting the internal protective gear out and ready. I would be giving her power to hurt me in ways I couldn't imagine, which could possibly lead to many, many possible other consequences. It was a lot like playing chess. I knew better than to ask for something, like the boy in *Oliver Twist* who asked for "more." The dolls I couldn't touch, the mother gave to my daughter, at age three, to play with. She gave the entire collection along with the antique oak glass cabinet to my daughter when she was ten. My daughter, knowing I was never allowed to play with these dolls, gave them to me.

But the mother did slap me that once. I don't remember exactly what was said. I'm guessing that the mother said something negative to me and I answered her with a sarcastic truth missile. She slapped me across the face. Now, at almost 11, I was the tallest girl in my fifth grade. My mother was five feet. I was taller. I also was very strong by then. It's still a video I can play in my head. As a reflex, I picked her up and pinned her, feet off the ground, against the refrigerator. I told her, "I have to put up with being hit from him. Never, ever hit or slap me again." She didn't.

— 17 —

Illness and Injury

Becoming ill or injured meant that I fared slightly better than animals in the parents' house. It was doubly not a pleasant experience as a child. It was doubly because as a child one feels miserable and in pain and also has to deal with questioning oneself as to whether one feels this way because one just wants attention or is the pain real. Sometimes, unless I collapsed or was sent home from school, it was just easier to keep going.

With my chickenpox experience and ongoing teeth issues stored away, I was basically terrified of becoming ill, experiencing pain and/or being helpless around my family. A simple cough would be interpreted by the father as my annoying the family on purpose by coughing for attention and keeping the family up at night. Everything I did was seen as being done on purpose. If you have ever tried to stifle or control a bodily function in the autonomous arena, it doesn't turn out well since becoming self-conscious only makes it worse. At least, as a child, I thought it became worse because I was so aware of trying not to cough. I would end up coughing so hard I would vomit. The cold could be over quickly, but the cough could go on for weeks.

Falling asleep at night had always been difficult for me, but by age ten it was even harder by my feeling so cold I would literally shake. Soon, besides getting into bed fully clothed, I was adding as many blankets and coats on top of me as possible. I was falling asleep at school. The school called the parents and then, magic! I got to see the doctor. This was the first medical visit where a physician talked at length with me and not the parent. It was all about being so cold at night and not sleeping. It turned out that I was anemic. In addition to vitamins and foods rich in iron, he wrote out a prescription for an electric blanket.

In 1955, I had never even heard of an electric blanket. To the parents' credit, they did purchase one, and I was warm at night for about four months. Apparently, the father was cold at night as well. He took it.

Being cold has haunted me all my life. My childhood experiences began my habit of dressing for bed. I didn't use pajamas and never nightgowns. Clothes, lots of warm clothes, and sometimes even hats, were necessary. Wearing clothes to bed served a double purpose. I walked in my sleep on and off until my early 40s and being dressed gave me a modicum (i.e., illusion) of control for an area of my life where I had none.

As the only recognized infirmities at our house were the mother's migraines and the brother's asthma, these sometimes month-long coughing sprees went untreated. At age 12, one such cold/cough refused to leave, resulting in several public episodes of what was labelled "fainting." Because of school, I eventually did get medical attention and was diagnosed with mononucleosis. Besides the cough, which turned out to be bronchitis, my red blood count was very low. I was seriously anemic, and the family doctor recommended hospitalization. The parents refused. Again, I found myself in bed, shades drawn, no reading, and no lights for weeks. It was not pretty. I was trapped and lonely. I missed five weeks of school. As a young adult, I discovered these coughing bouts were a form of asthma.

My 12th to 13th years were eventful physically as well. On a very cold day in January, three months before my 13th birthday, on my way to go ice skating, I fell. It hurt to walk. I hobbled home. The ankle continued to hurt, and three weeks later the school called the mother. My ankle, foot and leg had swelled to past double the normal size. Another doctor visit showed a bone fracture in the ankle acerbated by walking on it for three weeks. There were lots of complications for healing. We were referred to orthopedic specialists, as the bone healed twisting. Worse, the uninjured ankle and bone had congenital deformity issues that should have been addressed in early childhood before walking.

The prescription was for what I called "mud brown old lady shoes" with a metal brace and straps that went to my knees. They had to be custom made in Boston. They were the ugliest contraption ever seen by an adolescent girl whose only desire was to be invisible. The estimated cost, even in 1958, was

$600. I spent weeks of listening to the parents fighting about spending this money. The real issue was that too many outside people now knew. They knew the parents had ignored the limping child for three weeks, who walked, in pain, back and forth one-and-a-half miles each way to school. This was serious. It was money. Lots of money. I was not a good investment. But their dirty laundry was hanging outside for people to see.

Disgusted, the throwaway child solved their dilemma, leaving them blame-free. I told them not to bother spending the money as I wouldn't wear the shoe braces. I would correct the bones myself through exercise. The father responded that he would make me wear them. I responded that there wasn't anything he could do to me that would prevent me from removing the shoe braces and walking to school barefoot, thus bringing more attention to them. He conceded, and the parents were off the hook for neglect. They consoled themselves that the child was incorrigibly stubborn. I didn't need anyone's pity.

~ *18* ~
The Island

The island, when we first went there in 1948, was overgrown, and both it and the house on it had suffered from neglect. By the end of the second summer, the father had both tamed. My brother and I were totally unsupervised there and had mostly minor mishaps other than the drowning incidents. The father taught us how to target shoot, load and unload a .22 rifle and handgun and clean them. After dinner and on rainy days, the parents taught us card games: canasta, rummy, hearts, spades, cribbage, whist, poker and then bridge when we were a bit older.

For me, those six summers were overall the best. My island memories somehow remained positive despite incidents. The brother and I were rough and tumble kids: scraped knees, bruises, puncture wounds, cuts from digging clams with our hands, bug bites all over our bodies (the green head flies were vicious) and stings from lots of wasps and hornets. I was terrified of wasps, bees and hornets.

The island years ended the winter before my tenth birthday. Father's friend died and never deeded the property over to him. The widow of this man wanted the father to buy it, which he tried very hard to do. However, the bank wouldn't lend him the money as the parents had only recently bought the new house. Friends of the parents introduced them to another friend of theirs who would lend him the money. However, this man went behind the father's back to the widow and bought the island for himself. The father was furious. The brother and I were sad. The father sold all the boats and bought a big old sailing yacht.

Although my story paints the father as the bad guy, I really thought of him as a victim. We had more shared interests than either of us had with the mother or the brother. Rage-man was terrifying, but the father had a wealth of knowledge and skills, and I was mostly the one who helped him with yard work, building things, sawing wood or "manning" the coal furnace. The brother never got dirty. There were many interactions where the father was less volatile and more seemingly open and expansive. Despite the abuse and reign of terror he often perpetrated, I always knew he was a real, three-dimensional being. Dozens of times I took these more open times to try to talk to him and get him to see how his reactions and behaviors were so scary. And sometimes he seemed to respond and would cry and apologize for these episodes. But it was as if I was dealing with many different people. There was no change of behavior. Later, watching him, I realized that he could turn the tears on and off. Eventually I just gave up trying to reach him.

Many more changes happened after that last summer. The father stopped teaching and was recruited by a large company to develop a personnel department. His days were much longer and probably much more stressful. He was rarely happy before, and now he was even less so when at home. This is when he started drinking more and everything got worse. He spent most of his weekends in the spring, summer and fall working on the boat at Cape Ann.

There were some fun times on that boat. The father had converted it, so it was almost like a 42-foot houseboat that had power. We anchored on the river at the mouth of the little river where the island was located. We still could enjoy "our" beach at low tides, swim, dig clams and fish. Since the father moored his boat near where the lobster people had theirs, he made lots of acquaintances. We would be anchored at our spot, they would go by with their catch, the father would throw them beers, and they would throw him lobsters. There were lots of scary times too. A 42-foot boat is very close quarters for two adults and a 12-year-old and a 10-year-old. The father drank most of the time. Drinking never made his mood or personality better. I could be somewhat safe if I stayed outside on the deck—at least until dark, and even after if the bugs weren't too bad.

— *19* —

After the Island

eing home for the summer was a great new adventure. Friends could be seen daily and whole new territories could be conquered. The town parks department ran free "day camps" at the many local ball fields and pond areas, and the brother and I discovered new neighborhoods and friends. There were Little League games at night and tons of fun things to do, like playing "red light" or hide and seek with neighborhood kids in the dark with no adult supervision. It was heaven at ages 10 and 11.

With no island available, the parents sent us off to camp. My brother went to a camp in New Hampshire for four weeks. I went to a camp on Cape Ann, not far from the island, for two weeks. It started out okay. But I was sent to the nurse on the fifth day there. I had some sort of infection on my behind. What probably started out as a boil had changed and spread. The nurse called it impetigo. The camp tried calling the parents to come and take me home. Again and again, every day, for the next eight days.

Impetigo is plain yucky-looking, itchy and painful. It's highly contagious. It can appear anywhere on the body, but usually attacks exposed areas. Children mostly get it on the face around the nose and mouth. Most cases are simple; some get complicated. Children with poor hygiene and compromised immune systems are more susceptible. There are two types: strep caused and staph caused.

Those eight days the camp attempted to contact the parents were not pleasant. Basically, the camp quarantined me in a room in the infirmary. The infirmary was a separate building some distance from the mess hall/activity center and the cabins. The nurse was there during the day. No one was there at night. No one saw or spoke to me, other than the nurse who checked on me several times a day and brought me food. For eight days.

The day the mother came to pick me up, the nurse told her to take me to the doctor right away as the impetigo was not responding to treatment. She didn't. We went to the father's boat instead for almost another week. By the time I saw a doctor, the impetigo had spread into my rectum and vagina. In extreme cases, impetigo develops into ecthyma. I'll spare the reader and myself any detailed description of the symptoms and treatment. But just imagine what kinds of treatment might have been necessary that were given to a child who had been sexually and physically abused.

Hopefully you have never visited that place one can go to where one's self, one's core, is very, very far away, encased in a protective cocoon—so far away that one is not behind one's eyes. One is aware, on camera mode, recording and filming the visual passage of events in time, but not present living it. For one's core self, time has stopped. One becomes a robot. One wants nothing. Both life and death are irrelevant. The only solace, the only real, is running, jumping, flying through the air...movement, over and over and over, or curled tight in the cave...the nothing. The self waits and watches, hovering until one's core or a reasonable, acceptable facsimile (RAF) can safely emerge again. One can be above, filming down, or below, filming up. It's a dissociative protective response reaction from prolonged exposure to pain and abuse. One is grounded to nothing. Sometimes, in safer surroundings, one tries on the RAFs like new clothes in an effort to be and not be destroyed. It won't matter if someone destroys a reasonable, acceptable facsimile.

Fragments of a Puzzle
Parts and pieces sneak in the black
Shunning the light for shadows
Hiding after flight, like bats shy to the day.
Dreams silent incantations to the night.

****

The warm and the safe
Reaching inward islands of thought

Holding tight…a cocoon.

Separate parts that have never met,
Like proper, well-raised enemies,
Never acknowledging each other
But sitting politely at the same table.

Cautious in the same clothes,
Wearing the same mirrored
Smiles of derision,
each alone…
a piece of the puzzle.

—jp, 1976

20

Margo

The epiphanistic events described here are the ones that stand out against a background of daily minor cruelties and indignities. The brother and I were rarely supervised. On non-school days, because it could be unpredictably dangerous to be around the parents, we were almost always dressed and outside after breakfast when we could. Our nana's house was next to a school playground on one side and houses that were on a cul-de-sac on the other. The cul-de-sac ended in a large fence that extended along the top of a steep hill to another cul-de-sac and eventually to Margo's backyard. This became a well-worn path.

I spent almost every moment I could playing at Margo's house. She had one brother who was one year younger than me. Their father was a successful professional, and they had every toy, wheeled vehicle, board game, sports equipment and appliance that a child of the late 1940s and early 1950s could want. They got a television when I was four, and that acquisition lured the brother into the mix. They had a huge house and yard. My guesstimate was that their house sat on two acres. Their backyard seemed bigger than a ball field. But my mind's picture of their property is a four-year-old's picture. By the time I was eight, I spent what seemed like every other Friday sleeping over at Margo's house and almost every afternoon after school when she was home. Every other Friday was her father's poker night. There would be tons of edible goodies, and we would stay up playing and then sneak down to the kitchen to get food.

Margo only slept over once at the new house, never at Nana's house. She also never played over at either of the houses we lived in. It was never the subject of any conversation with either Margo or my family. In retrospect, I'm sure Margo's mom must have had her suspicions that things were not okay at my house. I spent 60 percent of my play time at her home, up until age ten, except for the summers we were on the island. My brother played there 50 percent of the time until he was 11 and threw a rock that caused damage. This caused lots of tension with the parents for a while but only disrupted Margo's and my friendship for a short period. The father was very angry. But he was almost always angry unless he had company or was out of the house. He had to pay the bill. Margo and I both had other friends from school and activities like Brownies, Girl Scouts and lessons, but she was my best friend until I started high school. I loved her.

Margo was of Mediterranean ancestry with dark hair and dark, almond-shaped eyes. The relationship became physical when I was 10 and Margo was 11. It lasted until I was 14 and a freshman in high school. She told me we were supposed to do what we did with boys and not each other anymore. I didn't question it. Other than Margo, I didn't want anyone to touch me. I liked playing sports and games with boys; they did things. They were competitive, whereas most girls, not so much. But I didn't want boys touching me, unless we wrestled. After Margo told me basically to date boys, I did.

My first crush was on a gorgeous sophomore football player. We dated for several months. During that time Margo confessed that she had slept with him. I told her I didn't mind. What she and he did, didn't have anything to do with me. It wouldn't affect our friendship, and she might as well as I wasn't going to do that with him. I never considered what Margo and I did together as sex. Sex was a male thing. It was something they used as a power move, to hurt and control you. What she and I did seemed natural and mutual, warm and affectionate. It just happened.

It was after this first dating relationship experience ended when I was 14 that I took a long look at the boy/girl dating thing and made several decisions. Since I wanted to be a mother at some point, I would get married, so it would be okay to meet and date guys. This was the late 1950s, early 1960s, a few years before the sexual revolution later in the 60s. Couples did not live together unmarried in my small town, nor did women live in public view pregnant without a husband. That meant I had to address how babies were made and be okay with it. However, I didn't like the "dating dynamics" I observed when watching my peers or that were portrayed in books, movies or television. I also couldn't stand reading romance novels of the time where females were presented as simpering idiots. I still can't, although now they are not so obviously simpering.

From the time I was nine or ten, the father would announce to the dinner table that he couldn't wait until I came home pregnant so he could throw me out on the streets where I belonged. Because he knew I would be a slut. I say "announced" since no one else talked during dinners. The brother's head would be in his plate, and everyone else would be tense as we knew what was coming. The father would bait me and the mother throughout the meal, working himself into a rage, tear into the mother, calling her a "cold roll of barbed wire" and worse. At least weekly, china dishes, silverware and glass would fly in her direction. I KNEW I would rather die than let him be right. I also couldn't tolerate when his rages ended up hurting the mother.

Having no clue what good relationships looked like, I made my own rules. There seemed to be two basic types in relationship personalities: distancers and pursuers. Pursuers seemed more like victims, obsessed with pathetically endless discussions around the minutia of the object of their affection and endlessly riding an emotional roller coaster of ups and downs; he loves me, he loves me not—emotional masturbation. Distancers seemed to make the rules and be in control of the relationship dynamics, have multiple other interests and appear far less mentally deranged. Any relationship I envisioned had to be as close to equal as the situation demanded with absolutely no ridicule, mocking, swearing and demeaning insults or physical force or abuse. I would not settle for being a victim.

However, there were obstacles. I didn't like being touched. Simply making the choice to date boys did not change this preference. Not liking being touched didn't even come close to the experienced reaction. It was visceral—total gag, almost seizure visceral. A simple light touch to my arm could be painful, as if I was burned. For years I thought this reaction occurred because of the abuse, as I had never known a time when touch was perceived as okay. I thought it was part of my early warning system.

I also didn't understand the sexual attraction theme that the world around me seemed obsessed with. I didn't think I had been sexually attracted to Margo. I liked the closeness and affection with her because I loved her. But I didn't mind sharing her with others. So much of this type of relationship was portrayed in books, movies and television as proprietary. I didn't want to own anybody, and I certainly was never going to allow anyone to own me. Being a child was barely tolerable.

I didn't mind that others might find me attractive. It was a power of sorts, energizing but not flattering. It was not flattering in the sense that I was already aware how deceptive people could be, flattering even, when they wanted something from you. After all, I'd been watching the father, other relatives and people for years. I'd already had enough of being treated like a thing and thrown away. This was on a personal level. In general, everywhere I looked with upside-down, damaged child eyes, men were exploiting females and children. Later, it changed to both males and females exploiting anyone who seemed weak, who had no power, money or someone powerful to protect them.

~21~
Abuses—Physical and Sexual—and Trauma

I've never read any description that adequately or even closely eluci-
dates the second by second, minute by minute, agonizing hourly, daily,
monthly, yearly, decades-long internal hell that is the legacy of sexual
abuse to a child. People may observe the subsequent behaviors that come
from and are the results of abuse to a victim. But they mostly ignore and/
or dismiss the continual internal pain a child lives with and fail to permute
or extrapolate the colossal consequences to their developing minds, psyche
and souls.

The younger the child is, the longer and more virulently the damage grows
until it permeates every cell of their existence and becomes their identity. Add
physical abuse and/or emotional abuse to the mix, and you multiply the dam-
age by powers. Add the abuse being perpetrated by a parent or trusted caregiver
to the previous, then square that result.

Sexual abusers inject an iniquitous poison into the bloodstream of their
victims that permeates into every cell, penetrating every organ, even to their
marrow, eating into their souls…twisting, turning, burrowing deeper, leaving
their prey pierced and shattered. Sexually abused children feel different. They
behave differently. They think differently. They are different. They have little
idea of who they are or why they are. The abuse interferes with achieving
every development milestone necessary for developing self-worth. They try to

hold onto anyone and anything. They react. But it's not by choice. Not because they are manipulative. Not because they are dramatic.

It's not because they want more attention. Not because they purposely misbehave. Not because they are too loud. Not because they cry too much. Not because they can't concentrate. Not because they can't sit still. They react because they want someone to take it all away. They want someone to see they are dying, torn apart and consumed from the inside by a soul-eating virus. They want someone to come and fix it. They want to not be rejected, to not feel so totally alone. They want the nightmares to stop. They want the terror to go away. They wish they had never been born. They wish not to be. They wish to die. They want someone, anyone, to notice that they were robbed, that their childhood was stolen. Their trust was stolen. Their bodies were stolen. Their minds and emotions were stolen. They want their souls back. They want to trust someone again. They want control of their minds, bodies and emotions back. They want to feel whole. They want the Mark to be removed.

Mostly they want not to hurt. Fighting back against a soul-sucking, insatiable, invisible enemy, they mistakenly direct their anger at themselves in an attempt to destroy the invader. They fight…some by turning their anger on others, some by fire, some by cutting, some by pills, some by alcohol, some by grabbing someone—anyone—to substitute the illusion of love, some by sex, some by stealing, some by death.

Tragically, along the highway of survival, they learn negative coping styles and behaviors and ways of relating to people that only reinforce the isolation, pain, rejection and alienation originally experienced.

They are the "thrown away," marked for life. Only God can remove the Mark. But for so, so many, the Mark has removed God as an option.

Unfortunately, any form of sexual abuse and any age claims pieces of what was just described. Very few survive to adulthood without substituting something, such as drugs, alcohol or sex, to cover the pain. Some go on to perpetuate such abuse. Many suffer from anxiety, depression and panic attacks along with post-traumatic stress disorder (PTSD) or complex-PTSD due to developmental trauma. (See the internet for the American Psychiatric Association's current Diagnostic and Statistical Manual of Mental Disorders *[DSM-5] criteria.)*

Most have managed to come to terms and learned to manage (and/or avoid) their "triggers" and resulting reactions. Their lives play out in a voyage that attempts to chart and avoid all the hazards particular to their history. Some do achieve some success in reducing post-traumatic stress disorder to a more manageable post-traumatic stress reaction or response.

But one cannot control everything. Eventually one relaxes, momentarily forgetting to monitor the people and/or situations around one and something occurs seemingly "out of nowhere" that triggers a flashback. It is not the flashback or memory itself that is devastating; it's the surge of old toxic neurochemicals that are released that are devastating. Instantly, everything changes. The world that was light becomes dark. Everyone and everything become suspicious. Others' facial expressions, body language, vocal tone and attitudes become constantly highlighted, scanned, coded and replayed. Hypervigilance takes over. Anxiety increases. Negative motives are attributed to ALL. Everyone and everything are microscopically analyzed into exhaustion.

My first reaction was identical to my reaction at age three: RUN. Trust no one. Especially don't trust relatives because if they are culpable for the original abuse and/or a subsequent trigger, then the surge can be a ten on the pain/toxin level. One's startle response drastically increases. One tries to go on with the daily schedule of life without appearing vulnerable or giving any clues to the chaos and confusion of one's internal environment.

Emotions feel shut down, constricted. Experientially, it feels like going from three-dimensional to one-dimensional...almost robotic. It becomes difficult to think and process all incoming information. It is a painful and exhausting response that eventually can give into depression and suicidal ideation. Even knowing that what one is experiencing and feeling is not real in present time, battling the neurochemical bath of darkness can be, in a short amount of time, exhausting.

One of my saddest and most pivotal work experiences as a child and family therapist was at a locked, residential treatment program for latency age (5- to 11-year-old) children. This was the population—the children and families—I chose to work with. These were children in the custody of the state and placed in a residential treatment facility after psychiatric hospitalization because their behaviors could not be managed in a home environment or group home; they were an ongoing threat to self and others.

Most were throwaway children. Some of these children had brutalized animals, siblings or peers; self-mutilated; set multiple fires and molested other children. A few had killed. Reading the histories of these children and what they had endured and been exposed to by parents and/or caretakers was shattering. Trying to positively impact the future outcome of these throwaway children, to give them hope, was daunting. Getting them to shower and brush their teeth regularly was a major milestone. Most were so angry and damaged that they no longer cared what happened to themselves or others.

A few, some as young as ages five, six and seven, no longer felt anything at all. Staff did not last long working in this environment. It seemed as if each new child intake history was more horrendous than the previous one.

Since part of the job description required working with the families of the few children who might be able to be discharged home eventually, it entailed driving hundreds of miles weekly, and I used that time and took up yelling at the God I had thrown away as a child. This was 1986. I was not only realizing just how angry I had been and now was, but I was also feeling it. I knew no person could handle it: not even my therapist of 11 years, who fired me for being too angry four years previously. I was also in the process of trying back on the concept of a God and aligning Him somehow with my existentialist and nihilistic views, reprocessing and reconfiguring many choices and decisions made when a child and teen. I thought if God couldn't handle my anger, this was going to be a short journey. The search began in books. I've been in His face, one way and now another, ever since. God not only handled it, but He also later took me on the ride of a lifetime.

~22~
Ages 10 to 12

From age 10 to age 12, besides wandering the halls, rooms and cafeteria of the new high school where my nana's house had stood, I also began wandering to other towns and cities, trying on differing roles as RAFs. These RAFs weren't alters in the current DSM-5 criteria or any psychiatric literature. These were roles I consciously made up. If you know or ever heard of the story of Ferdinand Demara as an imposter, what I did was somewhat close, but on a kid level.

The bus stop at the head of our street beckoned. At this time, my dance instructor's understanding of my intense dislike for ballet allowed for reducing my time spent on it to 15 minutes, which left 45 minutes for tap and gymnastics. I must have been decent at all three genres as she had some of her pupils dance at private functions all over the area. We were the entertainment. I don't think there were too many youngsters in the 1950s who had taps on their toe shoes and did gymnastics in a tutu.

I have no clue if I had talent or not. I have no memories of anyone ever telling me as a child, "Good job," or even if I did something well. I got tons of the opposite. I know that I didn't expect praise or look for it. I didn't even notice others giving their children praise until I had children of my own. I had read tons of books on child development even before having children. I had an intellectual understanding of the reasons that praising a child with "job well done" was a good thing to do but little understanding experientially of why. Back then, if many books said it, it must be true-ish until it proved otherwise.

However, this was the age I did start to get compliments—mostly from men, not boys. And the father, after the beatings stopped, would try to get friendly, saying in a sweet voice, "Come here. No, I mean closer." "I won't hurt you; you can trust me, I'm your father." "All fathers touch their daughters like this." "I'm supposed to check to see how you're growing." I became queen of the saying, "Fool me once [your bad]; fool me twice...." Once usually did it. Except for the brother. I've always given him another chance. I don't know why. And since compliments and attention started coming from men, I simply didn't believe any of it. Anyone who used "trust me" or "you can trust me" as a reason for belief, I knew was selling me something and/or wanted to take something from me.

I was very careful. I was always aware of the Mark. There were minor incidents seemingly weekly of men exposing themselves, trying to grab me or just saying lewd and lascivious things. There was even a local police officer who tried unsuccessfully for years to get me into his squad car. I remember reporting a few of these to the mother, but I was on my own.

Taking a quarter every week from each parent at nine years old transitioned into 50 cents, then 75 cents and eventually a dollar by age 12. I was babysitting by now and saved every little bit of money I earned. Although the yearly carnival was still a motivator of sorts, the rides had ceased to be the priority. Paying for gymnastic lessons was the priority. Once the middle school years were over, the mother stopped the dance/gymnastic lessons. I had no instructor.

Through Girl Scouts I had met another Girl Scout leader who was also a dance/gymnastic instructor, who lived several miles away. She agreed to give me private lessons, and we negotiated a fee of $2.00. Even by 1957 prices, that was a deal. It was a one-and-a-half to two- mile walk each way, but well worth it. Later, at ages 14 to 15, the mother would give me a ride as a friend lived across the way and she would visit. No one ever asked how I paid for these lessons.

Having almost survived seven years of parochial school scathed and wary, I could hardly wait to put those eight years in my past. Fortuitously, the latter half of seventh grade found me still participating in Girl Scouts. Our little troop had a wonderfully patient leader, Mrs. Jentry. Once a month our troop had swimming at the local YMCA. This one time, I went to change into a bathing suit and found blood. Panicked, I found Mrs. J who not only had all the needed paraphernalia, but who also explained the what and the why of what was happening. She made it seem like such a wonderful thing.

I couldn't wait to tell the mother. Silly, silly girl. Another memory video frozen in time. The mother was scraping and peeling vegetables for dinner. I told her. She never stopped what she was doing or even looked at me. Eventually, she said, "That's nice." I said, "Don't tell the father." But she did. It was his topic of conversation at dinner for weeks. Something Mrs. H made wonderful, he made an ugly, shameful weakness. I was reduced to a dog in heat.

Any reader might think, "Well, that sucks, but get over it and move on." I know at the time I did. It was just another hurdle. Unfortunately, that menses thing has a goal of arriving monthly. And, given a speck of acquired/innate motherhood responses (AIMR), most mothers, even in 1957, provided the necessary paraphernalia to deal with this "wonderful" event in their daughter's life.

Reacting with confusion, humiliation and shame at the lack of (AIMR) and provision of necessary paraphernalia and from the subsequent providing of old sheets and towels to be stuffed in one's underwear, like the Vaseline cloths of early childhood, it was very much an I CAN'T DEAL WITH THIS EVENT at age 12. I don't remember ever thinking about it. I don't remember crying about it or getting angry. I never told anyone until age 15, and then it was only out of necessity.

I only got my menses twice more at age 12. The second time produced the old torn-up sheets and towels again. The third time the mother's response to my asking, "Did you get me any sanitary napkins?" was, "No, you don't have your period; you have bleeding hemorrhoids." I never got my menses again until I was 15. And then, they only came once or twice a year until after the birth of my first child at age 22.

But my reaction at 12 was very uncharacteristic. I mean, I usually stole much of what I needed or didn't have. But not this. Or underwear. It never, ever even occurred to me to steal underwear and sanitary napkins. It never entered my mind until I was writing this chapter that I hadn't taken care of this myself. The shame and humiliation must have been so much more overwhelming and pervasive than the teeth events that I couldn't come up with a survival plan. And I never did. Anything to do with that area of the body seemed to totally disable and nullify my competence. Eventually a solution was provided to me at 15.

I know I was incredibly ashamed of what happened. The whole situation was too weird for words. It was frankly bizarre. I don't remember how it happened, but my guess is I got my menses while with my boyfriend, DB, at age 15. That I can't remember the details tells me how horrifically ashamed I must have been. My boyfriend was 18, a senior in high school, had his own car and worked a part-time job. He was my best friend. I must have panicked and told him since he bought sanitary napkins for me until I got my first real job and could afford them for myself.

Another major event in my little life at ten years old was the arrival of new neighbors next to our house. They moved in that summer. They were a mom and dad with a six-month-old baby girl named Elli and her 18-year-old sister, Jen. Being careful but intrigued, I would sit one foot behind our property line and watch this baby girl when her mom Becca put her in her playpen outside. This little girl and her parents became a huge focus and influence on my life. Eventually I was invited to come closer and interact with the baby, which slowly morphed into helping care for Elli. Becca and her husband Will were surprised when, 18 years after their first daughter, Jen, was born, Elli appeared. Will was the vice president of a big company on the 128 Industrial Belt, and both he and Becca had a very active social life and were avid golfers. They were, however, absolutely delighted with their second daughter, and Becca re-acclimated to staying home with the baby.

Both she and Will were high school sweethearts originally from California. As I remember their story, she worked and helped put Will through college. He was as handsome as she was beautiful, both on the inside and out. She was a gourmet cook, sewed her own and her baby's clothes, and loved gardening. They had been Jitterbug champions in their adolescent and young adult years in California and proudly displayed all their trophies. They were warm, friendly, affectionate and loving with their children and each other. I was privileged to watch them and be a small part of their family for four years.

Now home for the summers and with Margo away at the Cape, I slowly became Becca's helper with Elli. I learned to change, feed, bathe, read stories and dress her. I watched her while Becca cooked, sewed and worked in the garden. Somewhere in here, she taught me to cook and sew and seeded to me a lifelong love of landscaping and gardening. Both she and Will taught me to dance and do the Jitterbug. I would feed Elli while Becca cooked dinner, and Will taught me to make his martinis "just right" shortly before he came home.

Amazingly, they really liked each other. They were happy together. They were the closest thing to "love" I'd witnessed. There was no yelling, hitting, swearing or rage-man. They were real for four years: approximately 1,460 days, 35,040 hours, 2,102,400 minutes of my life. During that time, not a very long timeline in a lifetime measured against the abyss, they gifted me something priceless: hope.

However, hope's seed mostly lay dormant through the teenage years, lost in multiple layers of multi-directional shadow lives, of trying on selves and lifestyles as if they were clothing stacked in a dressing room. Just months before they moved, I met the 17-year-old boy who would become my husband seven years later.

The teenage years were an immense challenge. In many ways the wonderful people living in the house next door from ages 10 to 14 had been an oasis in the ongoing storm. Morphing from a child to developing female in the late 1950s and early 1960s required every survival skill previously acquired.

─ *23* ─
My "Get Out
of Jail Free" Card

The majority of my parochial school classmates in the eighth grade were going on to Catholic high schools. There were about six of us who were going on to our local public high school.

Personally, I was elated, and for years I described the event as being able to play my "get out of jail free" card.

All of us graduates of eighth grade had to have an exit interview with the Monsignor of our parish. Mine was memorable. After eight years, I had a formidable reputation. Some of it was earned; most of it was just legend. The nuns pretty much left me alone. The last "big" incident I remember occurred in the sixth grade.

During an exam, I was accused of cheating, along with four others in my class. The paradox was that I didn't cheat on this exam. I certainly had cheated on many others, and I thought I was a skilled cheater. I had planned to cheat and even prepared to cheat the night before the exam using multiple tools of the trade. However, in mid-preparation, it occurred to me that all this time spent prepping for cheating was work. The whole idea behind cheating was not to work, but it was work, so I might as well just study. So I did. As my life would have it, I was accused of something I, for once, didn't do. My exam was seized, as were four others. I did protest my innocence this one more time. This was my subsequent and only protest of disagreement with a nun since the second incident in first grade of being called a liar.

At the end of the exam, the Mother Superior and the Monsignor were called. The five of us were all called to stand in front of the class where my nun teacher ceremoniously handed the Mother Superior each exam, and she in turn handed each exam ceremoniously to the Monsignor. Each accused cheater was called forward as the Monsignor dramatically tore up the exam in front of the class. All four cried. Caught up in the exquisite irony of the surrealism of the drama, I laughed, went back to my chair, and sat down. The four other classmates' parents were called. No one called mine.

I said very few words during my exit interview. Other than confirming that I was going on to public high school, the Monsignor did all the talking. Basically, this is what he said: "When you get to high school, I would ask that you do me a favor. When you get into trouble, which I know you will… and they ask you where you went to school for the last eight years, I would like you to lie."

How did I feel about myself? By the end of my 13th year, very mixed. When I allowed myself to feel anything at all, it was mostly fear, sadness, pain and shame. Or at least I thought it was shame. I didn't have an emotion language. I didn't know then that repeated, ongoing humiliation could result in shame if internalized. I didn't feel that I was bad, though. I thought the parents and the brother were bad. What I felt was closer to "I was nothing."

Whatever the emotion was, it felt like the aftermath of being hit by a semi. It had some terror in it, as if I was about to be annihilated. I wasn't aware of naming much then, and shame is just the name I gave it much later. I didn't feel ashamed of what I did. Whatever it was, it was the big, black hole, the abyss that I'd find myself pushed towards. It was about not being, not existing. Sometimes I just wished it would swallow me up and get it over with, but on some level I always knew it was something to fight against. Once swallowed, I would never come back. I knew to stay busy, move, run, think and read.

There were the unexplainable-to-self things, like counting all the time or waking up in the morning with clothes and shoes on and wondering where I went at night. There was crying at night until I made myself sick and spending hours wandering the halls, classrooms, gym and cafeteria they were building where my nana's house once stood. This last one I did understand. It was still my nana's space. I would pick the locks on the out-of-the-way doors and then jam them with small objects when I left. The months before the high school opened, I would help myself sometimes to the ice cream already stocked in the freezers. But I always left a nickel or a dime on top of the counter, as it would have been stealing from my nana. Kid logic.

I did feel ashamed sometimes of things I didn't do, things I had no control over. I felt ashamed that I looked like a ragamuffin kid, especially standing out against the background of my surroundings. I was ashamed that eventually my teeth were green, as no one ever told me to brush them. Ashamed that my clothes never fit and were rarely clean or were ripped and stained. Ashamed, when I looked around and saw other children who were clean and seemed cared for and happy, and I was a throwaway. Ashamed that my defects of constant toothaches, infections and boils cost the parents' money and they looked at me with disdain. Ashamed that my very being was "too": too ugly, too fat, too stupid, too clumsy, too lazy, too loud when I talked and too quiet when I didn't. Ashamed that I never saw the same dentist more than a few times as they wouldn't pay the bill. Ashamed that the parents didn't want me. And I was as ashamed of the parents as I was afraid of them. I didn't want anyone to know that they didn't care for me. I was ashamed for them.

I wasn't ashamed of the lying and stealing I did; that came much later as an adult, after my daughter was born. The only time I remember being caught was by a peer when I was in high school, which was more embarrassment at getting caught. I was 15 and took something on impulse at a party. It was a 45 RPM record. It was impulsive; I'd broken my own code. I rarely did impulsive things, or so I thought. Back then I thought I was just doing what all the throwaway kids in books did to survive.

But I never told anyone. I never talked. I didn't talk until well into my 30s. And, even then, I never spoke of more than one incident and never to the same person. Sometimes, up until then, I would have another repeat dream: I would be talking about the things that happened as a child in our house and all my teeth, one by one, would start to disintegrate. The disintegration would slowly spread to claim my body, part by part, until I woke up screaming. I didn't understand until my daughter died that I might not make it past the abyss and all the memories it held, past the many times the parents and the brother told me they would kill me if I talked. It wasn't until writing this book that I realized just how often these statements were said to me well into my adulthood.

~24~
Teeth

My real-life teeth nightmares began on the island when I was four years old. Tooth pain is the worst. You can't get away from it. One tooth starts hurting and pulsating, and soon that entire side of your mouth is pulsating. At that age the problem was abscesses, and the parents would simply find a dentist and have the tooth from the infected area pulled out. I remember some strange infections. All of my fingernails fell off once, and the fingertips oozed for weeks. Once I broke out in boils seemingly all over my body.

My teeth were not only an ongoing shame-based horror, but they also were incredibly painful. They weren't just painful when abscessed or had cavities; they were painful when either hot or cold beverages or food was in my mouth. The irony was that my teeth were straight and perfect-looking. I dreaded toothaches. They were doubly dreaded as the parents' reaction was accusatory, as if I had purposely gotten a toothache and/or abscess infection to punish them. Or worse, as if I purposely had a toothache to get them to give me attention. They had no idea the time and mental effort I spent as a child scrutinizing my behaviors to ensure I would never do anything for attention. It was one of the worst sins I could commit besides costing the parents money or talking about what went on at home.

Even at 15 years old, when I had my first job and was able to find my own dentist and negotiate a fee schedule I could afford, it was still very difficult to talk about. It still is. Dr. S was a wonderful dentist and person. He never asked a lot of questions; he never mentioned billing parents; he always joked about wanting to "fix me up" with a dental student, and he fought long and well for more than 20 years to save as many of my teeth as possible. Because the infections and abscesses would flare up day, night or weekend, I had his home number and permission to even have him paged off the golf course (I only did it once). He took me seriously and treated me with respect, consideration and kindness.

As a child, other than one-shot visits to have a tooth pulled or abscesses lanced, I rarely saw the same dentist more than a few times. The majority was only once. The parents were big on giving me paregoric for toothaches along with codeine, whiskey and bourbon to dull the pain. (Ironically, all opioids and their synthetic act-a-likes cause me to become violently and relentless ill for hours. Whiskey and bourbon are okay.) There was one dentist, though, when I was in the second and third grades, whose office was across the street from the school. I think my mother liked this arrangement as I could go all by myself after school and she didn't have to participate. By age eight and nine, despite plural novocaine injections failing to dull the pain, this dentist used nitrous oxide for a tooth extraction (after I bit him). Apparently I must have been more compliant, as he used the nitrous oxide for every appointment thereafter. It was fine with me. This dentist became fun. Not too many seven- or eight-year-olds got to "trip" in the early 1950s. It was a win-win for both me and the dentist. I was able to construct whole other worlds to play in on nitrous oxide; I could speed up, slow down or distort sounds and make them dance. These were my first positive flashbacks. It seemed a long time before trips to this dentist ended. I'm guessing it was because the parents failed to pay the bill. I don't think they ever opened the bills and read them. They were furious when they found out they were being billed an extra $5 every time this dentist used the nitrous oxide.

After my first daughter's birth at age 22, the fight to save the teeth became more intense. Sometimes my entire face would swell, and the pain would be unstoppable, even with serious pain medications. By the time she was 18 months old, I had been on antibiotics for the previous four consecutive months. Some of the antibiotics were still in experimental stages. Then I discovered I was pregnant. Many physicians had multiple opinions and recommendations. The ob/gyn was concerned about possible fetal damage from pain meds and experimental antibiotics, recommending immediate stoppage; the oral surgeon recommended continuing antibiotics and terminating the pregnancy. This was 1969. The husband provided no input; surprisingly, the father did. He announced that my dental infections were very similar to what led to a brother's death from a brain infection. His brother had had lifelong dental abscesses. Not willing to terminate the pregnancy, I made the decision to terminate the teeth.

The operation was scheduled as day surgery at a local hospital. The plan was surgery at 7:00 a.m. and discharge by noon. When I woke up and it was dark and I was in a hospital room with all sorts of tubes and an IV, I knew something unscheduled had occurred. When the surgeon removed the teeth in the upper right of my mouth, he found a congenital defect. The roots of these teeth were imbedded into the sinus cavity. A plastic surgeon was called in to graft skin to close the hole left by the extraction. A one-hour operation had turned into an eight-hour operation.

This removal reduced dental abscesses and infections by 70 percent.

~25~
Male Friends

By now I already knew from experience that throwaway people had a big Mark on them that was only visible to abusers and other throwaway people. The world was filled with perverts, and the likelihood I would attract losers was a given handicap.

However, besides endorphins from practicing gymnastics for hours, observing others' attraction for me was the first people power I ever experienced—especially since I had never had any traits labelled by anyone prior to junior high/high school as positive, and even then I didn't believe them. That was mostly because any compliments came from males. I didn't trust males. Nevertheless, I wanted to have fun. Guys could be fun as they did things, or activities.

I don't mean to pick on males or single them out. I didn't trust females either, but for very different reasons. I had no fear of females physically. By adolescence, I was way past the "children are safe" of childhood. No one was safe. I only trusted myself.

Guys putting the moves on me was a definite downer and could be dangerous. Remember, girls' gymnastics in the 1950s and early 1960s was more like male gymnastics than now. By high school I was practicing not only floor exercises but also rings, bars and the pommel horse. I was mostly muscle and very strong. If girls had been allowed to wrestle, that would have been my second sport choice. Besides being strong, I was amazingly flexible. Then it was called double-jointed, which made little sense. I could have been a contortionist in the circus.

There were a few guys, bigger and stronger, who tried to use force and physically abuse to get what they wanted. Fortunately, I had an awesome early warning system: my Voice. I relied on it and took it for granted. I thought everyone had one. And there was always a much larger guy friend who would later advise this person personally of his error.

Up until age 14, I was mostly treated by my male peer as friends, measuring how well I could catch or hit a ball, work the pommel horse, catch fish, run fast, shoot baskets, knock down pins and drive a car. At 14 and 15 years old, I was the designated driver for many male outings to the drive-in movies or other outings where they wished to party and not drive, including multiple excursions with girlfriends where we borrowed a parent's car. (Imagine this: It's 1959 or 1960. You are the parents of a 14- or 15-year-old girl. It's a Friday or a Saturday night. A car with four or five guys, 16 to 18 years old, drives up and they honk the horn. You don't know the last names of any of these boys. You let your daughter go off for the night with them. Charming father yells out, "Be home before the milkman." Right…not if you're a parent in your right mind.)

Wow, what an education on the teenage male, and it so easily extrapolated to all males of all ages. I not only heard the most amazing stories regarding their physical abilities relative to size and distance (girls certainly didn't have those types of conversations or contests), but who knew vacuum cleaners could be so versatile. Their mothers would have passed out! The absolutely great thing at that time was that they forgot I was a girl. I was just one of the guys doing them a favor driving them safely back. The second greatest thing is that I got to drive their cars at 14 and 15 years old.

The best thing, though, were the friendships, whether I drove them while they partied or if we went bowling or played miniature golf or if I needed help with something or someone. They talked to me and shared their lives: what they wanted to do or who they wanted to date or the troubles they were having at home. And they listened to what I wanted to do, and we joked and laughed and played poker for pennies. Some went to private school and drove Corvettes, and some didn't have much. Most were into sports; some weren't. They were my first real experience of being treated as an equal. It was my first experience with respect. Many of these guys remained my friends into my 40s. There were some who attempted crossing the lines I laid down. Once. Most didn't.

Very few girlfriends related and/or interacted this way. At some point during junior high, most girlfriends became a total paradox. I couldn't handle sitting around talking badly about other girls, who were friends one day and not the next, or clothes or boys, incessantly. It was hard not to extrapolate that most friendships were just a veneer and at any moment friends could turn on a whim to get you. My rules: One on one, okay; threesomes, not good. Female groups: danger, danger, be very careful. Bullies abounded, from the subtle dismissals and cruel rumors to the blatant attacks, so never give anyone information that could be turned and used against you. "Loose lips sink ships" became a life mantra. In life, like with my family, one didn't want to stand out too much. It was better to be quiet and invisible.

∽ *26* ∽
Searching for the Truth

The summer before starting high school was euphoric and powerful. I was free and 14 but could look 18 or 12, depending on who I hung out with, the RAF of the moment, how I dressed and if I wore makeup. I was forbidden by the father to wear makeup until I was 16, which of course made it a given that I would wear it until I was 16, at which time I stopped.

The transition from age 12 to 13 had made the shame of my lack of clothing much more apparent to me. However, it was not as apparent and important then as it became in public high school. How one dressed, even in a small parochial school on the wrong side of the tracks, was a strong representative statement of who one's parents were and what their placement was in the social scheme of things. There was not much representative wealth in my parochial school. My small town was a money town. In my pre-teen and early teens, it was still a subtle but visible demarcation of status. By the end of adolescence, that demarcation was glaring to me. It may never have been subtle. It may have been just my awareness increasing of the world around me.

Money and status were always important to the mother. She mentioned her own wealthy status growing up seemingly at every opportunity. Or, at least to my upside-down ears and eyes, the background of my own reality made such references stand out. And the father too. Although neither one of them had many civil words to say to each other, they often would say positive things about each other's perceived status. The father was obviously impressed by the mother's ancestral lineage dating back to America's earliest settlers. Surface-wise, she was his trophy. The mother was impressed with the father's looks and his having been a commander in the Navy, as well as his dancing ability. In later years, after the father's death, she would refer to him as "The Commander." Such surface things by anyone who is impressed with wealth and toys caused my eyes to bleed and my mind to scream.

By age 12 or 13, despair ever present, the obsession of looking for the truth and what was real had become a mission. It must be somewhere. Margo didn't have it. The people next door had something. I couldn't name it, but I experienced it. It was real. I thought my nana may have had it. There was a friend of my nana's who sometimes babysat me when I was little, Mrs. W, and she had it. My family didn't. So I took the RAFs and travelled. Sometimes I went to a city in the north; sometimes I went to a town in the east or west or south. Basically, I reached locations that had public transportation in an approximate ten-mile radius to my hometown. I was just looking for truth and people who were real.

In retrospect, I must have been looking for someplace I belonged. I felt like I was an orphan—not merely parentless, but an orphan of humanity. It was a dark and desolate place I ran from. In all those other towns and cities, just like in the movie *Grease* in the late 1950s and early 1960s, there were biker groups, hot rod groups and gungi groups (sort of a cross between bikers and what would now be gangsta); there were nerds, jocks, and preppies. It was a lot of different clothing for the RAFs. I was learning to meld, blend into the surroundings of the day, always watching.

Having some money also was important to me. My stolen allowance plus earnings from odd jobs allowed me to have access to and purchase some needed and fun things, like bus and train fares. I also was able to purchase some clothing, but clothing was expensive. At 14 years old, my monthly income was approximately $12 to $15, minus $8 for gymnastic lessons. This left only $4 to $7 per month to save for school lunches and everything else.

There were no secondhand stores in my little town. I didn't even know they existed. Or for that matter, the Salvation Army stores in the big cities. There were the church rummage sales where the mother got most of my clothing, but I would have rather died than go there. So I often became a lot larger and heavier when I left a clothing store.

I was talented at shoplifting. In fact, I was so talented that I trained a small group of like-minded friends. We worked as a group. Someone would distract and the others would sweep. My small team was good. It was a rush. It all ended one day at age 1, at the five-and-dime store. They all got caught. I didn't. It is etched in my memory: me, standing in the store in a raincoat with inside pockets filled with stuff, watching my friends in slow motion get tapped. It was like I was invisible. The police came. They were arrested. Their parents were called. I just watched. None of them ratted me out to the police, but they did to their parents. Thus, they couldn't hang with me anymore. I was not welcome at their homes. I always wondered why no one ever bothered to tell the parents, but I was grateful they hadn't. It would not have been pretty.

~27~
High School

Ninth grade in public high school not only improved my social life but also made me feel like I literally had gotten out of jail and the entire world was now opening to me. And, since the school was built on the site of my nana's house and property, I already knew my way around from haunting the hallways and rooms years before. It felt safe and seemed to predict hope for the future.

Most freshman classes were mandatory and preselected. All were okay, except home economics. Even that would have been okay if I could have taken carpentry. I wanted to learn how to build things. My first week, high with hope, crashed and burned when the guidance counselor told me I couldn't take a shop class. I was a girl. Girls do not take shop. Girls take home ec. I went to the vice principal. No. I went to the principal. No. My response: If I couldn't take carpentry, then I wouldn't take home ec. Anyone who could read could cook and sew. Their response: No girl has ever refused to take home ec. Home economics went on without me.

I loved high school. It was a small-town high school where 85 percent of graduates went on to college. Classes were small. Graduating classes were well under 180. One could know almost everyone in their own level and many of those above and below their level. There were cliques, and the most dangerous time and places were lunch in the cafeteria, seconded only by the locker room before or after gym. Bullying and rejection were both obvious and subtle. If one was smart, one didn't call too much attention to oneself and had friends or at least a friend in each clique group if possible.

Most peers, however, kept to friends in their own grade level. There was always the "in" group of six or seven girls in each class level that were tight and defined what was happening. Then there was the larger group of maybe 20 girls who were alternately in or out of the smaller groups at varying times depending on the activity. Sports were huge, and jocks were highly represented in the "in" groups. All the "in" girls dressed the same, and all the wannabe "in" girls dressed just like them. It was a four-year-long episode of *Grease* sometimes interspersed with *Mean Girls*. Although not without a few minor upsetting moments, it was the happiest four years of my life so far.

No one at home was beating or molesting me. I had some power. I had a toe in every class and clique. I had friends, and very few bullies messed with me more than once. It was a "to thine own self be true" time, which meant being cautious, careful, watching, waiting and aware, but also having more fun than I had ever imagined. I also apparently had an attraction. Guys liked me. Now, knowing this wasn't that big of an ego boost. Early on I became aware that guys of all ages liked females. And guys liking females sometimes made them act real mean or real stupid. Guys weren't necessarily picky, so it wasn't much of a compliment.

But it was a power with unpredictable rewards. The benefits I liked the best were that it got me lots of cars to drive as well as first dates and enough second ones. When a girl was popular with guys in the 1950s and most of the early 1960s, rumors might spread that she was "easy." I wasn't ever easy in any area, but I was fun. There was one great guy, a senior, who took me out my freshman year and wanted to "teach me how to kiss." I loved his line. So, we negotiated. In exchange for playing kissy-face and only kissy-face, he would let me drive his car to the carhop restaurant two towns away and back. He had a really "souped up" car. We both thought it was a win-win at the time, and he ended up being a good friend for 40 years.

Another benefit, if you were a girl who attracted guys, was that you got included and invited to a lot of outings and parties by other girls because you brought the guys. These other girls didn't even have to like you. I think the motivation behind this is that there is only one of you but lots of girls and sharing eventually happens.

The power that I had wanted back at age ten had died an ignominious death after wishing a girl would break her leg. I didn't want to hurt people; I only wanted to keep people from hurting me. Although by this time I had physically defended myself and was aware I was capable of violence, but it was not something I ever instigated. People getting hurt literally made me ill.

In class at school I sat in the back with friends and did not participate much. My major focus was socialization with peers in class. After seemingly eight years of suppression, I went to school to be with friends. I was there for fun and sports. I had no interest in performing academically, but I did okay my freshman year. Or, I did at least well enough to qualify for sports. I liked English, history and gym. Life was improving. I had friends, a handsome new boyfriend and seemingly endless activities on the weekends. I was rarely home. It was a win/win time for a while.

Once a week there were CCD (religious education) classes at night at the parochial school I had attended. The mother would drive the brother and I and pick us up. It was fun to get out, and I liked challenging whoever led the class for that week. I would question everything from what made Mary a saint and why would anyone pray to her, to playing devil's advocate on birth control and abortion as babies were parasites. That got lots of reactions.

We had gym twice a week. The biggest challenge and downer was getting the parents to buy the uniform required. Most of the girls had at least two sets: one to leave in one's locker and one to take home and wash. They weren't expensive. No uniform meant being marked absent even though one was there and having to stay after to get credit for attendance, once one had the uniform. Since the mother was a gym teacher, she eventually succumbed to purchasing my uniform. This was mega-embarrassing at 14 years old, but it also ended up a plus.

The assistant gym teacher had early on ascertained my exposure to and love of floor gymnastics. She began working with me during gym classes, introducing me to the parallel and uneven bars, the pommel horse, the rings and the springboard and vault apparatus. With about 14 gym class-es to make up after school, this assistant gym teacher started training me three to four days a week. It was amazing. Even though I had caught up credit-wise by that December, I kept working with this teacher two to three days per week until shortly before the end of my freshman year. In April of 1959, this teacher informed me that she was on the Olympic gymnas-tics outreach committee and that I was invited to spend the summer at Springfield College training for tryouts for the women's gymnastics team to compete in the 1960 Olympics.

This was beyond any expectation. I cried happy. I was amazed and hum-bled. I never felt so honored. But I tricked myself. I actually believed that the parents might be proud of my accomplishment. Silly, silly little girl. I couldn't wait to tell them…couldn't wait to ask. The mother said nothing. The father laughed derisively and said, "Girls are only good for making babies." End of topic. It was never mentioned again. A piece of me was mortally wounded and slid off to the cave. For the next 30 years, someone fought tears through every televised Olympic gymnastics event.

It was a never knowing in the "I could have been a contender" category. I was competitive, a fighter, and that girl label kept getting in the way. I would have been competing with other girls as skilled but likely more skilled than I. I just wanted the chance. I held on tightly to the thought that I was a real person, but nothing I ever did or didn't do seemed to make me real to my family.

I don't remember as a child or adolescent ever thinking that the parents did or didn't love me. It wasn't even a category. Nor did I think about if they liked or didn't like me. I never thought any of their words or behaviors towards me were personal. It was just the way it was. I was alone, a ragamuffin girl, a thrown-away speck among thousands of thrown-away specks. I thought they thought I was a thing.

After this blow, it wasn't that I became angrier. I don't think it was bitterness, either. It was something much lower. I think it was indifference. Something inside got a lot more numb. I ceased to care. I kept up the lessons until I was 16. I still practiced for hours every week as it helped me feel okay about myself, but it was never the same.

~28~
Sophomore Year

That fall, my sophomore year, I tried out for the gymnastic cheerleading squad and made it. We performed at halftime at the football games. I have no clue how I did. No one ever gave me any feedback one way or the other. There were no pictures anyone took of me except group photos in the yearbook or town paper. It was another huge hassle trying to get money to pay for these uniforms, which were expensive. I no longer had the energy to fight to look and play the part of normalcy in my community.

In sports attitude is important. I no longer cared about much. I think my general attitude towards adults and my sarcasm apparently showed, and I was asked not to participate in the cheering squad any longer. I just wanted to have fun. If I didn't do sports, it didn't matter what grades I earned. Life got very simple. It was about fun.

The winter of my freshman year, a guy friend had tried fixing me up with a friend of his, DB. It was one of those catastrophic dates. Obviously this guy was way past nervous, and the date was a disaster. We did, however, become friends before springtime. He planted himself in my life space. I was 14, a few weeks short of 15, and he was 17, a junior with his own car and a very lucrative (for 1960) part-time job. I had just mastered the art of smoking. He had cigarettes. Forty years later, I realized he stalked me. He was just everywhere I went then.

He filled a huge void in my life. The people next door and Elli had moved to New Jersey in March 1960. I was going through the crash and burn of Olympic disappointment. DB and his friends liked to do activities and go places. There were ball games and miniature golf and bowling and just driving around. We'd take the train to Boston Garden for Bruins games. My job was to smuggle a big GIQ of Narragansett in my pocketbook along with cups. A close friend of DB and the brother owned and ran the parking lots at Fenway Park. We went to tons of games. We went to the beach. We laughed. It was fun. I was mostly with DB and his friends that summer when I wasn't dating someone. I was rarely home. During my sophomore year, DB was my ride everywhere. He appointed himself chief transporter, rescuer, boredom deflector and friend. Sometimes we just rode around in silence but listening to music on the radio.

The fall, winter and spring of my sophomore year I skipped 52 days of school, from October to May, and never got caught. Nobody ever questioned the absences. Nobody ever questioned my written excuses. The only challenged excuses were the ones the mother wrote because I was home ill. I had only skipped once in freshman year. It was only a class. Big mistake. Teachers took attendance every day, in every class. Duh. But learning from one's mistakes being a skill of mine, it never happened again.

The skipped time during sophomore year was spent mainly with girlfriends, listening to music and their talking about boys, and laughing. These were mostly girlfriends from my class, but upper-class girlfriends were a bit more risk-taking. There were some excursions to Boston with more adventurous girlfriends who were interested in college guys, but the majority of time was spent in my hometown at girlfriends' homes whose moms worked. There was the occasional "borrowing" of a parent's car and riding around town after school let out for the day to show just how cool we all were, but 1960-61 was a very different time. No one whom I knew disrespected the police, and we were often escorted home by a police cruiser and threatened with "we're going to tell your parents," but they never did.

Once such excursion to a Boston university with a friend named Ann almost ended in rape. With little information other than she was meeting a new boyfriend at his apartment, off we went. After a quick introduction to this guy's roommate, my friend and her new boyfriend disappeared into a bedroom. The roommate stood about six feet and five inches, weighed about 240 pounds, and was on the university football team. Without much talk he picked me up like I was a sack of potatoes, announced he planned to rape me, took me into another bedroom, and threw me on a top bunk. Now, obviously I was scared. This guy was way beyond my area of experience, and I pretty much froze from the lack of immediate coping skills. However, the picture of both of us on the upper bunk bed with him trying to remove my clothes and banging his head and shoulders repeatedly and becoming more and more frustrated totally struck me as hilarious. I couldn't stop laughing. Soon he couldn't stop laughing, and he gave up and we moved to the living room and just talked. I never went on another anything with this girlfriend.

There were many "close calls" during my high school years as I was so often somewhere I shouldn't have been doing something unwise but fun. I think at the time I just assumed I survived relatively unscathed because of caution or luck. I took the Voice for granted. In retrospect there are just too many incidents to be coincidental where this Voice impacted an event or issued a warning. Except for two occasions, where I doubted the reality of what I heard, I always listened and followed through. During the high school years, it most often proclaimed loudly, "Get out!" Which I did, and almost always either the police or a parent or both would appear on the scene, and I'd watch my friends and everyone else get into trouble.

Maintaining a D average wasn't easy. It required a precision of sorts. I was no longer playing team sports, so it didn't matter to me. One didn't need a C average to play intramural sports. Plus, when both parents were or had been teachers and were totally into maintaining their "image," it was a way of reminding them of my existence. I don't remember my report card being a big deal with either of them except for their feeling that they were "losing face." I say that because I never got in trouble for bad grades or had consequences. I know I was surprised that neither one even noticed the 52-plus days of absenteeism. But it could have been obscured by the number of days I was late to school. It would have been better to list the number of days I was on time.

We lived five minutes from the school. It started at 8:00 a.m. I got up at 7:30 a.m. Homeroom was from 8:00 a.m. to 8:20 a.m. I apparently decided that showing up for homeroom wasn't necessary. That fall I got tagged by the guidance department, probably because of the discrepancy between testing scores and actual grades and teacher reports of attitude and sarcasm levels. Mrs. D was a hoot. For three school years I had weekly sessions where we talked about every other worrisome student in the school. There were some students we helped. We spent a lot of time on one girl, Nora. At 15 years old, she was clearly on the road to self-destruction. Her dad was a minister. I had my own assumptions of what was going on, but no one listened and there was no deflecting her. She ran away eventually and, after years of drug abuse, was brutally murdered at 22 years of age.

However, Mrs. D did make me wonder. I never had really thought about whether I was smart or not. I'd certainly been called dumb, stupid, worthless, retarded, idiot and other flattering names by the family. And while I automatically dismissed their opinions, there always was an elephant of doubt hanging over my head.

My academic performance for the past seven grades had not been stellar. Gradually I was impressed with the necessity of having to find out if I could do the work to get the marks. So for one whole quarter in my sophomore year, I studied and did the homework. I earned Bs across all courses. Having satisfied my criteria, I reverted to just having fun.

The home life was much the same. The father would yell, scream and swear at the mother that his underwear wasn't ironed right, and then he was out the door by 7:30 a.m. and gone until at least 6:00 p.m. The drinking was worse, and the nightly barrage at the mother at dinnertime continued. He still threw dishes and utensils, but I stayed out of it. I no longer volunteered for resident punching bag. He was gone to the boat on weekends from April until November and mostly spent time in the basement when he was home.

One winter night at dinner, when the brother was out, the father launched into his well-used rant at the mother being "a f--king cold roll of barbed wire" and her refusal to have sex with him, etc. She responded with some remark that just fueled that particular "Let the Games Begin Marriage War," and I just was so sick of hearing it. I turned to the mother and said, "You know, maybe if you would just have sex with him, he would leave me alone." Dead silence. The mother kept eating, looking at her plate. I said, "Aren't you going to say anything?" Silence. "Did you know?" "I knew," said the mother. "You knew, and never said one word to me?" Quiet. No one said another word about this. Ever.

The following week the father announced that he had arranged to be transferred to an out-of-state branch of his company and would be moving that weekend. He did. I did not see him until that summer when the mother dragged the brother and I down to where he had his boat for a weekend.

DB now transported me to CCD classes, which I skipped. I'm sure they didn't miss my presence. However, in early winter the Monsignor happened to catch me sitting in the car with DB talking and smoking in the school parking lot, and he kicked me out of CCD classes. No one ever told the parents, and I continued to go out supposedly to those classes for the next two and a half years.

Late that fall, before the father left, I got my first part-time job at a local year-round candy and ice cream store. It was a dream job of sorts as ice cream had always been my most favored substance to eat. Ice cream had always felt like being loved, or at least it was the closest reasonable facsimile. Chocolate things were good, but I only wanted them in the winter.

There wasn't much of a reaction from the parents about my getting a job. The father did say, however, that I would have to turn my paycheck over to him for room and board and clothing, etc. My response was basically in the ballpark of "when was the last time you bought me anything" and didn't he remember the "he wouldn't give me a used postage stamp rant." My paycheck was my paycheck. I kept it.

Working a real job steadily allowed me to stop paying myself an allowance from my parents and drastically cut down my stealing from stores. I now had money that I earned. It was $1.75 an hour plus tips. It averaged between $25 and $30 per week. We wore uniforms and changed from our street clothes in rooms in the basement. I could now pay for my own dentist appointments, cigarettes, underwear, sanitary napkins and clothing. I didn't pay for all the ice cream I could eat or walk out of the store with. I'd like to say I stopped stealing. I didn't. It was a rush, and I was good at it. I was addicted.

I also was addicted to saving money. There were two sports I had always wanted to try: golf and skiing. Since it was winter, I bought myself the necessary ski equipment and went skiing with friends. That purchase and my learning how to ski opened a whole new world of ridicule. "What's the stupid bitch think she's going do now, try out for the Winter Olympics? Ha, ha, ha." Occasional bouts of teasing happen in most families, but this was not friendly fire. They took to calling me "Penny" after Penny Pitou from the 1960 women's Olympic ski team, and it went on for years.

With the father living in another state, the mother went back to work as a gym teacher. This was and wasn't a good thing, as the father ceased to support us financially. My brother's grades weren't sufficient to get him into a good college, so the mother applied to fifth-year private schools.

With DB, my friends, my job and my own money, I pretty much did what I wanted, when I wanted to. There wasn't any real adult supervision. I dated who I wanted, mostly upper-class guys and college guys. Everyone partied. Most everyone drank. I didn't. That was too much like the parents. Drugs, such as marijuana and heroin, were around too. I knew to stay away from it all. Somehow I knew that I would be prone to addictions. I remembered the nitrous oxide, and I was watching Nora, the girl in high school, ruin her life.

~29~
The Father Goes Away

With the father gone, the relationship between the mother and me changed. She began to treat me as if I was a friend, confiding all sorts of inappropriate information. Before the father moved, all my energy went into surviving living with him. None went to recognizing or questioning why the mother didn't behave like a real mother, or why her acquired/innate motherhood responses toward me were missing. Without the father, she needed someone to perform various functions usually done by the father, so she began treating me as if I was an equal and, at times, as if she were the dependent. This change colored our relationship until the day my second daughter died when I was 25 years old.

We never had a mother/daughter relationship. We never had much of a relationship at all. Very little of the needs a child wants filled from a mother figure were provided. I do have some memories of her making me clothes and dressing me up when I was three years old. I must have disappointed her terribly. I wasn't a doll. There was food, shelter and clothing (sort of). But there was no warmth, security, protection or approval, delight or love. Did I realize this then? No. I never gave it a thought.

DB's parents invited me to dinner one Sunday that winter, and, although I didn't realize it at the time, it was a kind of love at first sight. They had always wanted a girl while I, apparently, had always wanted real parents. I'll never forget the dinner. It was roast beef with mashed potatoes, peas and freshly made rolls, real butter and chocolate bread pudding with a sweet bourbon hard sauce. I never knew roast beef had a taste. Up until that day, I didn't understand why people went on about steak and roast beef. I thought all meat except ham tasted the same. I discovered that beef had a great taste if you didn't burn it and barely cooked it. Maybe other foods had a taste. It was a whole new world.

DB's parents were prim and proper, but not. They were so real. They were both wicked swear faces. But they didn't swear in anger or rage in front of me, like the father. They funny swore. They had ridiculous sayings like, "up Mike's ass." Swearing was also something I never did either. That would have been too much like the father, and that was never going to happen. They never said anything, but DB's mom started making clothes for me, knitting sweaters for me and teaching me girl stuff.

Now, the mother couldn't stand DB. She could be incredibly rude and cold in a subtle way. Although his family had an equally impressive lineage and played in more selective social arenas than the mother, she treated him as if he were barely acceptable. Once the father left, she'd ask DB to do things for her as if he was paid help. He was too polite to refuse. Eventually he realized she was using him, but it was okay. DB went to school with the brother. They were in the same class. She never asked the brother to help with anything. She was inexplicable to me.

DB was at my house a lot now. He drove me to school and back, took me to friends' houses, drove me to and back from parties, and picked me up from work. We would sit in his car in front of my house and talk or sit on the staircase or stand in my hall and talk and laugh. This made the mother weird. She especially seemed to dislike it when we laughed. She would walk by muttering things like, "familiarity breeds contempt," which, of course, caused us to laugh even harder.

These laughing incidents with DB were the first realization of the mother's reaction to my laughing. She'd walk by or walk into a room and zing me. Her insults and put-downs were much more subtle than the father's and, up until the father's leaving and DB's hanging around, didn't stand out. It was so obvious that, years later as a young adult, at a gathering where both friends of the brother and myself were present and the mother was in the kitchen preparing something, I made a wager that if they could get me to laugh, I could "make" the mother come into the room and insult me. The entire group went silent when she did.

True potential freedom cemented on my 16th birthday with my driver's license. Along with having a job, it was one of the greatest privileges received in my 16 years of existence. I had been driving since age 12, but now I could do it legally. It meant I could take care of myself; I could meet my own needs and never, ever have to depend on another person to survive. I may not have owned my own car yet, but I had no doubt I would someday. Small gains continued to blossom, like no longer having to go to church on Sunday with the mother. I now could drive myself to church. And, of course, I didn't go to church; I went and picked up friends and we went out to breakfast.

Well before the age of 12, I had totally dismissed the Catholic church as just another corrupt and amoral political structure, a magic act, which survived on the backs of the poor and ignorant. I didn't yet deny the existence of a God, but I had begun getting into Nietzsche, Camus and Sartre. I was an existentialist, a "being" up against "nothingness" and having to define one's existence daily, and well on my way to atheism. I didn't quite know what to do with Jesus. His Father had thrown Him away. He was still a hero like King Richard, Gandhi and Martin Luther King, Jr. So I put Jesus on a shelf with the rest of my heroes and didn't think about it.

In my adolescent insight I had no clue how angry I was at the parents, adults and the Catholic church. How dismissive and disrespectful my behavior must have appeared, and why did neither of the parents or any other adult ever call me on it? No wonder at times I considered I might be invisible. Bringing books to read during mass was probably the least offensive thing I did, along with saying that I felt I was going to faint and leaving to sit outside. (I had and have fainted multiple times. It was something to do with standing motionless and low blood pressure.) By junior high age I was bringing manicure tools and nail polish and doing my nails during mass. Back then, if an adult had actually told that me my behavior was disrespectful, I would have dismissed their words as just another adult "trick." If I could have responded back then, I might have been really surprised that what I was doing was perceived as disrespectful and answered that I was trying to be good and not act out. I was just managing my behavior through distraction. I had no idea then what respect even was or what it might look like. Although, in retrospect, why did no one say anything?

I'm fairly certain that a great many of my behaviors would have been labelled ADHD or as somewhere on the "spectrum" today, but this behavior was actually how I managed to be quiet and not misbehave while sitting through something I didn't want to be at, was bored with or didn't want to do. As a child that would have been 90 percent of the time. It was my own behavior management coping skill. I still use it. I have never gone away from my home without something to read or sat still and listened to someone without my hands being able to do something. Knitting is preferred but picking lint off my clothes will do. With the advent of e-readers and smartphones, I no longer carry books in my backpack or keep them in my car. Waiting rooms before appointments are just another place for me to read. It's a win-win. I'm happy because I'm reading and not upset by the waiting.

My own children were non-stop challenging and hyper at home. But they were polite, respectful and well-behaved at school and in public. I could take them anywhere once they were past three years old. In contrast, the brother and I were quiet, still and well-behaved everywhere adults were from the time we were three and four years old, especially at home. We didn't act like children. We were very self-controlled in front of adults. We were not only not heard, but we also were rarely seen.

Looking back, I really didn't believe in much. But I must have believed in myself. I must have had hope. I know I believed there was truth to find if I read enough books. I must have been convinced that I would recognize this truth when I found it because I was so determined, or maybe desperate. I didn't know then that I was running just feet in front of despair until it caught me when my daughter Missy died. The three-year-old who ran away looking for someone to love her and keep her safe had ceased her quest in childhood. Truth was bigger and better. I'd given up on love. It seemed too quixotic, too esoteric. I only wanted safety and respect. I didn't believe that I was special or better or less than anyone else. I believed I was a speck among billions of specks in the universes, and the universes were indifferent to who won or lost. I was not indifferent to the throwaway people. I had a code and what was probably a negative identity. I knew what I wasn't. I would never be like the parents or the brother.

Even as a child, I knew from experience that if I walked into a room of 100 people, 25 percent would dislike me on sight, 25 percent would like me, and 50 percent would not have a preconceived opinion. It was just the way my life was, and I shouldn't waste energy trying to change the negative 25 percent. Nor should I take it personally. It just was. One can learn a great deal from crushing disappointment and pain as a young child.

My reading had morphed from Nancy Drew fiction and the classics like Shakespeare and Dickens to novels such as Sir Walter Scott's *Ivanhoe*, Dumas' books, *The Three Musketeers* and *The Count of Monte Cristo*, and of course books about my hero Robin Hood, to mysteries and science fiction in my latency ages. My pre-teen years of delving went into Freud and Jung and their psychological theories, which led to the thoughts and thinking from the great philosophers.

Reading was rarely one direct line though. One book might spark an interest that would branch off and branch off again in multiple directions that would years later coalesce into a bag of knowledge concerning the history surrounding a topic. For instance, reading a novel about Robin Hood branched off into reading other novels about King Richard, which branched off into reading about the real King Richard, which branched off into reading novels about the Crusades (what led up to and ended them), to the crimes of the Catholic church and its popes, to the slaughter of the Knights Templar and the crusade against the Cathars, to the Children's Crusade, which then jumped to the Inquisition and then branched off to reading about the Muslims, then Mohammed, and eventually into reading the Koran.

~30~
Junior Year

T hat summer before my junior year, I had my first weekend at DB's mother's family's old farm. The farm itself was at the base of a mountain. The dirt road leading to it was named after her cousin. The cousin's house was down the road, and their barn and farm were beautiful. I loved it during the day. I was terrified at night. Other than *Dracula*, the few scary horror-type books I had read all took place in this state. There were no streetlights or neighbors close by. There were all these animal and insect noises I had never heard before. Who knew the woods and wilderness was noisy?

That first night sleeping "at the farm" was epiphanistic in its own way. Not all epiphanies are positive or insightful, and some can become a PTSD reaction. This one began a reaction that has and can appear suddenly again in my present life. I slept in the back bedroom closest to the woods. The room itself was rustic, with beautiful old pine slats. The double bed was grand, made of pine and hand carved by DB's mom's great-grandfather. The other furnishings were rustic and simple. The house was only used in summer.

I went to bed around 10:00 p.m. That was early, as DB and I were getting up at 5:00 a.m. to go fishing on the pond about one and a half miles from the farm where his mom's brother and his cousins each had a camp.

113

Sometime in the middle of the night I woke up and opened my eyes. I couldn't see. I was blind. I became hysterical and woke the entire household up. They turned on the lights. I could see. I never slept in that room alone again. There were no nightlights at the farm in the early years of my visits. I would sneak into DB's room and sleep in the other single bed there and get up early (but light out) and tiptoe back into that room. He thought it was funny. I'm certain his parents knew.

Up until that night, other than on the island, I had never been at a location at night that didn't have streetlights in proximity. In my memory, I had never not been able to see my own hand in front of my face. Thinking I was blind, even for only a few minutes, engraved such a profound emotional reaction, like drowning, that it will never be forgotten. I reference drowning because it took me well into my 30s before I could get my face wet in the shower without triggering a flashback of those childhood incidents. Subsequently, even now I still must remain aware and manage the present moment when showering. Otherwise, relaxed or not, getting my face wet can trigger a flashback once again. So, I have a plethora of nightlights. They are not in the bedroom itself, but in bathrooms, along the staircase, etc. It's just enough light so it's never really "hand in front of your face" dark. I have little packets of them. They travel. Oh, and I have an automatic generator.

Nevertheless, I had so much fun that first visit to the farm. DB did get me up at 5:00 a.m. to go fishing and insisted on cooking a bacon, eggs and toast breakfast for me even when I tried to explain to him that eating in the morning made me ill. Not wanting to make a big issue and appear ungrateful on my first weekend with his parents, I ate the breakfast. We went to camp and, out in the boat, I got sick. He rowed me back to the beach. I drove back to the farm. He never pressured me to eat breakfast again.

I really liked my life. I liked my job. I had my own money. My teeth were getting fixed. I had sanitary napkins, underwear and clothes. The father was still in another state. I had girlfriends, DB and as many boyfriends as I wanted to deal with, and I had my license. By that summer, I was working a lot of hours, 35 to 40 hours per week, which netted about $60 per week. That was a lot of money for 1961. Later that summer, the mother started going for the weekend to spend time with the father every few weeks, and the brother and I were on our own. More freedom.

The only negative at the end of that summer was that I had attracted a stalker. That wasn't even a word used back in the early 1960s. This guy would call when the mother and the brother were gone and I was alone. He would say that he was watching me and knew my every move and when I was alone.

Back then you reported such phone calls to the telephone company, and they would call the police. From the years of terrorizing and abuse by the father and the brother, I had a somewhat atypical response to fear and terror. I got really angry. The last time he called and said he was "coming to get me," I responded, "Right. I keep leaving the door open, and you never show up. I'm waiting." I then called the police and a girlfriend's mom who came and took me to their house. The police got him.

The mother was back teaching gym in September. We were hurting for money. The father had stopped giving her money when he left the previous winter. She had sent the brother off to a fifth year at a private high school in the western area of the state. I know the father refused to pay for any of it, so she must have taken out a loan. In New England, the average cost of a fifth year today, at a good private school, is $30,000. At a great school like Concord Academy, it's $52,500 per year. Back then my best guestimate for cost would be approximately $8,000 to $10,000 for room, board and tuition.

—31—
Work

School started and my work hours had to be changed. A month into the new schedule, I noticed the manager, Ned, putting me on alone with him on Sunday nights. When asked why, he responded that "Sunday nights were slow." Okay, as I got all the tips. But soon warning lights were going off. He was standing a little too close and getting a bit too touchy. The last Sunday afternoon I worked there, I came in and went downstairs to the small dressing cubicles to change into the uniform. The uniforms were khaki colored with white collars and cuffs that buttoned down the front with a small white apron, like a maid's uniform but tan instead of black. Have I ever mentioned how much I hate surprises? They don't elicit my best responses. That day was no different. The silly manager literally jumped me and tried to remove all my clothing.

Working for the past eight months at an ice cream store had added 30 pounds to my frame. Plus, I was still doing gymnastics and had turned the weight gain into muscle. I was very strong and no stranger to fighting to protect myself. He didn't succeed. I incapacitated him for a short period of time—enough time to grab my clothes and stuff and leave the store. I walked home in shock.

Here's the scene when I got home. The mother's in the kitchen. I said, "Ned tried to rape me." She said, "Are you sure?" I said, "He ripped the uniform off." She said, "Oh." Nothing. I left the kitchen. She never mentioned it again.

So, poof, all my security is gone; I have no job, no money. My solution? Within the week I had a new job at the local hospital in the kitchen cafeteria. It was the best job ever. I was now earning $2.25 an hour. I had work experience. Actually, it was mind melting. I had only cooked one meal ever. That's the good news. The bad news was, unbeknownst to me, three weeks later, the mother rented out a room in our house to Ned, the rapist manager. No lie. No kidding. Unbelievable, right? At the time, I do believe I accused her of being out of her mind. She rented him a room in the attic. "The man in the attic" was back. When I slept, which wasn't well, it was with two knives under my pillow.

I'd like to say I got a lot of support from friends and others. I didn't. That was no one's fault. I only told DB. I swore him to secrecy. He told his parents. I was too ashamed and embarrassed once again to tell anyone else. I had no explanation. I was caught up in an illogical conundrum maze with no exit called cognitive dissonance. I thought the mother was evil. But for there to be evil, there had to be good. Good led one to a conception of a "being greater than oneself," i.e., a God. At this point in life, even considering for a moment the existence of a God caused my eyes to bleed and my mind to implode.

I didn't even begin to deal with the mother being evil until the early 1980s. Reading M. Scott Peck's book *The People of the Lie* in 1983 gave me the most insight. I had never heard of malignant or pathological narcissism before graduate school. One story shared in the book was eerily similar. Not similar in the story, but in the level of evil. It described a family who had been referred for treatment because their youngest son had attempted suicide. His older brother had committed suicide the year before, shooting himself with a gun given as a present by his parents. The next Christmas these parents gave this youngest son the same gun his brother had used to kill himself.

Ex-manager Ned's rental stay did not last long, just a few months. The good news was he was gone before Christmas. The bad news was the mother stopped ordering fuel. Up until well after my younger daughter died and the relentless unfolding of all these memories began, I had never questioned the mother not having enough money to heat the house that winter.

I had to shower at school (without getting my face wet), which meant I had to wash my hair in the sink at home. It was so cold at home. On New

Year's Eve day, DB and I were going into Boston that night to a huge party given by his glad-handed brother, CB. What did I mean by glad handed? My definition was a bit different. It maximized the emphasis on being two-faced and insincere, but with great charisma. In other words, "not real." There was great energy behind his eyes but no real heart, just faucet heart, easily turned on and off. CB would have made a great politician.

Now our house was huge, with 19 rooms. It was stucco with massive Victorian-style first- and second-story porches. Coincidently, DB's paternal grandmother had been born in this house in the same room I slept in. But the house itself was in another location when she lived there. The house had been moved by oxen in the early 1900s from about one and a half miles away. His grandmother delighted in showing me pictures of her "before" house and my sharing my "after" house.

The house, in 1961-62, was heated with coal. The coal furnace was in the basement and was huge and thoroughly fascinating to watch. This was an automated coal furnace. The coal itself was small and almost pulverized and sat in a large bin that had a window-chute access from the driveway. In the winter, big trucks would back down the driveway and fill the bin in the basement through the window, which was about a ten-foot drop. The coal itself would be gathered by a conveyor belt that ran through the coal bin and out, travelling to the furnace where it dropped the coal down into the furnace flames until it burned to ash. Air was blown through this flame pit, forcing the ash from the burned coal upwards. A flat metal rod circled the flame pit and knocked the ash out of the pit down through a grate where it rested until someone shoveled the ash out into barrels.

I mean, it was exactly what every 15-year-old girl in my now afflu-ent little town knew how to do: manage and maintain an old coal furnace delivery system. This particular New Year's Eve, the weather prediction was for single digits that night. The mother became panicked; the pipes might freeze. The coal yard was closed. The mother played helpless, and her silly daughter bought it. Silly daughter called her DB to the rescue. Silly daughter got on the phone and, not knowing who else to call, tried the town police who called the police where the coal yard was located. Those police called the owner who sent someone to open the yard. By this time, it was approximately 6:00 p.m. at night and officially New Year's Eve. DB pulled the backseat out of his car, loaded the car up with as many barrels that would fit, and he and I (the silly daughter) went off to the coal yard with shovels to meet the man. We couldn't take the barrels out of the car and shovel the coal in. The barrels had to stay in the car as, once full, we couldn't lift them. We had to pull the car as close to the coal as possible and shovel little by little into the barrels in the back seat.

Now I can only imagine, of the people who might read this someday, the great numbers who have spent time in their youth in a coal yard at night, on New Year's Eve, with the temperature falling into the teens. Everything in a coal yard is very, very black. Everything that goes into a coal yard not black comes out very, very black. Covered in black coal dust, we headed back to the house and unloaded the coal, bucketful by bucketful into other barrels in the furnace room. This was not conveyor belt-size coal. It was too big and would break the machinery.

The house had three huge basement rooms. The first, with the entrance from the driveway, was about 20 feet by 20 feet and had old slate washtubs and the ringer washing machine. Back then we did not have a clothes dryer. A small woodstove, table and chairs and an upright piano also sat in it. The second basement held the furnace and coal bin. It was approximately 20 feet by 20 feet with floor-to-ceiling shelving. All the pipes and the furnace itself, inside and out, were covered in asbestos. So now the silly daughter (me) must build a fire in the furnace. DB couldn't do it. Poor baby. His family had an oil furnace. Piece of cake, right? The mother couldn't do it. She was too short and nowhere to be found. The house temperature was now approaching the low 40-degree mark. It was a very dark and cold New Year's Eve.

This furnace was ten feet tall with a circumference of approximately six feet. The inside "hearth" itself was round with about a four-foot circumference. As noted before, the hearth had an iron/steel bar pole about 15 inches tall that moved around the circumference of the hearth when the furnace was running, skimming the hot ash down to a grate below where it fell through to be shoveled into barrels to be disposed of.

Starting a small wood fire was no easy task. There was no getting close to start the fire unless one got in the furnace. The trick was to get a small fire going just enough so that when one turned the furnace itself on, triggering the upward draft, this draft did not blow the fire out. It caught. Now the task was to shovel enough coal into the fire to burn and not smother the fire, adding increasing amounts until it was hot enough and large enough to bank it.

It was my second most memorable New Year's Eve.

~ 32 ~
Being Real

Fearful that the mother would rent out a room to someone more dangerous than the rapist manager, I brought home a new friend. Jody was new to our school. She had lived in a neighboring town with her mother and mother's boyfriend. Her mother's boyfriend had been sexually molesting her, and she came to live with her dad and his girlfriend, but it wasn't working out well.

The solution: I brought her home, introduced her to the mother, and informed the mother that Jody had no place to live as she was being sexually molested by her mother's boyfriend and so Jody would now be living with us in the third-floor bedroom. The mother said hi to Judy and that was that until she left at the end of the school year.

It probably challenges credibility that the mother never discussed or even mentioned this arrangement, ever. But, remember, the mother never discussed anything real. Menses could be hemorrhoids and up could be down. Even more startling, that February school vacation, the mother took Jody and me skiing for the week in North Conway, New Hampshire. Lots of snow, lots of fun, until I fell during a lesson and tore a ligament in my right knee, putting me on crutches for a few weeks. Fortunately, I did not lose my part-time job.

Working at the local hospital was spectacular. Initially I worked in the cafeteria's kitchen, prepping lunch and dinner for the hospital employees. I got lots of positive feedback from supervisors, and I made lots of new friends of all ages and backgrounds from other towns. By the first of the year, I had received both a raise and a promotion and soon was working from 7:00 a.m. to 7:00 p.m., Saturday and Sunday, basically being in charge of prepping now for lunch and dinner.

Weekend food preparations were a lot slower than for the rest of the week with fewer staff on but more hospital visitors. Down in the basement by ourselves, our work breaks could get hilarious. Our favorite game was "jousting" in one of the long corridors. This jousting required upright dollies maned by someone strong pushing the "jousters" who were holding long cardboard poles from packaging materials. The goal was to destroy the opponent's pole.

I must have performed my job well, or else they were very short on staff, as just four short months later I was promoted again to weekend charge of the special diet kitchen, all by myself. I was honored, humbled, flabbergasted and, frankly, at barely 17 years old, too inexperienced to be even scared that a girl who couldn't wash dishes or vacuum correctly, who was too stupid, lazy and clumsy, who didn't even deserve a "used postage stamp," and who had only cooked one meal so far in her life, was deemed able to prepare meals for patients with special diets—and get paid to boot. Miraculously, no deaths or poisonings were ever brought to my attention.

Being "real" and knowing the "truth" are a pivotal gauge in measuring my perception of people safety, as in trust. Many profess to be "real"; very few live it.

The Velveteen Rabbit talks about being "real":

"What is Real?" asked the Rabbit one day, when they were lying side by side near the nursery fender, before Nana came to tidy the room. "Does it mean having things buzz inside you and a stick-out handle?"

"Real isn't how you are made," said the Skin Horse. "It's a thing that happens to you. When a child loves you for a long, long time, not just to play with, but *really* loves you, then you become Real."

"Does it hurt?" asked the Rabbit.

"Sometimes," said the Skin Horse, for he was always truthful. "When you are Real you don't mind being hurt."

"Does it happen all at once, like being wound up," he asked, "or bit by bit?"

"It doesn't happen all at once," said the Skin Horse. "You become. It takes a long time. That's why it doesn't often happen to people who break easily, or have sharp edges, or who have to be carefully kept. Generally, by the time you are Real, most of your hair has been loved off, and your eyes drop out and you get loose in the joints and very shabby. But these things don't matter at all, because once you are Real you can't be ugly, except to people who don't understand."

"I suppose you are Real?" said the Rabbit. And then he wished he had not said it, for he thought the Skin Horse might be sensitive. But the Skin Horse only smiled.

"The Boy's Uncle made me Real," he said. "That was a great many years ago; but once you are Real you can't become unreal again. It lasts for always."

Besides "real" being a pivotal gauge, there was love, which could never be just words spoken. Love must always be a choice as well as an action and a behavior. How could something so elusive be forever? How could someone who loved another, abuse or kill that loved one? At ages 15 to 16, I had already spent years thinking long and hard in trying to define what love was and is. I read hundreds of books every year trying to understand relationships between people. The people next door, from ages 10 to 14, I was almost certain, lived it out in front of my eyes for four years. They didn't pretend to be what they weren't. Their behavior showed that they liked each other. They were affectionate but not possessive. Their relationship didn't isolate but pulled everyone in around them. They didn't change personalities depending on who they were with or what life threw at them. Will cried on my 12-year-old shoulder when the telegram came that his oldest daughter had eloped. They had plenty of material wealth but were down to earth. They didn't pretend they were better than anyone else. They drank alcohol but never became mean or cruel or drunk, from what I observed. And I was in their home from morning to night when not in school.

I was definitive about what love wasn't. I knew it didn't live where I lived. I knew words meant nothing. I knew love had little to do with sex. I knew love didn't take, use, lie, ridicule, abuse, possess or kill. However, knowing what love wasn't didn't help me much to know what love was. Love's impossible quest had changed to truth.

Over time DB had become my best friend. I liked him. We had fun together. We did active things together. We laughed a lot. I could relax and be me. He didn't make demands. We didn't like the same music. He tolerated what he called my "rah, rah" music (rock), and I came to love his jazz music. We both loved Sinatra. We talked about cars, driving, work, music, sports, guns, hunting, fishing and guy stuff; we discussed his life, his friends and his family's lives. Rarely did we talk about me, past, present or future, or the parents or the brother. I didn't explain or apologize for them, and he didn't ask. I liked his parents, and, surprise of all surprises, his parents acted as if they really liked me. Our relationship had slowly morphed into something resembling girlfriend and boyfriend.

DB and his family were part of my outside life. My family was part of my inside life. My outside life included school, work, DB and his family, friends and sports and activities. My inside life included the family and time spent in their company, in the house or on the father's boat. There were few activities that overlapped both inside and outside. As a teen, the overlap had grown to reading, music, gymnastics and intake and elimination activities.

This compartmentalization of my life inside to outside is important relative to understanding how I interacted/reacted to and with both environments, how I processed information, interactions and events, and just how separate from each other they were. If possible, I was always busy, moving physically or reading. Amazingly, through some sort of intellectual visional/auditory osmosis, I managed to learn and take in information from school and surroundings. All the fragments seemed to be made of sponge material. They soaked up all information visually and auditorily to be sorted and filed later. Alone, in safety, "inside," I could view all the data recorded. Since "outside" was never as safe as alone, access to data could be limited. If I was afraid, I was limited to no access. Depending on the degree of fear, I could be literally frozen to complete shutdown except for fight or flight.

The boyfriend/girlfriend interaction with DB was more difficult than imagined and more fun. It was much more complicated than just dating. Dating was a delineated period of time, hours that could be limited to once or twice weekly. One could set it up as having a beginning time and an ending time. One, meaning me, was in total control or the date was over. Boyfriend/girlfriend was a relationship. It was ongoing. It had many more parameters than dating or fishing or bowling and a lot more expectations. There were deficits and perks.

The deficits were being touched and dealing with reaction(s) at the time and aftermath reactions when alone. Inside emotions in the here and now and later unknown acceptable and expected responses to kindness and generosity were downsides, along with sharing details and information and confusion when feeling not in control. The perks were feeling liked, feeling included, being part of DB's family, being able to count on continuity in someone, and the beginnings of trust.

Being touched proved to be the most insurmountable problem. All the time and research spent earlier convincing myself of the idea that physical intimacy between males and females was a normal biological function like eating and elimination that would somehow just happen, was far easier to think than actualize. The reality of being intimately touched by a male of my choosing, who I liked and did not fear, proved to be daunting. Being touched by a male was an instant out-of-body experience, an enveloping numbness. However, being touched by a male was not the only event that would trigger this response. Loss and betrayal, emotional blindsiding and the weapons of egocentrics could send me spiraling down. If one qualified being human as being three-dimensional, then my response was instant reduction to one dimension. It was a sudden morphing into just a set of eyes and a mind, absent vulnerability to any incoming stimuli. This is something that now I would describe as a computer with streaming video. Sometimes it went into a withdrawal as far as the cave. Its name was "Somewhere's Else." It was a child's response to a trigger to trauma memories before I knew what trauma triggers were and what they could replay.

The Cave
The land was clay red except for the caves
Which pulsated warm and welcoming.
Glowing soft neon, alive inside.

The first was large and empty
Like life.
I would be cold from its size.
The second was smaller

And I could see loneliness
Hanging from its walls
As more than one person had died there.

The last was so small
I had to crawl and squirm to get in.
I knew it was mine
As it did not hurt and felt warm enough,
Fitting my body like fluid.
It had everything I wanted.
I played inside

A CHILDHOOD DERAILED

Without moving or thinking a thought,
As it knew me.

Someone called my name, catching my breath
Reminding me I could breathe.
I struggled to push myself out,
Stuck, then panicked,
I could not reach who was calling me.

The cave contracted telling me
There was no one out there
That could give me what it would.

I slid back into the warmth of everything's
Nothingness.

The voice stopped calling my name.
I could always go out. Maybe.
Later.

—jp, 1976

The above was written from a dream when I could access the right words that came closest to painting a picture of not only the emotional tone but the physical and visual impact as well. Many of my writings were birthed by rather surrealistic dreams.

Before and after a visit to Somewhere's Else, I would feel really, really bad. I couldn't describe it. There were no words that I could access in explanation to DB's s's asking what was wrong. I could only respond, when it happened with him, that I felt funny. But it wasn't a humorous funny. It was a bit like feeling dizzy, another little bit of feeling that some of you, like a leg or arm, were present while the rest of you were in another world or dimension, and a lot like feeling out of control from far, far away. It was like bits and pieces were spread all over the place, but all of the pieces were watching. This is the closest I can come to describing it now, many years later; I was fragmented and sometimes literally unable to move or speak. It was an eerie and scary conglomeration of feelings and nothingness floating outside of time. Later I was able to recognize that they were most likely pieces of dissociated memories of feeling states from early abuse, split off and unfiled.

There were no references or descriptions in the late 1960s or 1970s of ADHD or spectrum behaviors or reactions. Very little had been written about dissociation and its relationship to trauma and abuse. Although I thought the abuse trauma was the cause of my reactions to touch and intimacy, I now think such strong visceral reactions and sensitivities may have preexisted or paralleled my childhood abuse.

I was 16 and just wanted to be normal. I wanted to have a boyfriend one liked, who liked and respected one back, who came from a family one was starting to love, who appeared to give what one gave right back to one. I wanted it all—the normal, as defined by the standards of the late 1950s and early 1960s—and I was determined that I was going to be able to compete in life with my peers who were not so handicapped. This sadness that I couldn't compete on an equal playing field was very close to the same terrible wound of never being able to try out for the Olympic team in gymnastics. I just wanted to be able to try. I didn't question back then why I was never crushed by defeat for too long. I just refused to be defective. I didn't want there ever to be another arena where I might never even get to try. But I despised being touched.

~33~
High School's End

Despite this handicap, the years when I was 16 to 18 were a stable time in my life. The father was still living out of state; the brother was off to his fifth high school year and then college; DB was going to a technical college; and I was still working part-time. The mother and I were very civil. There were very few incidents after Jody moved into our house.

The most telling event was taking the SATs. Both the brother and I were brought up to believe we would be going to college. It was a given. Both parents were college graduates. I never questioned it. Ninety-eight percent of the peers I knew were going to college. Their parents went to college. That Saturday morning of the SATs the mother woke me up, I dressed, walked to the school and got in the check-in line. My name was not on the list. The mother never sent the paperwork in with a check. Another lesson learned. It was pointless to ask why. I could have even made a case back then for why I ought not to bother taking the SATs because of grades or even because of money. I could have paid for it myself then. But it was hard to understand why the mother would let me go to take the test knowing it couldn't happen. Did she not think I might be embarrassed in front of the teacher monitors and my peers?

I didn't ask why, and I never questioned why I didn't. I didn't question the constant little omissions and commissions then. As for the big ones, like the father touching me or the mother renting a room to the rapist, my actions or non-actions were, at the time, self-protective on a physical and emotional level. Those were skills I'd taught myself. But as for the others, the little wounds that linked together to form the abyss, refused the light of truth until my daughter died when I was 25.

So many of my past and current ways were birthed back then. So many seemingly silly, but harmless things I do to mimic comfort and stability and mock chaos, like eating the same thing every day for weeks or saving every bit of change every day to feel secure or eating ice cream before going to bed to feel loved. They were someone small's version of magic. There were many versions of magic. Later, in the years when clothes still needed to be ironed, feelings of great accomplishment and well-being came because wrinkles were out of multiple blouses. Today, it is mowing my lawn to perfection.

Cigarettes were magical as well. It took me weeks of practice, at age 14, to look cool while smoking. Smoking managed and magically submerged anything I felt. Smoking was my comforter, my solace. It was the first thing I picked up when sad, angry, happy or stressed. Ironically, when taking any of those "Are You Addicted to Nicotine?" questionnaires that one found in doctors' offices or in magazines in the 1970s and 1980s, I never scored as addicted. I didn't have a cigarette until after noon. I didn't smoke at all during my first two pregnancies. And I never had difficulty stopping. I never went through withdrawal. Four times I went three years or more without, only caving during times of great stress and/or loss. Cigarettes were my drug of choice.

They were my magic ritual. They managed everything. And then there were clothes. Clothing needs its own chapter. Although I treated smoking cigarettes as magical, I did understand the chemistry of nicotine. Back before ADHD was a diagnosis, I knew that nicotine helped me think logically. Later I discovered that it released acetylcholine. How does acetylcholine influence human behavior? It plays a role in arousal, memory and learning. It also helps to engage sensory functions upon waking, helps people sustain focus and acts as part of the brain's reward system. Acetylcholine helps maintain rapid eye movement (REM) sleep, the part of sleep during which people dream. Caffeine can have a similar effect. Coffee and a cigarette…it was homeostatic nirvana.

~34~
Clothing

I never confronted the mother or even talked to her about clothing. I can't imagine how a woman who reportedly, by her own shared history, had the best of everything growing up, didn't notice that I had very little clothing that fit or wasn't damaged and had no underwear. I never knew if her not noticing was purposeful. That torn dress and missing buttons incident, when I was four, was representative of the state of my clothing until I was old enough to repair, alter or steal clothing from stores, and later, when working, purchase my own.

I had apparently internalized that my needs did not matter. The brother was always well dressed. He still is impeccable. Only on the island did I ever see him messy or his clothes dirty. Even as a child he was meticulous. Me, not so much. Somewhere between the ages of four to five, the mother lost interest in what I wore or any hygiene issues. Maybe it was because I wasn't interested in girly things. Maybe it was because I was messy. Maybe it was because she just wanted a life-sized doll. Maybe the snakes, frogs and salamanders in my underwear drawer pushed her over the edge. I don't have a clue. Whatever it was, shades of it lasted until I was 44 years old.

As a child I didn't think about it. My stance at four years old over the torn dress and missing buttons never happened again. Protesting to the parents wasn't healthy. I don't think I was a "thing" kid. I don't remember wanting much. Besides, wanting something would have left me vulnerable to being bought, and I was so not for sale. The only things I remember wanting were a horse, a bicycle, a portable record player, records and gymnastics lessons. I got the bicycle at five and the record player at 15. I bought my first horse at 33 years old.

The town attracted professionals. Most residents were middle class to wealthy. The parents were probably on the lower end of middle class financially. But, after my nana's death, they owned her house: no mortgage, just taxes. Even though I played mostly with Margo who, in retrospect, had more toys, bikes, games and clothes than anyone else I knew, I wasn't self-conscious that I didn't have those things. She was my best friend, so I kind of did have all those things. Margo had no problem sharing.

By mid-elementary school the mother obtained most of my clothing from rummage sales at churches or hand-me-downs from friends. She may have been doing this all along and I just didn't notice as I didn't care up until junior high age. Nothing ever fit me, but the clothing was never too small. It was always too big, way too big, or somehow deformed. In parochial school we had to wear dresses. There wasn't much I could do about them, but by sixth grade dresses morphed into skirts.

By the junior high and high school years, I held up the skirts with clothesline rope or old belts that I cut and made new holes in with scissors. The blouses could be covered with bulky sweaters as mostly just the collars mattered. I must have had some decent clothing that fit as one couldn't always wear sweaters. During the sixth grade, I taught myself to sew, and I hemmed and fixed holes as best I could. I had commandeered the mother's old sewing machine and attempted to make skirts with some success, but there was little money for fabric. Shoplifting was easier. The downtown center had a mid-sized department clothing store, higher-end stores, and several smaller women's boutiques as well as one men's store, while many more department-like clothing stores were in a city seven miles away by bus. A lone child would have attracted attention in my small town's retail stores. In the city, not so much. But occasionally I took a chance in the local Woolworth's or mid-sized clothing store.

It still makes my mind bleed that I never thought to steal underwear. I always thought that the most shameful things I dealt with were my teeth and sanitary napkins. It was one thing to hear the father say over and over that he "wouldn't give me a used postage stamp" and quite another apparently to delve into one's perceived level of worth at the age of 12 . That abyss had to wait until the death of my second child.

By high school, in 1959, it was not only not cool to not wear a bra, but it also was considered not proper. Elvis was considered decadent and a sign of the moral decay of America. I did ask the mother for bras, and she did give me her old worn and tattered ones that I had to hand sew to repair and alter. Changing for gym class was the real challenge. I knew to never, ever let peers see the state of my underwear and device machinations that held my clothes up. Getting dressed or changing clothes without baring any skin is still an operational skill. I can change clothes anywhere. Ironically, by the 1960s, skirt lengths were slowly going up, and I was not the only girl using devices to hike them up.

Once I was working steadily part-time, my perceived need to shoplift clothes ended. That, coupled with DB's mom making me clothes, added significantly to my wardrobe. I had clothing that fit. The mother never seemed to notice either any new shoplifted clothing or items made by DB's mother. I only mention this because my own daughter went through a shoplifting phase in her late junior high school years. I knew what I had purchased for her and washed versus "new" items in the laundry.

Clothes were magic too. They bestowed value and identity. They created the illusion of belonging to a group. Eventually all the RAFs had to have their preferences. They each had their own style. How did the mother miss these warning flags? It is mind-boggling when one strings together everything that was missed. Fortunately for me, such stringing didn't happen until I was an adult. Even then, I barely made it through all those strings intact.

By 18, shoplifting was an addiction. I stole mostly clothes. It's hard to tell as I simply never thought about it. It wasn't a constant thing; it just seemed to pop up, impulsively. It still was a high, like the endorphins from gymnastics. It wasn't even a predictable thing. It could be many, many months in between those moments. Retrospectively, it was most likely a response to feeling needy or badly about myself. Stealing was a rush and endorphins the result. It never caused any bad feelings until I was 32 and the Voice kicked in.

DB's mother continued to make mine and my children's clothes through the early years of my marriage to her son. I also had a sewing machine by then, and there was never a year past 14 when I didn't work, at least part-time, or from the house. Having no clue how healthy marriage relationships worked, I just went along. I never asked for much in the early years, never had a clothing allowance for myself or the children. I just had money for food, and not much money for that either. Food shopping was a challenge, and I learned to add items in my head rather than be embarrassed in my small, wealthy little town. So, meats like roast beef or ham, I stole. Turkey and chicken were inexpensive enough and too big to steal. It still was a feat to smuggle a roast beef or ham under one's clothing when one only weighed roughly 100 pounds.

The father, when I was growing up, had controlled the mother by withholding or threatening to withhold money. I had given up as a child asking for much of anything. Life when married to DB was always a drama on the verge of bankruptcy. I believed him. He handled the money. And I didn't ask; I just stole what I needed. Although I don't specifically recall actual details, I most likely helped myself to his loose change or one-dollar and five-dollar bills. It was the "MO" of how I saved from childhood.

I don't remember DB ever buying me any piece of clothing, giving the children a toy, or willingly participating in any of their sport activities. I don't remember him giving me gifts, which later became a huge issue in our marriage. It wasn't about gifts in and of themselves, but the gesture. Near the end of our marriage, he did give me $300 to buy something for myself. I bought a clock for the house.

At age 32, in 1977, the Voice struck after a very productive clothing run on a local discount designer chain store. This time the Voice was accompanied by a picture of the headlines in the local paper showing my picture after being arrested for shoplifting and the consequences of this on my children. I was horrified. I never stole another thing. It wasn't easy. I also decided, as a mother, that I needed to be a role model to my children and became super honest, with some funny results.

The day I made the choice to no longer steal things, I went food shopping at the "stupid market." I disliked food shopping so much that I only did it every other week at this time and later only once a month after I bought a freezer. The food purchase amount was about $200. I wrote a check, handed it to the checkout person, who then handed me back the receipt and my check. I was out of the store before I realized that she'd given me back the check. So, after I put the groceries in the car, I walked back inside and gave her back the check. It wasn't easy.

The following day, I headed to southern Maine to see my therapist. Rather than seeing him at the college, I saw him at his office there. Besides the privacy factor, he lived with a view of the ocean that was worth the drive, and being able to regularly purchase fresh fish, lobster and shellfish rocked. Stopping at the local seafood market on my return, I bought fresh scallops and lobster, handing the person a $50 bill. She handed me back change as if I had given her $100. I corrected her mistake. Something like both incidents happened almost weekly for the next several years.

~35~
Post High School

The school year 1963-64 found me attending business school in a city in New England. The mother did pay for the first year. It was a two-year program. I couldn't work part-time anymore because traveling to and from school took one and three-quarters hours each way by bus. But I had enough money saved by 1960s standards for an 18-year-old. I did work on weekends at the beginning of Christmas season and during weeks for break at a local store in town.

That fall, life with the mother was mostly quiet and uneventful. Most friends from town were off at college and any socializing was with friends from business school. The brother was at college near Maryland. The father was still living out of state. He would come back occasionally when we all went to visit the brother. Visiting the brother in college was okay for two reasons. First, I got to drive all the way from our small New England town to almost Washington, D.C. and back. Second, the brother was in a fraternity, and I got to date some of his friends. It was a whole new level of partying.

Business school was an eye-opener. I really liked it. I had lots of fun and friends. We played bridge every day during lunch. I loved card games as well as board games. They were a respite from all the storms and an equalizer. Playing bridge in high school during cafeteria or study hall time had somehow put me on the adult substitute bridge player list in the town teams when a regular adult couldn't play. That, again, was amazing. The mother must have been the most trusting person in town. Some adult would come and pick me up and bring me home. She never knew the person or whose house I was in.

The surprise of all surprises was how well I did in business school without much effort. It was here that I discovered I had an eidetic memory. I thought most people could remember just about everything they read and on what page sought-after information could be found. I had never even used a bookmark. I got straight A's in all subjects. Because my GPA was so high, I was excused from final exams. A few of the teachers suggested that I should consider going to college. But my understanding then was that because I hadn't taken the SATs in high school, that was a closed door.

At the end of the first year, as I was in the top five in grades of first-year students, I was eligible to be placed for the summer break at a business. It was full-time paid employment, and I was hired by a law firm.

So many new experiences. Through a friend who briefly dated a race car driver, I became enthralled with formula car racing and became part of a local driver's pit crew when racing in New England. I so wanted to drive. There were plenty of teachers willing to show a girl the ropes, but racing was so expensive and sponsors for women drivers few. The love of speed and performance were an addiction of their own.

That summer, another new world opened. I rode the train, Monday through Friday, with other young people whom I knew who worked in the city as well. I also walked a lot. I walked to my local train station in the morning and back.to work So I walked approximately three miles, five days a week, in three-inch heels. That didn't include miles walking to stores and back, mostly discount designer stores, on my lunch hour. I'd found clothing heaven.

I loved my job. I really liked my boss, who specialized in real estate law, and most of the other lawyers and secretaries who worked at the firm. They treated me well and fairly. I opened my first checking and savings accounts. Other than clothes, train fare and lunches, I had no expenses and so saved whatever was left. At the end of the summer, they offered me a full-time position and a raise with one condition. I had to seriously consider going to college Mat night. I agreed and took the job.

DB had graduated from technical college in June. He had signed up for and was off to flight training school by the end of that summer. Flying jet planes was his dream. Watching the jets take off from the roof of the city's airport in the early 1960s was a frequent date. This was the time of Vietnam, and it was better to sign up than be drafted.

Unfortunately, DB was unable to finish basic training due to physical reasons. He was discharged from flight school and sent home to await active status for the armed services. It never happened. Unable to find a job locally, DB was hired by a company out of state and moved there in the winter of 1964. The move soon strained our relationship, and we broke up.

I continued to visit DB's parents regularly, depending on my being able to use the mother's car. By the spring of my 19th birthday, my life had morphed into a predictable schedule: school, out with friends and dating. A fraternity brother of the brother, whose parents lived 30 minutes away, asked me out on spring break, and we began dating steadily after his graduation in May.

Kevin was a great guy. I liked him a lot. He was smart, steady, sincere and safe. He got serious very quickly. At 19, I didn't want serious. I wanted fun. On Friday, July 3, 1964, I phoned a girlfriend who said she and a few other friends were leaving that afternoon to go to a music festival for the weekend. Without a single thought, I wanted in on this and said, "Pick me up."

Did I call Kevin and cancel our plans for the weekend? No. I just left. In many ways, I've always felt this was one of the worse things I'd ever done to anyone. That was mostly because Kevin seemed to be a decent, sincere person. Our plans were dinner Friday night at his parents' home, later bridge, and then on Saturday, dinner with his parents followed by fireworks. At 19, that sounded so boring.

~36~
Drew

The music festival was amazing. But not from the music. I don't remember much about the music. I remember we had to park miles away and walk to the outdoor arena. On our way through this parking lot to the admission box to buy tickets, my friend Mary spotted an old boyfriend. They talked and talked. Bored, my eyes spotted a guy lying on the top of a car, listening to the music. He was the most gorgeous male creature I had ever seen. Without a single thought, I walked over and said hi. His name was Drew. He turned out to be Mary's ex-boyfriend's friend. He was from a town just six miles from my home. In a split second, I decided that this was the man whom I would lose my virginity to.

Now for some readers, saying I would "lose my virginity" may seem odd since so much of the abuse implied when I was a child was sexual. Dissociation of extreme abuse is so powerful that I believed I was a virgin.

I have no recollection of the particulars, but I do know that we never went in to the festival. We stood in the parking lot for hours talking and just gazing into each other's eyes. Who knew that could be fun? Then we just left in his car.

I don't remember ever saying anything to my friend Mary or whether Drew said anything to his friend. I just remember leaving and ending up on a beautiful beach all night with Drew and sharing a sleeping bag. It was so totally romantic. I wasn't scared. I wasn't anxious. Time just seemed to stop. I was literally enthralled. This was the night.

And nothing happened. We talked, gazed at the stars and the moon, and talked some more. On Saturday we wandered around, ate probably, gazed into each other's eyes, and talked. Saturday night was a repeat of stars and moon and sharing his sleeping bag on the beach. On Sunday we went over to where the father docked his boat. Somehow, in my enthralled, blurred memory of this great love, besides the romantic flavor of the entire weekend, the only other thing I remember vividly is taking Drew to introduce him to the parents. The parents liked him. That should have been the first warning.

I'm sure I must have told them his name and where he was from, but I don't remember. What I do remember was that the parents never asked any parent-like questions. I told the mother I didn't know when I would be home and asked her to call my work and tell them I was sick. And she did it. So Drew and I wandered all over for several more days, and we meandered our way back to home and my house.

I remember nothing real and concrete about the time with him. I don't remember if I had a change of clothes, if I showered or when I ate or even if we ate. I came home knowing Drew drank tea, worked at a business in his hometown, and liked classical music. He was 26, and I was 19 and still a virgin.

We did date for several more months. We drank lots of tea, listened to hours of classical music, talked, parked a lot and kissed. Nothing else, just kissing. I was really frustrated. Not sexually frustrated—I had no idea what that even was. I was more frustrated that I couldn't seem to influence him to make a move. I met his family and visited their beautiful "summer" place in the mountains. It was an idyllic summer. However, I didn't sleep much.

Saturdays and Sundays I slept until 2:00 to 3:00 p.m. and did my laundry. During the work week I was up at 5:30 and in bed by 2:00 a.m. I lived on coffee and snacks when I realized I hadn't eaten. I kept that schedule going until the end of November when reality began to encroach on thralldom. This whirlwind schedule of sleep deprivation, coffee and food as an afterthought dropped my weight down to 100 pounds. At five feet, six inches, I was thin and a wonderful size two. This was the time when thin became in and Twiggy was the rage in the UK and here.

What should have sounded alarms didn't. The mother liked Drew. I mean, she really liked him. At times she behaved as if she were dating him. In my more aware moments, she seemed "in love" with him as well. She hovered with a girlish demeanor, waiting on him and listening attentively to his every word discussing art, music and theater. She never hovered with anyone else I ever dated. Drew was amazingly polite even by mid-1960s' standards. In many ways he was right out of a British Victorian novel. It was the only time I remember when something I did and someone I was involved with elicited her approval. I never shared with anyone that he was an ex-felon, and I never asked what he went to prison for.

It all ended right before Christmas. I never knew why; he just moved on to a woman with three kids. Although I was immune to rejection by others, this was different. I felt it. That first boyfriend in ninth grade who slept with my best friend Margo was a great lesson and hardly left a mark compared to this. Besides this, that boy's trading me in for a senior with a sports car was a minor ego blow. I moved on. But this breakup was somehow different. Maybe it was because I chose him. The others had all chosen me. The protective bubble had some cracks.

~37~

Its Name Was Grief

I was depressed, although I doubt I named it that at the time. It just felt heavy, like sinking into quicksand. It was a very yucky feeling. Doubly troubling, I became aware that a shade of this feeling reared its head every year at Christmas time, becoming increasingly stronger as New Year's approached. I never had given it any thought before, never wondered why. So, I gave it thought. I knew I had never understood why people made such a big deal of celebrating New Year's. I had just put it in the file with dancing around a maypole, another weird custom. But New Year's was a custom with an edge. It really annoyed me. There were plenty of things and holidays I considered useless, but I didn't get feeling all yucky and irritated at them.

I just wanted it to be over with. I ust wanted this New Year's thing to get started, pick up speed and sail far past New Year's Day. It was like treading water, caught in a void. Treading time, waiting for an end. This yucky feeling had an anchor attached, making it hard to move on. Suddenly, I wondered, when had Nana died? I asked. The first of January was the answer. Did knowing this make the yucky feeling any better? Yes and no. Yes, because the New Year's anchor was now attached to something solid: death, loss. And no, because how could one be depressed about the loss of someone one could hardly remember? However, it took the sting out of losing Drew. Maybe his rejection wasn't the heaviness. He had nothing to do with my nana. But they both were gone.

This epiphanistic realization about the loss of my nana put the blow of losing Drew into a much more manageable perspective. So, that New Year's Day I went to visit DB's 's parents. Sitting in their living room chatting with them I eventually asked how he was doing. His mom's response was, "He's here. Why don't you go up and say hi?" He had come home for the holidays, and his car had died. It wasn't worth fixing. He wanted to buy a new car but needed a down payment. We talked for a while, and then he asked if I would lend him $1,000 for the down payment. I said yes. He also announced that he was leaving his job and getting one locally. He did. And although we just started hanging out as friends after his return, it morphed into dating again.

I loved the car he bought. It was all performance. Turbo, manual five speed on the floor, and moved low to the ground like a cat, it cornered like a formula one car. There were several, very curvy roads in our little town that were used as a racetrack for those minded to do so late at night when they were little used. We found out this little car could really move.

Late that spring DB asked me to marry him. What he said was, "Shit, or get off the pot." My response was, "Let's just live together." He wouldn't, saying his parents would have a fit. It just wasn't done in our little town in 1965. He did inform me that if I said no, he was leaving for California. I don't remember exactly, but I eventually said yes as I know we told the mother in June and she said that no, I couldn't marry him. I asked, "Why?" She never did have an answer as to why. My response to her was, "Fine, we'll elope."

I totally dreaded getting married. I thought the dread had nothing to do with DB and more to do with the concept of marriage as viewed in the mid-1960s. I never wanted to have even the appearance of being owned, and that is how I viewed marriage. To anyone. Mostly it had to do with anyone having any power over any aspect of my life. There was no way to explain how I felt to DB; there was no way he could possibly understand. One had to have experienced the darkness of my family, the void and the control and chaos. I needed to be free. He wouldn't just live together so I kept begging him to elope. He wouldn't.

Growing up in a wealthy little town comes with a plethora of expectations one absorbs from not only one's family but also from friends and teachers and family friends. That included being cared for on a certain materialistic level, access to medical care and opportunities like one's peers become seemingly a given, along with the normative celebrations of certain milestones in one's life. As every encounter with milestone markers involving the parents had been missed as well as scoffed at, I knew down to my toes that my wedding held the potential of parental drama on a scale of humiliation not previously experienced. And I wasn't wrong. They had power again.

I had never stopped to add up all the milestones and celebrations not attended by family. I'm assuming that the parents were at the piano recitals at ages five to eight, but I have no memories of them at dance recitals. No family ever saw or supported my gymnastic events. The mother went to football games and track meets as the brother was on those teams in high school, but no one came to games when I was on the cheerleading squad. The mother did go to my high school graduation. The father never went to anything.

My wedding would be added to the list along with the shame of my teeth, the untreated medical issues over the years, the lack of underwear and the misfitting clothing, no sanitary napkins and not being worth "a used postage stamp." However, weddings were very public. There would be no hiding the level of venom my family expressed towards me from my friends and DB's parents and family. I was terrified numb.

That fall and winter the mother slowly came around as my eloping would have been a narcissistic blow. Both parents announced that there would be very little money for this event. I would have to pay for it. They would plan and dictate the event, but they refused to share those plans with me.

DB's mom gave him her mother's diamond for my engagement ring. It was very old and would have to be recut to be reset as a solitaire. I didn't want it touched. I designed an "old style" setting and had it made. It was beautiful. I was so used to not having any expectations that it never occurred to me, and no one pointed out, that my designing and paying to have my own engagement ring made maybe said a lot about my future husband, money and success of our marriage. But even if someone had pointed it out, I doubt I would have been able to grasp any implied warning.

Even by age 21, relying only on myself was so deeply imbedded in my personality that whole interactional, culturally normative expectations and boundaries were never absorbed or erected. The plus side of this was being spared a great deal of disappointment and discouragement. So, going shopping all by myself and paying for my wedding dress fell right into the no expectations of my early life. I didn't realize most daughters didn't pay for their own wedding dress and wedding for years. But I was in the middle of a living hell of drama, where one week the wedding was on and the next it was off. And DB still refused to elope. Denial and dissociation can be useful tools for survival.

145

It truly was six months of drama hell, and it had almost nothing to do with my future husband or his family. I loved his parents. I know he and his brothers' wives thought they were difficult, but they had no idea what difficult really looked like. I know that when his dad got angry, they all scattered like chickens. At one time, long before I knew him, he reportedly had been an alcoholic. His angry outbursts didn't even register on my rage-man scale.

~38~
Getting Married

Poor DB. I told him I would marry him. I did love him as much as I was capable of defining love as a construct with parameters. But I also told him our marriage had to be a different kind of marriage. I would respect him if he respected me. We were equals. I would never obey him, and I didn't know if I could be faithful. That was sort of a strange thing to say considering I was a virgin and had no interest in sex. But I didn't mean the faithful thing in a sexual context as I didn't have a sexual context. I had reduced sexuality down to an animalistic biological function and a choice. I considered it closer to the digestion and elimination of food, another necessary inconvenience. It occupied the third lowest possible rung on the ladder of life. It was necessary back then for procreation but had no higher or grander meaning or context. It was a freedom thing. I couldn't be owned. I needed to be free.

The reality of my childhood had been a seemingly unending trap, an enslavement. I can never capture in words what freedom meant and means to me. I so worshipped at the altar of free choice and free will. So much of that part of my childhood and adolescence had been marking and treading time waiting for moments, days and years to end, waiting until I had control of my own life and who came in and out of it. Every cell in my being screamed to be free.

It's probably impossible to imagine what the experience of living as if you were invisible to your own family entailed. I mean invisible in the sense of who you really were. I cowered in a dark space, my essence tightly wrapped and protected, deflecting the parents and the brother's projected poison from touching me with the darkest, most hidden parts of their own souls, so that they could never see who they really were, forcing me to carry the weight of their abuse and rejection for them all. The psychology of abusers has called these behaviors projection, displacement, scapegoating and gaslighting.

The parents insisted on my marrying in the Catholic church. If getting married in the Catholic church brought me one step closer to being free, I would do it. I just wanted the whole thing to be over. If anything, my attitude toward the Catholic church was worse at that point than when I was younger. I don't think the priests were very keen on performing the ceremony for me either, especially since I was marrying a non-baptized person. Basically, a pagan. Of course, that classification totally delighted me.

My pagan fiancé was not pleased to have to go through these pre-Cana classes or at being married in a Catholic church. But he still refused to elope. The six weeks of classes were not too bad, considering that even taking them was a lie in and of itself. I had no intention of raising any child or any creature in that church. By age 20, I was basically a nihilist or, if there could be such a thing, as an existential nihilist. I alone was in control of my life; I alone would define who I was and what I believed in, in the day I found myself in. I was an agnostic with atheistic leanings. I had no compunctions about lying to a priest. I just wanted this marriage thing to be over and move on with my life.

The only person other than myself whom I had any expectations of was DB. I believed he loved or liked me enough. I had tested him for years. I believed he had my back. He'd seen me when I was In and when I was Out. PTSD wasn't a named entity in 1965. So it was that some days I just felt "funny" and would withdraw.

The spring and summer before my marriage in September were dissociative. The parents made the decision that the reception would be in the yard. And to the father's credit, he did an amazing job with the gardens and its design. The parents, despite continual, repeated declarations that they were not paying for the wedding, eventually ended paying for most of the reception. But it was like being a living yo-yo, being yanked up, down and all around, day in and day out. It was a seemingly never-ending cycle of "go away, come here." One day stands out in memory. Tired, I took a hot bath and several hours later I seemingly awoke, sitting up in cold water. It was a summer of lost time. A summer of dissociation.

The wedding dress bought in June was a size four. It had to be taken in professionally by a seamstress twice before the wedding. I was basically a size zero by my marriage date. Everything I owned was too big. I weighed 88 pounds. If they had BMI calculations back in 1966, mine would have been 14. Was I anorexic or bulimic? I don't think so. I neither gorged nor purged. I was nauseous most of the time and never even thought about eating or food as I had stopped feeling hungry.

Two weeks before the wedding, the father dramatically announced that he would not only not walk me down the aisle and give me away, but that he also would not contribute any more money and would not even go. This was the first time DB's parents had ever seen me come close to being upset. They didn't seem that surprised by the father's pronouncement. DB must have shared seven years of exposure to the parents. His dad graciously offered to walk me down the aisle, and I thankfully accepted.

The father waffled back and forth. The parents argued and fought. I spent as much time away from the house as possible, "treading water" until the moments I found myself in, passed.

And the time did pass. The day did come. I don't remember much of it, except, of course, I got my menses. The father did walk me down the aisle. Apparently the organ broke as we walked. I didn't hear it. I was way too busy concentrating on not fainting and not wetting myself. People told me the reception was great.

I was mistaken in my panic. There were too many of the parents' friends and associates at the wedding and reception for them to publicly shame me. They kept the drama close to home with just a family audience. It was over.

~39~
Post-Wedding

I am not sure if I drank too much champagne at the wedding, was exhausted, neglected to eat for who knows how many days, or all of the above. But I became ill in the hotel dining room when I tried to eat and fell right asleep when we got back to our room.

Off we went the next morning to the farm, still a virgin. DB had no money for a real honeymoon, and I'd spent all mine on the wedding. We only stayed at the farm for a few days. It became a bit tense. He tried, but I was still a virgin. I had never heard of panic attacks.

We had rented a small house about 40 minutes from where we grew up and one and a half miles from the train station. We only had the one car, which DB took to work. I still worked in the city about an hour away. . I remember walking home from the train station often, but DB did pick me up at the station much of the time.

By the Columbus Day weekend, I was still a virgin. Although back then neither DB nor I knew what a panic attack was, that is the closest description of what happened to me when we attempted to consummate the marriage. However, my reaction was much more visceral and physically combative. I tried to stop this reaction, but it would have been easier to stop hiccups.

That weekend, DB had had enough. Technically, he raped me, if you color in using restraint and force. But I never used that word until now. Nor did

I ever hold it against him. I didn't blame him, but I think he blamed himself. We never really talked about it. We, who as a couple for years, talked about seemingly everything, did not talk about this or about much. He didn't touch me again, for 15 months.

No one has ever accused me of talking too much, except teachers. I literally lived the maxim, "loose lips sink ships." I didn't talk about how I felt or about other people or share my opinion. DB and I talked about the things we did or wanted to do, like sports and activities. We went to as many Red Sox and Bruin games as we could afford. When the Boston Patriots started up and played in Harvard stadium, we went to every home game. We talked about fishing, hunting and bowling and boats and cars. I had had few positive female role models. I had never observed either gender actually discussing much, let alone something important. Fighting, yelling and arguing, yes. I don't think we knew how to really talk. Neither one of us had ever talked or expressed much feeling. I did not even know I had any.

We had several close couple friends living nearby whom we saw practically every weekend. Playing bridge one night with the wives in early December, I happened to mention that my shoes had become tight or no longer fit me. This prompted dozens of questions from all three girlfriends who concluded I was pregnant. Impossible, I insisted. After all, I was the girl who only had her menses maybe two times a year. I was the girl whose doctor told her she may not be able to have children and would need to see a fertility specialist when she wanted to have children. I was the girl who had only had intercourse once. And, ultimately, I was the girl, a child really, who was two months pregnant. I also had toxemia and nausea 24/7.

I, the girl who never felt hungry, was ravenous constantly but couldn't eat any processed foods, deli meats or canned foods. I absolutely could eat no foods with salt or any type of sodium. Hard-boiled eggs and ice cream became the staples of my diet. I worked, drove, relaxed and slept with a wastebasket with me always. My mouth and tongue felt alien, as if they belonged to someone else. I kept some type of lozenge in my mouth almost constantly as the taste of my own tongue caused ongoing, unrelenting, intense nausea and vomiting. The only chewable thing that tasted right, besides ice cream, and fought and defeated the nausea, was Bazooka bubblegum. I bought a case.

At four months, I was almost hospitalized for dehydration after a weekend of nonstop vomiting. The doctor put me on medication. DB and I wanted children someday, but we were in no way financially prepared for one so soon. We needed the two incomes. Fortunately, the house rental agent let us out of our lease and, by the sixth month of pregnancy, we moved into the third floor of the parents' house in March. The space was a huge area. We had a living room, which basically ran the length of the house, approximately 12 feet by 25 feet, a bedroom 10 feet by 15 feet, and another room 10 feet by 12 feet. All the rooms, including the hall, had large walk-in closets, while the living room and large bedroom had built-in drawers. We only lacked our own bathroom. That was the good news.

The father was still working and living in another state. He rarely came up to visit. The mother was still working and visited him on the weekends. The brother was working for a company in Boston and had an apartment in Cambridge. DB and I almost had the house to ourselves.

My due date was June 17th. I was terrified. There wasn't a day that went by where I didn't say to myself, "A child shouldn't have a child." But I was also excited. I wanted children. I was over the top when I first experienced quickening. Despite the constant nausea, vomiting and toxemic food restrictions, I liked being pregnant.

DB's mom was knitting and sewing clothes, I was painting walls and furniture and buying little outfits. We basically had all used furniture and not much money. I still went to work every day by train, walking to and back from the train station. Despite the severely restricted diet, toxemia persisted, and, by the sixth month of pregnancy, I weighed almost 150 pounds. My feet had swelled from a size six shoe to a seven and a half. Still, I was basically happy and looking forward to life. I stopped work the first week in June, two weeks before my expected due date. And waited... and waited...and waited.

I was basically nine months pregnant, huge, uncomfortable and home by myself all day. We still only had one car, which DB drove to work and back. The mother's school vacation started at the end of the second week in June, and she was off to the father's boat for most of the summer. I had basically no preconceived ideas about pregnancy and delivery and had been programmed as a child to never ask questions. I had no idea what to expect.

I was bored, alone and did I mention uncomfortable. Sleeping was difficult because I was huge. I weighed by then about 175 pounds. I saw the obstetrician every week. Not much was happening. I had some minor cramping, but nothing I thought was noteworthy. By the end of June, nothing still was happening. Remember, despite the doctor's doubting me, I knew the date of conception. Average gestation period is 280 days or 40 weeks, but I was naïve and figured the doctor knew. No one questioned doctors then. Wrong. I should have looked it up like I looked up everything else. But I didn't. Doing so never even entered my mind.

~40~
My Sally

Most people do not spend much time examining where the sense of their self-value comes from. If they have that sense, it feels as if they've always had it from the inside. If they don't, it feels like they never will, and they look for someone, anyone and eventually anything to give it to them. One needs to be taught as a young child the ways to care for oneself or, at a minimally practical level, be exposed to the ways and means of appropriate hygiene and self-protection. Value of self does not arrive intrinsically. It is a gift conveyed by the action, behaviors and words of others.

Some of the most difficult tasks I've struggled to learn centered around taking care of myself, learning and accepting it was okay to do so, and doing so. Like sports and any new achievement, it meant practice, practice, practice. But it also remains a self-taught skill; it was not an inner garment worn from the inside out but rather something identified on the outside and put on, like a coat.

It's still a difficult topic for me to try to even think about. It's like a group of selfhood sinkholes. Over the years I've been able to fill in so many of the holes. But some still seem to sneak up on me, and all I seem to be able to do is skirt the outer perimeter, peer over the edge, recognize the depth and erect warning lights. It's still difficult to recognize what is an unacceptable level *of pain or illness that necessitates a need for a physician or an emergency room visit. I still automatically default to questioning if I am actually ill or even really in pain.*

By the beginning of the second week in July, I was beyond restless. At almost 200 pounds, "uncomfortable" had left and "miserable" had moved in. Sleep was impossible; moving was arduous. Constant minimal cramping interfered with any position. I didn't know anything about Braxton Hicks contractions and had even less of an idea what a real contraction would feel like.

By mid-July, due to worsening of toxemia, the obstetrician induced labor. DB dropped me off at the hospital, went to a friend's house, and partied that night, showing up 40 hours later after the baby was born. Sally was an eight-pound, eight-ounce, 21-inch beauty. (See Chapter 7 for the full description of the fun labor and delivery.)

DB's parents were beyond overjoyed. She was their Sally. My mother-in-law made her dresses and sweaters and coats and mittens and everything in between. She knitted several one-piece snowsuit-like outfits that we zipped Sally into that were beyond adorable. She gave me a year of private yoga instruction to get "my figure" back and made me more sweaters and clothes. Both of DB's parents wanted Sally as many weekends as we were willing to send her.

Back then, one stayed in the hospital for three to four days, depending on all being well with mother and baby. Once I could get her awake, Sally drank four ounces of formula every four hours that first day. Once home on the fourth day, she drank eight ounces every six to seven hours and slept through that first night and every night thereafter. Sally rarely cried. I had to wake her up in the morning or later I'd find her in her crib quietly watching her mobiles move in the breeze from the open window. She stayed awake most of the day, and I would talk to her constantly as I did chores. By six weeks after her birth, I was back to weighing 100 pounds.

I interacted with Sally almost constantly during the day, but sadly I wasn't a very affectionate mother. In all my research and head knowledge of parenting, I missed the affection thing. It wasn't that I wasn't affectionate just with her; I wasn't affectionate with anyone. I never craved being held or touched. I avoided it, stiffening when anyone touched me. I had always assumed this was from the abuse as I had an unusually strong startle response, ducking as if I was about to be hit, but, in retrospect, not liking being touched or held may have preceded the abuse.

After her birth, DB and I headed to the farm as often as we could, at least every other weekend. He decided to winterize it as much as possible for the fall and deer hunting, closing off the upstairs, shutting of the water from the well, and draining the pipes.

By that fall, we had moved to an apartment on the other side of town and our lives settled into a routine. The family below us were Mormon. They shared an enormous amount of reading material with us, which I enjoyed. It was fascinating what people believed. Life was without any crises of significance. I apparently fell down the stairs walking in my sleep and sprained an ankle. The mother also wanted overnights with Sally on the weekends. Her house was not as safe or as clean as DB's parents' house, so that did not happen for extended periods. She usually got Sally for drop-offs after dinner on a Saturday and a pick-up in the morning when the father was not there.

Sally would touch me a lot, and by age six months would do some curious actions toward me that I didn't really understand at the time. She would suddenly poke me in the eye or stick her hand in my mouth, which, of course, caused me to pull away. I didn't know that back then, as far as visual emotionality goes, I resembled Spock on Star Trek. She apparently just wanted a visual emotional reaction. She didn't let go of wanting such a reaction for 20-plus years. The town nurse in this small town visited new, first-time mothers once a month and documented a child's progress. Sally said her first words at six months. No kidding, no bragging. It was documented. By the time she was one year old, she spoke in paragraphs.

We used to joke that once she started, she never stopped. She talked constantly. Her father and I would jokingly and lovingly refer to her as Ms. Motor Mouth. Car rides were hysterically noisy. She voiced an accompaniment on long trips that ran nonstop until we arrived at a destination. It went like this, "Awgadydogadyawgadydogadyawegadydawgady," for hours. We played our music tapes loudly.

She also never crawled. One day, at nine months, she just stood up, wobbled a bit and then ran. From that point on, Sally was nonstop energy, night and day. She didn't sleep much, would eat anything, including dirt and worms, and bounced in place watching Sesame Street and Mr. Rogers. The joke in the house was that if we could get her to lie still for five minutes, she might fall asleep, but only for a little while. But she was so, so happy. She loved life and the world around her. Keeping her safe became a challenge.

One of the more dangerous escapes she had at 14 months was somehow getting out of our second-floor apartment, making it to the driveway, getting in our station wagon, pushing the clutch down, and rolling out of the drive-way. Doors and car were now locked. Her roaming the house at night while we slept was not safe. Her pediatrician gave us a prescription-authorized safety harness to keep her in her bed. She could roll over, sit up, and play on her bed, but she couldn't get out. The Arnold Arboretum and Poison Center in Boston knew me by first name, and I learned to identify almost every poisonous plant in New England. But she was so happy.

— 41 —
New Cousins

One of DB's cousins, Roger, started coming up to their family place next to the farm the summer of Sally's birth. The house had fallen into disrepair, and none of Roger's other siblings had tried to keep it up. They would come up to the family cemetery down the road on Memorial Day weekend and say hi, but that had been their total interest for years. For whatever reason, at that time Roger and his wife decided to pay some attention to the old house.

Roger and his wife had six children. Three were mostly grown and either on their own already or about to be. The younger girls ranged in age from 8 to 14 when we first met them. Roger owned his own business. They started coming up every weekend and working on the house, making it livable again.

DB and I didn't become friends with them until the winter of 1967-68. With his parents taking the baby for every other weekend and with limited money, we'd just go off to the farm. Gas was still cheap and cars a lot easier to fix. Once deer season passed and the snow came, it was cozy, like camping. The farm was on one side of the mountain and skiing on another. Skiing wasn't as popular as it was to become in the late 1970s and early 1980s, so ticket prices and equipment were reasonable. The ski area at the mountain was still small and family-owned and operated.

Late afternoons would find DB and I over at his cousin's place. Eventually, our visits grew into cooking dinners with them and playing penny poker and having lots and lots of laughs. Roger owned the first Ski-doo I ever saw, and he and his wife would go off for long rides through the mountainside and pastures. That winter flew by. Despite being new parents on the poor-ish side, life was wonderful and beyond. I was married to the only being in the world I trusted. I so loved these cousins of DB's. They were simple, down-to-earth, "a spade is a spade" type of people. I loved their children. It was a wonderful time. We visited them for weekends at their home and they visited us.

Winter at the farm was beautiful and peaceful, carpeted in snow. And cold. It was a happy time, not a lot of bills, not a lot of stress. I was happy. The only elephant in the room was our physical relationship. There wasn't any. DB didn't make any moves or indicate interest in any way. On our last weekend in March at the winter farm, I told him, "Come here. I want to make another baby." He did and we did. And Missy was conceived.

When I was approximately six months pregnant with Missy, Roger and his wife announced that they would not be going to the farm any longer. Other relatives of Roger's were demanding shares of time at the farm but were not willing to contribute to its upkeep or reimburse Roger for all the renovations he had completed. They were leaving and buying a camp on a lake. I had no clue, up until this news, how attached I had become to these people. I didn't know how much I considered them my family. I started crying and could not stop for days, triggering premature labor, which required medication to stop the contractions. Another loss.

Words cannot possibly describe how I felt about being pregnant with Missy. Elation maybe, joy possibly. That was even with the morning sickness and toxemia again. She was special. Not that Sally wasn't; Sally was so special, she was everyone's baby. I had to share her. And, I hadn't planned her. Her pregnancy was a surprise. Missy was planned, and she would be mine. She was the second-born and would never be least. She would never be thrown away. I loved her the moment I gave her a name, even the moment she became a thought in my mind. That moment, days before she was conceived, I loved her, and I dared to step out and call it love.

∼ 42 ∼
Endings and Beginnings

The summer of Sally's birth, DB had bought a small used boat, trailer and outboard. With plenty of babysitters offering to care for Sally, DB and I would take the boat on hot weekend days to my old flounder/ sole fishing holes on the coast. At night, we went striper and blue fishing. I didn't care much for eating striper or blue, but landing them was a rush.

Somehow, along the track of survival, I had learned to trust my own judgment from a long history of my life depending on me and no one else. The last fishing night adventure was at midnight in July of 1969. The stripers were running. The night was beautiful, a full moon summer's night. It was flood tide time. All was fun until DB refused to listen that he was outside the river and over the salt marsh. He wouldn't believe me until the motor died. Cotter pin death, and we had no spare. At least it wasn't a nor'easter this time. We had a very long row back to the mainland. It was the first real ding in trust.

Now, my trust level resembles a fluid, living, breathing entity. It is a hypervigilant, nonstop part of my radar system. My trust, tentatively given, takes a lot of hits as it scans my environment constantly and affixes category and weight to all. Some hits are miniscule and eventually discarded with time as the unintentional "slings and arrows" of life. The ones repeated are filed and watched. Those that possibly threatened my safety or the safety of someone I love, weighed the most. DB, ignoring the knowledge and experience I shared regarding ocean water and flood tides, placed both of us as parents and myself, pregnant with our second child, in potential jeopardy.

This action on DB's part caused me to pause, consider and adjust. I probably would have dealt better with him cheating on me. I would have been hurt by the disconnection, but I wouldn't have taken it personally. I would not have experienced it as my lack. It would have been about him. Danger, however, was personal. This was danger to myself, danger to my unborn child, and danger to Sally in the sense of her becoming an orphan. It was "mother think."

How he handled the episode was another deep concern to me. I saw a display of anger never directed at me before. The first red flag flew. Dismissing important information, not just the failure to listen but total dissing as in disrespect—a second red flag flew. Anger and potential rage at a circumstance one is responsible for was another flag. No admission of error, another. Emotional loss of control when clear objective thinking is called for, so not good. He didn't display shades of the father at this point, but hues.

The spring of Missy's conception, DB's mother's brother died, leaving her his small ranch house in our little town. His estate being settled that fall, she gave this house to us as a gift. It was a great little house nestled between two huge Victorian houses that her grandfather had built on the avenue named after him. We were surrounded by houses this grandfather had built. Pictures from the early 1900s showed a beautiful, interconnected compound with little mini-parks and strolling areas. However, this house was a small ranch with two bedrooms, one bath, an almost galley-sized kitchen, living room and den. It was very rustic but ours. We started turning the den into a nursery for our new baby.

Determined not to have another 40-plus-hour labor and delivery, I had a new obstetrician whom I liked a lot, and I read up on labor and delivery, discovering the "Lamaze" method. This method from a French doctor was not a recognized method in 1969 in my little town hospital. No one I spoke to had ever heard of natural childbirth. However, my new obstetrician was okay with giving it a try.

After eight long months of battling toxemia, off I went to the hospital to be induced. Shots given, the labor started almost immediately. After about one and a half hours of labor, a nurse came by asking if I wanted something for the pain. I declined. After two and a half hours of labor, my doctor said that he and another nurse were going out for a smoke. (It's hard to believe, but most doctors smoked back then.) They weren't gone three minutes before the contractions picked up speed. The urge to push became increasingly strong with contractions coming every 30 to 45 seconds. Every time I tried to call out, it turned into a long but loud groan. Thankfully, the woman in the next labor room heard me and was able to get a nurse who in turn got my doctor and another nurse. What transpired next was a scene right out of a 1950s sitcom. The doctor quickly established that the baby's head was crowning. He immediately told one nurse to get the gurney to take me to delivery. She did. He was on one side and the two nurses on the other. They were trying to calmly say "hurry" to each other. However, the doctor pulled one way, the nurses the other. After three or four attempts to get me into the gurney, I sat up and announced, "I'll do it myself." Minutes later, out popped Missy, all 8½ pounds, 24 inches of her, and healthy. I had three and a half hours of labor. Not bad. Me, on the other hand…there was no episiotomy, so I was torn end to end. Baby doing well, the doctor sewed me back together.

My Missy was beautiful and mine. No one rushed to see her or hold her or take her overnight. But she was fussy. She hardly slept more than two consecutive hours. Everything I learned that comforted and worked with Sally didn't work with Missy. She didn't tolerate her formula. She projected it into the air. She screamed. Holding her, she arched her back and winced. The new formula, soy-based, was okay for a week. She liked to have her back rubbed. She was uncomfortable with being held. Then, the same thing happened: projectile vomiting and screaming inconsolably until exhausted. I tried meat-based formula. The same thing happened. I went back to regular formula for a week, and then the same thing. This went on and on until Thursday, February 19, 1969, the pediatrician put in a referral to the breast milk bank at her three-month checkup. No problems were discovered. She got her first round of immunizations, the DTP shots. She was very fussy the rest of the day and night. I rocked and walked her until 2:00 a.m. Exhausted, I fell into bed.

— 43 —

Desolation Arrives

Friday, February 20th, at 7:30 a.m., I got Sally in her highchair eating breakfast. I went to get Missy for her bath. She's in a strange position… blue, not breathing. I started mouth to mouth, and I ran with her to the phone. I called the police, continuing mouth to mouth. The rescue was at the house in minutes, and they ran in. They took over resuscitation. I heard them saying, "I think we've got her…." Got her what? My neighbor, Jane, came in, immediately rushed to Sally and started throwing Cheerios around to distract her. I called DB and his mom and left a message for my mom at her school. Jane stayed with Sally. DB and I rushed to the hospital. The doctor came out and said, "We got her breathing for a minute, then she was gone." We're told that she died of interstitial pneumonia. What's that? My known world collapsed irrevocably.

DB's parents came to the house. DB's 's brother and his wife came to the house. Our friends came to our house. Neighbors brought food. The mother came at 4:00 p.m. but neither the father nor the brother came.

I was shattered. Fragments of myself slowly fell into a deep, dark hole. Painfully numb and not behind my eyes, thought stopped. My dead baby. I wanted time to stop. I think I wanted all life to stop. But, only mine did. Everyone offered platitudes: cutesy, timeworn sayings like, "God's will," or "she's in heaven," or "time will heal this," or even "there will be other children."

I knew they meant well. But none of it helped. I wanted to hurt them. No way was I putting my baby in the ground in a cemetery on the other side of town. I would bury her in our cold cellar. Who knew there were laws against doing that? It seemed so cruel and heartless at the time. Who knew there were tiny white coffins?

Missy's memorial service was on a rainy cold day in February. The minister of the Unitarian Church, Jack Z., was amazingly real. He came to the house after the service and personally interceded, keeping the fake platitude people at a distance—the ones who don't really know what to say to help so they pat you on the back of your hand, looking sad, while they murmur the well-worn words and then go eat whatever's offered, thanking God that this never happened to them or to one of their children. In retrospect, I'm not sure who Jack was really protecting, me from them or them from me. But he was real.

Those subsequent weeks after Missy's death remained painfully numb. However, the pain was distant; it was removed somehow, but still there. I was basically one-dimensional, just a mind and more robotic than even Data from Star Trek. I literally went through the motions of a life, emotionally vacant. My mind, however, could not wrap itself around the interstitial pneumonia as the cause of death. So, of course, I went to the library to research this diagnosis. "Interstitial" literally means "between the spaces" of something. Coupled with pneumonia, it didn't seem to be logical. I went to our pediatrician and asked.

That is when the term "sudden infant death syndrome" dropped like a boulder. I'd never heard of it before. However, when he then added "crib death," I recognized it. Back to the library I went to research. I found the National Foundation of Sudden Infant Death. I don't remember if I called or wrote them. Most likely I sent a letter of inquiry. They sent back to me as many facts regarding SIDS as they had in 1970.

Everyone around me was encouraging me to get pregnant again as the quickest way to heal. You know the type of things people spout, like when one's dog dies and some people tell one go get another puppy. That suggestion of getting pregnant again literally made my insides cringe. But I didn't hurt them. However, it was a moot subject because, surprise: I stopped getting my menses. So when friends and family inquired, I would just smile and respond that I wasn't pregnant yet. Now I was more two-dimensional, all intellectual stimulation receptive, and off I went working closely with the National Foundation for SIDS, working to create a local chapter. Paperwork was completed and filed with the state and a board was chosen. I spoke to area police and agencies and even appeared on a Boston TV talk show. There were articles in newspapers that brought many inquiries to my attention as well as parents who had experienced the death of a child to SIDS. I began to work with grieving parents to help understand SIDS and help them deal with their sorrow and loss. I had no realization that I hadn't dealt with my own or any, ever.

Fast approaching a year after Missy's death, and still not having any menses, my ob/gyn recommended inducing them, so an appointment was set for the end of December. Much to my surprise, he refused to induce my menses. Why? Because, at his best guess, I was at least three months pregnant. I was stunned, for I was not nauseous and amazingly had no toxemia.

I made the decision not to continue my involvement in the SIDS chapter and stopped around the eighth month of my pregnancy. Although at the time it was a purely intellectual decision, it proved to be the right one. Intellectually, I was prepared for this subsequent child, but emotionally, I was still vacant. I didn't know the terms "dissociation" or "denial" in 1970 and 1971. That knowledge would come a few years later while pursuing a degree. What I did know was that I didn't want to be talking about dead babies when I was caring for my new one.

~ 44 ~
And Next

This was, without a doubt, the best pregnancy experience of all. I had stopped smoking and drinking any alcohol when the pregnancy was discovered in December. By the end of January 1971, the nausea had set in once again. However, my husband and I and most of our friends were invited to the weekend wedding festivities of a close friend in Connecticut. We drove down with friends who started "partying" on the way. They were all smoking. I was miserable for the first hour into the ride, trying to fake my participation in their fun. I couldn't do it.

What did I do instead? I said, "Give me a beer and a cigarette." It was a very fun trip and weekend for me and everyone else. Just for your information, there were no drinking and driving laws or open container laws in the 1970s, nor any prohibitions against the same. This was the only pregnancy during which I drank alcohol and smoked cigarettes. Although repeatedly offered, I was able to avoid "just trying" any type of recreational drug for years, using pregnancy, breastfeeding or caring for my children as an excuse. Although researchers were just beginning to test and discuss the effects of alcohol and tobacco on developing fetuses, I wasn't too concerned as I was well into my second trimester when I resumed using alcohol and tobacco. However, one of the warnings mentioned was lower birth weight from using tobacco. I wasn't that concerned on this either, as both previous babies were more than eight pounds. A smaller baby might be easier.

Toxemia showed up in the fifth month, and I was gaining weight rapidly. I went back on the "eat nothing I liked" diet: no salt, no processed meats and no canned goods. What fun. Nausea was back being a close companion. Still almost totally in my head, armed with all the published information I could find, I felt no anxiety about the arrival of this "subsequent child."

My only difficulty was this baby was extremely active and would manage somehow to land on my sciatic nerve without warning, and down I'd go to the ground, curb or stairs. The husband put up army cargo netting on the sides and ceiling of the cellar stairs. I fractured my coccyx bone (also known as the tailbone) twice on those stairs. However, by the seventh month I had started to dilate and the obstetrician scheduled me for weekly check-ins. (This was another new obstetrician, as the previous one, who I liked, ran away with his nurse. This new ob/gyn I loved.) Dilation continued to increase, and after an incident in the beginning of my eighth month (I collapsed in the center of a main street and couldn't use my legs for many minutes, panicking a nice man who stopped and tried to help me up), the obstetrician scheduled to have labor induced.

Off I went to the hospital in September, 1971, weighing in at a solid 200 pounds and seven fingers dilated. It should be an easy delivery, and it was. As this was to be my last pregnancy, I was planning on watching it. Labor was quick. The fluid retained during the pregnancy overwhelmed my bladder, necessitating catheterization. This should have been a simple process, but any new venture in that part of my anatomy produced an unintended consequence. Every time they went to insert the catheter, I fainted, which caused my vitals and my baby's to crash. They would immediately stop and revive me, only to have the process repeat itself. My solution was telling them that the next time I passed out, to first insert the catheter and then revive me. This worked.

However, the baby was breach, and the doctor ordered spinal anesthesia as he kept turning the baby physically. It would have been a huge OUCH. It was all over in 45 minutes. I had a beautiful, huge baby boy, all nine pounds and three ounces of him. And he was a month early. I thought, what would he have weighed if I had gone full term and not smoked?

Because CW was being breastfed, he came into my room every two hours to stimulate my milk letting down. The next morning one nurse began insisting that I give him a bottle of water after every nursing attempt, and I refused. Every article I had read on breastfeeding in 1971 emphasized not confusing a breastfeeding newborn by introducing a bottle nipple too early.

By noon, I was in tears. I was so upset, I called my doctor. After explaining the situation to him, he came in and discharged me and my baby from the hospital.

CW was a good eater. By the end of that first week home, he weighed 11 pounds while I had lost 50. By the end of the third week home, he weighed 13 pounds and I had lost 20 more. By the end of the sixth week home, he weighed 19 pounds and looked like a baby Buddha. I now weighed 99 pounds, was anemic and might lose my gallbladder. At a follow-up appointment with the ob/gyn doctor, he called CW's pediatrician and informed him the child was "killing me" and I could no longer breastfeed and to recommend formula.

During that sixth week CW became ill quickly. His temperature flew to 105 degrees in 90 minutes. He stopped breathing. I picked him up, and he was struggling for breath. I called the pediatrician. He came right over, checked him completely and wrote CW's first script for antibiotics for the next ten days. He recovered. Me, not so much. I found Sally in the hall closet, sobbing and shaking, terrified that her brother was dead. Three weeks later it began again. CW spiked a fever to 103 in two hours. I rushed him to the pediatrician's office. His glands were swollen, his throat was slightly irritated, he had some difficulty breathing, but there was nothing concrete. He got another script for antibiotics. I now checked him constantly. I basically strapped him to my body. Baby slings and carriers had not been developed yet. I took two bath towels and sewed them together to make a sling. CW went everywhere with me. He was either on me or my eyes were on him. He slept in our bedroom.

The pediatrician refused to give him his immunizations, saying that he just wanted to wait a bit as CW's immune system might be overloaded. His schedule was high fever, fever seizures, ten days on ampicillin and three weeks off, and then high fever, fever seizures, ten days on the antibiotics and three weeks off, until his second birthday. After almost a year of this rotation, I had a supply of ampicillin in the refrigerator and only called the doctor's office to let them know that he was spiking again and that I was starting the medicine.

By his first year, after multiple visits to the pediatrician's office or the emergency room for his increasingly higher fevers, doctors from both encouraged me to add putting him into a bathtub filled with cool water or giving him a tepid enema to bring his fevers down. I opted for the tepid baths and would sit, holding him in the tub, to slow the speed of the spikes. They were now going past 103 and approaching 105 to the point of his

171

having fever seizures. It was very, very scary. Before a seizure would hit, my little guy would hallucinate, seeing bugs coming to get him and crawling all over his body. I quickly learned that telling him the bugs were not there did not help and only increased his emotional upset, which would increase my anxiety. I learned that the calmer I remained, the calmer he would be, and one bug-filled moment a solution appeared. I spontaneously told him that I was picking the bugs off and crushing them. Now neither one of us got overly upset as I discovered more imaginary ways of disposing of his hallucinatory bugs.

I learned a great deal about responding to someone's hallucinations from my little guy, which served me well in future crisis situations with mental health patients. The fever-induced seizures were something else entirely. The hallucinations heralded an upcoming seizure. I would need to get the fever down quickly as I had only minutes once the halluci-nations began, and handling a seizure of a slippery child in a tub full of water was not easy. I was walking a continual, unending, emotional, anxiety-filled tightrope.

~45~
On the Edge

I was walking that emotional tightrope alone. Each physical crisis with my little guy left me weak and dreading the next one. I was no longer numb. Rather, I was back terribly behind my eyes. The possible loss of another child, my son, was unthinkable and tortuous. I barely slept, my breathing and my essence anxiously dependent and in synch with a little boy's breaths.

And the memories…horrible, horrific, unrelenting past childhood memory tapes filled my nights accompanied by their voices playing constantly over and over. Every photo memory of abuse, every scathing insult ever directed at my being, played over and over and over until I hoped for death. And the questions—horrible questions—arose that wrenched the blinders from my mind's eye and exposed the marrow of my being. None of it had been personal. They didn't see me. I wasn't real to them. I became the No Thing that they yelled at, insulted, cursed, slapped, hit, kicked, whipped, smothered, choked, drowned, hung, molested, not-worth-a-used-postage-stamp thing that they could take their evil out on. Their evil wasn't that they disliked and hated me and did those things to me as a toddler, child, adolescent, or adult; their evil wasn't that they didn't love me (whatever that was); their evil was that I had less value to them than anything else they owned. I was Nothing, the No Thing of No One and No Body.

During the endless nights when my husband and children all slept, I would sit with the earphones on, listening to music playing loudly in my head, sobbing until my eyes swelled shut, a knife, Jack and butts close by. But that lasted only for about 15 days into a month until CW vomited: his heralding signal for the 10- to 15-day illness cycle to begin and play to its end.

DB and I barely talked. I don't remember him much at all after Missy's death. He had said the most despicable thing anyone could have said to me after her death. I don't know if he meant it, but I don't think it really mattered if he did or didn't. What he said out loud could never be unsaid. I don't think we fought. I think we both went through the motions of living. I think I went on without him. He wasn't part of the SIDS outreach after her death and before CW's birth. Nor did he participate in any involvement with the Unitarian church or in Sally's activities or the care of CW.

It's as if the boy I had dated and had come to trust and the man I had married had slowly slipped away and been replaced by someone who no longer laughed or smiled. He became someone who had a nasty temper and went into rages. I never realized, in the tsunami of cascading losses, that his was the quietest and most deadly. His rages left me empty. They were nothing like the father's. I wasn't afraid of DB or that he could physically hurt me. It was more like he was dying and sucking the life from what little essence I had left. He became someone I no longer knew. I think we both may have retreated into different caves and only interacted when necessary.

The women in the neighborhood reached out and surrounded me from complete isolation. There were coffees at different houses in the morning in the winter and in the afternoon in the summer. I was already friendly with Kait and her husband and family who lived in the large Victorian house next door, our yards connecting. Kait was in her early 40s, exotically beautiful and colorfully dramatic. She appeared so vibrant and alive. Her husband, Jeff, was a physician. She had three children. Jane and her husband lived on the other side; their children were grown and in high school and college. Joan and her husband, also a physician, had three children and lived across the street from our house, and Karla and her husband and six children lived across from Kait.

There were other neighbors not in such proximity who sometimes attended. It was a very close neighborhood for many years. I tried so hard to enjoy them all. I appreciated that they were there, but there was so much turmoil swirling seemingly endlessly. I would think thoughts of, "If one more woman talks at length about the color of the drapes she wants or about a new couch, I'm just going to start screaming." But I also was slowly realizing that this was not the life I wanted. I so couldn't spend my life talking about children, husbands, drapes and couches. This was not any identity I wanted and not what I wanted to become. And I knew, deep in my bones, that I desperately needed to become someone other than who I was. Who I was would not live long. It's easier to know who one isn't than turning it around to create who one is.

At 25 years old, I was entering the most depressed time of my life. It didn't help that I kept repeating to myself that I was "a quarter of a century old." Unknowingly, I was sliding ever so slowly into despair, and repeating this phrase for an entire year didn't help. Immersing myself in Sylvia Plath's and Anne Sexton's writings most likely assisted my decline, but that was before I began to understand the power of a negative mind. Misery, which does like company, found a sister in Kait. . She lived through an abusive childhood as well and fought depression for more than 20 years. Another piece of my heart broke off.

I still attracted men like flypaper. I was aware it was the Mark they saw. I don't think it ever was an ego trip. It was a power trip, but a negative one. There was a great deal of anger toward any male who hit on me. If any of them ever complimented me on being attractive, I don't remember. But I wouldn't have believed them. DB never knew how many of his friends hit on me. I thought telling him would have been mean, and I had my own ways of punishing them. But I only did so if I thought they were despicable. Despicable occurred if their wife was a friend. I only mention this aspect as it was this 25th year that the Voice said, "Physical attractiveness is just a genetic accident, and its usefulness will decline as a tool over time." The Voice said that I was given "actual skills and gifts" that I was "responsible for developing" and that I would "need them to survive." I did listen.

— 46 —
Kait and Jeff

When Kait and I first became friends, she already had three suicide attempts in her past along with many hospitalizations. She took a lot of medication. She seemed to look at her hospitalizations as a time out from her family, mostly from her husband. The grounds of McLean Hospital in Massachusetts back then were lovely. She would stay in a private house on the grounds that would be staffed. It always sounded more like a spa stay than being hospitalized for a suicide attempt and depression. It never sounded as if it helped.

She didn't like her husband much, or mine. I don't believe that she liked men in general. But she did have things to say about the way my husband treated and spoke to me. She thought DB was abusive. But measured against the father's, DB's actions didn't register as yet. Kait was positive that her husband had been cheating for years. I thought her childhood abuse was the base of her ongoing depression. I liked her husband. DB and I socialized regularly with both. Jeff seemed gentle and quiet. He was interested in many things and was attentive to his children when he was home.

Kait had two boutique businesses in the Caribbean. Every three months she would go there for three weeks, and she hired me to feed her family and clean her house while she was gone. In July she went to their house on an exclusive island in the Atlantic with the children for most of the summer.

She was always trying to take me away from it all or educate me in more feminine exotica. She hated that I drank beer instead of wine or vodka. Although she seemed to grasp that wine was too caustic for my digestive issues, she never understood how beer soothed my stomach. She did give up on the vodka, though. It turned out that I was allergic to it. She moved to gin. That was a much better choice.

In the summer of 1972, she invited me to visit their island compound off the coast of New England for a three-day weekend. After arranging care for the children and scheduling the visit during the healthy weeks of CW's cycle of illness, DB drove me to a 6:00 p.m. ferry. Jeff and Kait were to pick me up around 8:30 p.m. The ferry became befogged and stopped halfway there. Fortunately there was a bar in the ferry and another female passenger, and we befriended each other. Life stories were exchanged. The ferry arrived at 2:30 a.m.

Kait and I stayed up for the remainder of the night talking. Their island house was magnificent. The grounds were lovely and meticulous with rental cottages on the property. She and Jeff treated me like royalty, and after dinner Saturday evening they took me to my first live concert: a rock band. This was an open-air concert in a field. More alcohol was had. The concert was amazing. I discovered very strong groupie tendencies. I got on stage with the drummer. My hosts thought it was amusing. I thought concerts were out until my kids were much, much older.

It was a great little vacation for me, a brief step into someone else's reality; it was a day or two to forget my real life. Kait was miserable in her marriage. Her children were independent and self-sufficient. It was sad. I didn't identify any concerns in my own marriage at that point in time. I knew I was depressed, but I pinpointed the cause as the death of Missy, the flashbacks and pain of my childhood, and the current ongoing illness with my son.

~47~
My Marriage

I don't think I had many expectations of DB. I don't think I had many expectations of anyone. I think I was completely and thoroughly focused on finding the energy to meet my children's needs but feeling like I was failing miserably. Like Kait, I too wanted to be gone. I was exhausted and slipping closer and closer to the abyss. After three failed suicide attempts, Kait wanted to know how I would off myself. I told her.

I remember lots of money troubles. DB had sold the boat, trailer and motorcycle. We had received a sterling silverware flatware service for 12 from his paternal grandmother as a wedding gift, and he sold that. He never asked me. There were a lot of US bonds I had bought, and others were given when Sally was born and on her birthdays. They were gone. He said we needed a car, and he wanted CW out of our bedroom. We temporarily moved CW and his crib in with Sally, which escalated my anxiety and sleepless nights. I constantly checked him to see if he was breathing. The two-bedroom, one-bath scheme no longer worked. Although we never discussed it, neither DB nor I ever considered putting CW in the small den where Missy died. Since the house had no mortgage, DB wanted to get a $20,000 mortgage to add a master bedroom and a bath and buy a new car.

DB's paternal uncle, Robb, was the president of the "in" town bank we used. He was very impressive. DB was terrified of him. We called him "uncle god." I was delegated to go see this uncle and ask to take out a mortgage. So I did. It was no problem; we had the money within a week. We looked for contractors and DB looked at cars. A VW bus was chosen. We received several bids for the construction. I only remember the contractor we chose. His name was Mark. He was approximately the same age as DB and me, was married, had four children and lived in a suburb 15 minutes away. Construction started right away during the summer of 1972. Mark and his men were at the house from early morning until 4:00 p.m.

Although we couldn't afford it after Missy's death, DB had bought me a dog, a small apricot poodle I named Cream. When CW moved into Sally's room, we bought Sally her own dog, which she named Kola after her invisible friend. Neither DB nor I realized that poodles needed grooming every six weeks or so. Since it was expensive, we did it ourselves. One grooming episode that took place outside just as construction was beginning, I was holding Cream while DB was grooming her when the Voice stated, "CW needs you." I immediately ran to find CW choking. This was a few years before the Heimlich maneuver was known. Tipping CW upside down failed to work, but long fingers did. I shook for hours.

Our yard was fenced in the back to keep Sally and her little dog out of the main street. However, the builders had taken down a portion of the fence to get the heavy equipment in the yard. This one morning, Sally went out to say hi to Mark, and Kola went with her. He ran straight into the street and met with a swift end. We were devastated. The builders felt awful. I think it was after that incident that Mark started talking a lot more to me. I believe the addition took about six weeks to two months. I was so focused on the children and putting one foot in front of the other that I really didn't notice his attention until the day he said, "I can't stand the way your husband speaks to you or treats you." I literally had no idea what he meant. I asked him. He described insults and name-calling and DB speaking to me with contempt and derision. I was stunned. I really thought he must be mistaken. So I monitored my and DB's interactions and conversations more closely.

Sadly, Mark was correct. I crashed and burned. The only person I had trusted, the only one I thought I loved and whom I thought loved me besides my children, was a lie. I had dismissed Kait's calling DB abusive, but I was becoming more and more aware.

Soon after Mark's pointing out the way DB talked to me, he began declaring his feelings for me. I may have liked the attention of actual positive interaction and communication. However, I only remember it making me uncomfortable. He seemed like a nice guy. I didn't want him touching or kissing me. I was so lost and overwhelmed from descending into oblivion in addition to DB's betrayal. I was just so numb, it was as if I was frozen. But the day Mark announced that he was going to leave his wife, the ice cracked. I panicked. I told him, "NO, I'm not leaving DB." That day I called and made an appointment for counseling at a local mental health clinic. And that was an education.

— 48 —
Counseling

I no longer remember exactly what I told the counselor, Mrs. A. But it was something like a *Reader's Digest* version on dead baby, subsequent baby son trying to die, exhaustion, not sleeping, feeling I no longer existed, husband verbally abusive and unsupportive, and contractor leaving his wife and four kids because he said he loved me. I also requested counseling for Sally, as she was not adjusting well to kindergarten. We lived within eyesight of her school, and one morning I found her hiding in the bushes crying rather than going down the hill to school.

Confidentiality was a major concern. The counselor and I discussed this repeatedly, and I had every assurance that this would be the case. Despite assurances, it was incredibly difficult to talk about myself and describe what was happening. I didn't really have any "feeling descriptive" verbiage. Apparently Mrs. A would ask me how I felt about something, I would describe it and then she would interrupt and say, "No, I asked you how you felt, not what you think." And I would sit there blankly for a minute, then answer that what I said was what I felt. I had no idea what she meant.

However, I really tried talking to this woman. But it was an agony. So many years of never putting those events into spoken words, so many life-long threats to never, ever talk, were proving impossible to overcome. I had no fragment that talked. Meanwhile, Sally had been referred to a Dr. G at the mental health center. She was a young child psychiatrist. Sally was five and liked to talk. She didn't mind going, and it was arranged so each of our sessions were at the same hour.

After several visits Mrs. A announced that Dr. G wanted to have a session with DB and myself concerning Sally. I did question if this was usual practice, and again she assured me that it was. I again questioned her whether our "talks" were confidential. Again, she assured me that they were. DB was so not thrilled, but he did agree, and a late afternoon time was set. The four of us adults met at 4:00 p.m. for the usual 50-minute session time. It didn't take long to recognize that Dr. G had an agenda and did all the talking. It was painfully, and I mean painfully, like being hit by that 18-wheeler, blindsided once again, triggered by Dr. G. DB said nothing. Mrs. A said very little, and that little was only when I would challenge her with whether she was "going to allow her to do this, or was she, as my counselor, going to stop her." She didn't stop her. At 5:00 p.m. Mrs. A excused herself (it was her office) and left. So then it was just the three of us. DB had no clue what was going on, but I did. Dr. G wanted to tell DB what I shared with Mrs. A, and I would tell Dr. G, "No, you are not going there." "That's confidential information." And off Dr. G would go, rewinding her buildup to be a big disclosure.

I was so beyond angry. I'd been betrayed once again. I was ice cold inside with a fire that burned white-hot ice flames. An hour later Dr. G did the damage. She told DB that I had had an affair with the contractor. And she, Dr. G, recommended that we all, as a family, go camping together to mend. That was her professional solution. Life was surrealistic again. Apparently she had missed the parts about the dead baby, the current baby that was ill all the time, my trying to die, my depression and suicidal ideation, and DB's s emotional and verbally abusive behaviors—AND the fact that the affair NEVER happened.

It was a very quiet ride home. I wish I could say it was a wake-up call for the marriage. It wasn't, but it did push me towards a pivotal wake-up starting point within weeks. I don't remember us ever really discussing this "affair." To this day, I don't know if DB ever realized I never followed through with it. The "affair" thing was happening in Mark's imagination, not mine. I was locked into dead baby, dying new baby, depression, anxiety and flashbacks of my childhood and now emotionally and verbally abusive husband world. I was literally and figuratively all alone. The whole point of seeking help was because all these events started to occur with Mark, and I had no idea how he got there when I wasn't even sure I was present.

What did I now know? I knew I was having a feeling. I was angry. I was back to a ten-year-old's, hide-the-whip-and-razor-strap angry. I wasn't that suicidal anymore.

I called Matt, the lawyer I used to work for. We discussed the whole Mrs. A and Dr. G event. He reviewed all the possible and probable consequences and unintended consequences if I chose to legally go after them for this breach of confidentiality. There were some I liked and a lot I didn't. He did suggest that I let the center know that I had contacted him. Basically, the bottom line was I wanted to hurt Dr. G. I wanted to hurt this person more than I had ever, ever wanted to hurt anyone in my memory. That my reaction was most likely the accumulation of a lifetime of abuse did not occur to me then. I did, in fact, have a viable legal case against this doctor and the agency.

However, the probability of legal action becoming publicly known was likely. And that would hurt many more than just myself. I did consider Matt's advice for quite a while. But I also called the mental health center's administrator's office to inform them that I was in contact with my lawyer, as Matt had suggested. "Considering" his advice is such a controlled, intellectual term. I was wrestling with that advice. I didn't feel depressed, suicidal or anxious. I was so agitated, so beyond anger. But I wouldn't let that anger hurt my husband, children or DB's family. I would just kill Dr. G—eventually, carefully, down the road in time to ensure not getting caught. I worked out an arrangement with the mental health center. We would never see these people again. Both Dr. G and Mrs. A would have their hands officially slapped, and Sally would get a new child psychiatrist to work with who would work with DB and myself as well at a reduced rate. We all saw this new doctor, Dr. R, at a satellite setting in another town. Eventually, when Dr. R left this mental health agency, Sally saw her at her home office.

One weekend many months after the "disclosure" incident, I became cognitively aware of possessing a great deal of information regarding Dr. G. I knew the town and street where she lived. I knew her spouse's and children's names. I knew what kind of car she drove and the license plate number on her car, and I knew her schedule. I also became aware that I was becoming increasingly paranoid toward the people around me and that I had an actual plan.

—49—
Walking Through

It was another epiphanistic moment. It was as if I tuned into a planning session where someone was "walking through" the steps necessary to carry out that plan. Except, that someone was me. There was no internet back then. I still have no memory of obtaining this information. But I recognized the "walking through" steps.

Anyone who has been seriously suicidal and made the decision to kill him or herself has "walked through" various plans. That "walking through" step is the last thought process before an attempt, whether the attempt is killing oneself or simply choosing to cut oneself. Also, anyone who has entertained the "walking through" knows it takes on a life and energy of its own… it begins to own you.

I was so shocked and alarmed, I froze. Even now I can picture where I was standing and where other people in the house were situated. It was as if I, simultaneously, was home in my living room but gazing into an abyss. And I heard the Voice, loud and clear. It said, "If you continue down these path choices, you may never be able to come back. You may lose yourself forever." And I listened.

Although neither a God nor forgiveness were in my awareness anywhere in my being that I knew of, I immediately let go of killing Dr. G. This decision did not fix the depression, anxiety, PTSD flashbacks and emotional pain then. But the paranoia left. I decided to focus on what was positive. I focused on what I wanted to do.

I was still involved with Rev. Z and counseling a few people occasionally and very aware that I had no idea what I was doing. I remembered this same feeling when I was working with sudden infant death syndrome parents, wanting to help but having little idea how to or what to do besides being there and providing what little information was known about SIDS. I always knew that I was not the only person suffering with horrible memories and devastating emotional pain. I still saw it everywhere I looked.

Two phrases repeatedly went through my head: "When the going gets rough, the tough get going" and "God helps those who help themselves." I didn't think much of any god, but I liked the energy the sayings gave. I wanted to go to medical school. I wanted to become a psychiatrist. I wanted what happened to Sally in school to never happen to a child again, and I wanted what happened to myself to never happen again. I wanted to bring an experienced broken heart to mental health. I wanted, I decided, to see about going back to school.

I didn't even know if I could do it. Just feeding my children took enormous energy that I didn't have. I was exhausted all the time from not sleeping. I weighed about 95 pounds. I addressed the lack of sleep first. After much thought, I set a new rule. If, after going to bed, I was not asleep after one hour of lights going out because of "stinking thinking," I had to get up and clean my oven or my toilets—two jobs I hated.

The unrecognized thing at the time was that I had no self-doubt that I would follow through with this behavior change. I never realized until many years later exactly how valuable all those years of practicing gymnastics for hours were, as they laid the groundwork for a self-discipline I never even knew I had. I know it sounds unbelievable, but it only took one toilet cleaning for my not sleeping to stop. You have no idea how much I dislike cleaning toilets.

Thus empowered, I signed up for a psychology class at the local community college and bought the Real Estate Licensing book for Massachusetts. I read it, took the exam, passed and found a part-time job selling real estate on the weekends and evenings.

Although the spring and summer of 1973 appeared to be going well, activity-wise, I was still massively depressed and suicidal. I just ignored it. That is such a simple statement for an incredibly complex set of choices: The first step was in acknowledging the feeling but not feeding it or acting on it. Thus the first step at a deeper glance appeared to be three choices. But each of those three had multi-level choices embedded within them.

Acknowledging the feelings of depression required identifying all the comorbid feeling states that comprised depression. Not feeding the feelings fueling the depression required an identification of all the fuels that, in many instances, crossed over to impact acting on them. *Ignoring the depression simultaneously meant not giving in to it on a feeling level while increasing the focus and awareness of it on a cognitive level.*

— 50 —
CW Again

O n Friday, September 14, 1973, DB and I packed up Sally and CW and headed for the farm for CW's birthday weekend. On Saturday, September 15th, CW woke up with a temperature that gradually increased during the day, despite having started him on antibiotics. By early evening we decided to head home rather than risk having to take him to the small local hospital as we were running out of antibiotics. It was just simpler and safer to deal with his possible seizures at home. On arriving home and calling CW's pediatrician, we discovered that Dr. D was still in Europe on vacation and that Dr. W was covering his patients. After speaking with Dr. W and explaining how Dr. D had been dealing with CW's reoccurring illness, Dr. W wanted to see CW in the morning before prescribing.

After being caught up on CW's history the next morning, Dr. W took some blood samples and swabs and wanted to wait and see where the illness would go without antibiotics. CW's temperature hovered between 103 and 105 all that night. He was lethargic and very hot the next morning. Dr. W called around 10:00 a.m. to say the blood tests and swabs were not significant and to just watch him and call back as needed.

After hanging up I went to check on CW and found him lying face down in a pool of blood. Have you ever experienced your entire being shaking in terror? It's not trembling. Trembling is subtle. There was nothing subtle about my terror. Time stopped. I could hardly walk. But I did. I walked to the phone and called Dr. W back. He said, "Take him to the ER." I called DB who was ten minutes away at work. Grabbing CW, DB and I headed for the hospital.

Apparently Dr. W had called ahead as CW was whisked into the ER when we arrived. We were asked to leave when they were examining him. They performed a cutdown intravenous on his ankle. They wouldn't let me in with him. His screams were heard loud and clear in the waiting room. Time stopped again for me.

CW was admitted. His temperature continued to climb to 106, and he started having difficulty breathing. They packed him in a plastic tub of ice and put him in an oxygen tent. I held onto his hand through the tent as I sat next to his crib. DB went home for Sally, then came back around 8:00 p.m. Since they didn't allow parents to stay with their child then, we went home at 10:00 p.m.

The hospital called at 1:00 a.m. CW had stopped breathing. They had performed an emergency tracheotomy and needed permission to do exploratory surgery right away. I gave it. I called the mother. The brother, who had been gone for six months traveling the world, had just come home an hour before. He came directly to the house to stay with Sally.

The five hours that CW was in the OR were the second longest hours of my life. The first were the days following Missy's death. Now, it was as if my mind and soul, my being, locked onto CW and breathed for him. No other thought, emotion or focus other than determination that CW would live crossed my consciousness. The ENT surgeon, Dr. K, appeared in the waiting room. CW was in recovery. He was in critical condition and would be going to the pediatric ICU. Some very long Latin name, unpronounceable and long forgotten, but basically a staph or strep-like infection, probably from exposure at his birth at this hospital, was the cause. The difficulty in diagnosis was reportedly from few incidents then, and no one younger than seven had had this infection this way. Previously those who were infected had all been able to talk. All the antibiotics he took for two years had just prevented the inevitable crisis from occurring. The surgeon had removed his tonsils and adenoids and the infected lesions from his throat and esophagus.

CW was in the pediatric ICU for ten days. The first five days he was tracheal intubated, and all I could do was hold his hand and sing to him. Mostly he lay there motionless, sleeping. When awake, his eyes would lock onto mine as tears slid noiselessly down the side of his face.

DB would get Sally off to school in the morning, and his mother would be at the house in the afternoon. DB would get to the hospital at 3:00 p.m., and I would go home, make dinner, feed Sally, save DB dinner and Sally and I would meet DB at the hospital.

The pediatric ICU nurses were more flexible with my staying in the room with CW once he was in his own space. I slept in a chair. It was a very scary and exhausting five days until the antibiotics took hold, they took the breathing tube out, and he started to slowly improve. Great was the day they closed off his tracheotomy and he could talk again.

51

New Beginnings

Settling CW back into a regular home routine was a happy challenge. Still depressed and suicidal but ignoring these feelings proved to be 25 to 75 percent successful, the effectiveness varying daily. I could pretty much "fake it" until everyone went to bed and I was alone. I was still able to sleep. Those percentages pretty much remained the same for the next ten years.

Meanwhile, my happy, outgoing, beautiful little girl was miserable in school. This was before ADHD and ADD diagnoses took over. Back in 1973 they called it "minimal brain dysfunction." I called it devastating. My happy little girl who said her first word at six months and stood up and ran before she was a year had a brain dysfunction. So not. She was very active and simply delightfully different. In 1973 it was "be neurotypical and fit in the square or be shamed and then bullied by one's peers." There was no "neurodivergent" or "on the spectrum" delineation then.

She loved the outdoors, animals and nature's tiny little creatures. We explored frogs, toads, salamanders and snakes. She was all girl, but so adventurous. She hated school. The schools tested and retested her. They singled her out and shamed her for behaving, they said, more like a boy than a girl. She wanted to run and climb. They wanted her to sit still. She cried a great deal. She still saw Dr. R regularly and was happy and active at home, but getting her off every morning to a place that made her feel horribly about herself was painful for both of us.

I channeled all the accumulated sorrow, anger and frustration from my childhood and Missy's death, my depression and anxiety, CW's two-year-long illness, Sally's struggles and pain adjusting to school, and the living death of my marriage into a determination towards getting a degree. I read everything I could find on child psychology and ended falling in love with D. W. Winnicott and the British school of psychotherapy and object relations theory. This is what I wanted to do. I wanted to be a child psychiatrist. I wanted to help children who were suffering.

CW was so not the same little boy after his hospitalization and brush with death. He was both more clingy and angrier. Reading childhood psychology books did not help my depression, but it did spur me to try to hide it more from both children. Pretty much everyone was in bed asleep by 8:00 p.m., so I had four to five hours alone at least five nights per week. I averaged only five hours of sleep at night, so this worked well for alone time to read, think and cry.

Discovering play therapy was amazing. At this point CW was continually playing out his hospitalizations. So, getting an inexpensive baby doll, spare clear tubing from our fish tank, and a small doll-sized baby bottle and crib, CW and I built a hospital room and rigged a doll-sized intravenous setup. Buying him a child's medical kit with a stethoscope and other instruments, he proceeded to play doctor to that doll baby for months. Being a doctor was all I ever heard CW say he wanted to be until his late teens.

I also had heard from a friend about a fantastic teenage babysitter who could run an entire household. Julie was a sophomore in high school. She was one of the most reliable and responsible people I had ever met. No one, and I mean no one, would babysit CW. Before Julie ever started, I explained CW's reoccurring illness and the steps necessary to prevent seizures. She had taken care of her two younger siblings and was more proficient than me in household duties and cooking.

The psychology class at the local community college was a breeze. This school thing could work. I sold two houses and had money. Julie was a whiz at everything. One time Sally opened the safety lock on the cellar stairs, and CW landed unconscious at the bottom. Julie called the pediatrician and had him all checked out before I could even get home.

Late fall of 1973 found my goal to go back to college in a pre-med program crystallizing. I was teaching Sunday school at the Unitarian church. Their beliefs were simple. They believe in the fatherhood of God and the brotherhood of man, and my doubting the existence of a God was not an issue. I was still helping with lay counseling with people referred from the church. College was going to cost money I did not have, and I knew I needed a more predictable income than selling real estate. I needed a part-time job where I didn't have to pay the majority of whatever I earned to sitters, and at this point I would only leave the children with Julie, their father or my mother-in-law.

I found a part-time job at a hospital in an adjoining town. My hours were 3:30 p.m. to 12 midnight three days per week, and alternating Saturdays and Sundays,7:00 a.m. to 3:00 p.m. in emergency admitting. So I worked roughly 30½ hours per week. Julie would come to the house right after school on the days I worked. She would cook dinner and feed the children, and DB would drive her home when he came home from work. She also would come alternating Saturdays and Sundays for four hours until 3:00 p.m. when I got back to drive her home.

~52~
The Abyss

I loved working in the emergency room until midnight. I didn't love being the person who took all one's information while one was in pain or bleeding. I did have one poor middle-aged man die from a myocardial infarction while in the middle of providing his insurance information. I loved working with the nurses and doctors. It's hard to believe now, but most doctors and nurses smoked then, and we smoked in the office.

It was in the ER that I discovered the *Physicians' Desk Reference*. Did I mention that I was still an obsessive reader? I found this drug reference book fascinating. I read it every chance I got in between signing patients in and out of the ER. Why did I find it fascinating? There were so many reasons. Foremost, it was basically new information in an area completely foreign and unexplored. It was a challenge as the chemical ingredients in the drugs were strange and complex. Once in the system of a person, a drug could have a whole life, a three-quarter life, a half-life, a one-quarter life, etc., and that drug could interact with other drug(s) having the same complexity of lives in wholly different ways on different days. The overwhelming variety of side effects with their possible lethality and statistical variances in testing populations was mind-blowing. But some fragment of attention particularly homed in on the information that a lavage and/or antidote for one drug could be contraindicated in another drug, resulting in death.

The thought of suicide as an option and a potential choice was quiet but still alive and well. I had been particularly horrified by all Kait's stories of her many subsequent hospitalizations after as many attempts. I knew that I would have found failing a suicide attempt to be humiliating and horrendously mortifying. Double-down mortification would have been to be hospitalized against my will. My worst nightmare was for anyone to pity me. Ever. Over anything. Even the death of my daughter. Such pity would be beacon signals of weakness pulsating like flashing lights. You might get kindness at first from people; most, though, would dismiss you as soon as possible. Pain, grief or any emotion deeply felt seems to trigger most people towards discomfort. That is, except for the feeders, like my family, and the people leeches who feed off other people's wounds.

I fully believed that it was my right to choose to live or to choose to die. Remember, I was still philosophically an existentialist and, spiritually, a nihilist. I thought I had found the answer to a successful death. As a result, I researched away. Drug by drug, I compared lavage and/or antidote recommendations and interactions where one was contraindicated by the other and slowly obtained a small but lethal cache of pills that would ensure that any attempts to revive me would in fact kill me. I would never be revived. This was in 1974. I threw them out in 1985.

Depression colors everything in an endlessly hopeless light. It is also exhausting. The mere thought of having to get out of bed at times can seem so overwhelming that hours might pass before that action can be accomplished. Anyone, and I mean 80 percent of people, who have experienced a major depression have more than just thought of suicide. Sixty percent of those experience the "thought" itself as a beacon of hope, I last-ditch relief choice. Fifty percent of those have a vague plan and 50 percent of these a means. Just because, like me, they decide to give life that last-ditch effort—that all-out, all-in, 100 percent charge—at living, doesn't mean that thought, that plan and that means go away. Rather, they're just safely tucked away, hiding in a fragment, an island feeling state, drifting unawares, awaiting that dark day or dark night on the edge of the abyss when the walking-through dance once again becomes reality and the abyss's beacon of freedom shines brightly. That thought has a power and life all its own, surprising one at many turns.

Inside, Out
We were there alone, you and me.
You were therefrom the inside, out at last; me,
I was on the outside as usual.
You lay there reproaching me with
your starved body and transparent skin, so I would
be sure to notice your bones; as if I were
responsible for your obvious neglect. You knew I
would hate you, I didn't hide it, as I could see you
hated me by your ugliness. Still, I would have fed
you if I had known of your hunger. You came out
at a bad time, I was busy; you knew that and how I
detest being late and your silent demands were
making me late. I'm sorry they forgot to feed you.
Still, I did try, but you were such an old infant and I
didn't expect the full set of teeth. If I hadn't been so
busy I might have wondered, but I don't really blame
you for biting me, I deserved it.
—jp, 1976

Believe it, those days arrive with shocking regularity, when, without warning, the bottom falls out of the world you're holding onto by the tips of your fingers. It doesn't take much. Sometimes it is just the mere incident of the 101st emotional paper cut. How did I cope? That depended on the strength of the blow and the depth of the cut. If it was bad, like a betrayal, then shock, followed by total withdrawal, could occur as soon as possible. Usually I engaged a cover in the form of taking a nap or feeling ill. But such a blow followed a path of felt pain, then a progressive numbness. It was a slow withdrawal into Nothinghood, but I had enough time to put a child to bed or finish making dinner before the dimensions of selfhood totally disappeared. What was Nothinghood like? Reread my poem, "The Cave," in Chapter 32.

Later, I had a Jack and a beer chaser. That is, I drank when the house was asleep. I didn't drink to numb the pain or as an escape, and I never used alcohol when sliding into a depression. Jack was my weapon to incapacitate and drown the final hope and call of nothingness. The energy behind the call of nothingness can be overpowering. It was as if I was wrestling against the pull of the abyss, against the pull of the No Thing birthed by my family, the one so unlovable that she didn't even deserve "a used postage stamp."

And then there was cutting. Unless one has been there, one can't imagine the overwhelming desire to pick up a knife and start cutting. The greater the pain inside, the stronger the lure to let it out. But I didn't. I fought it. I somehow knew that cutting would be more addictive than smoking cigarettes. It would take between a pint or more of Jack to immobilize myself, until I was too exhausted or too sick. Then I would sleep. The next morning I slowly resumed dimensional selfhood.

— *53* —

A New Life

O ne Sunday in February 1974, while reading the Sunday paper's want
ads, I noticed an advertisement from a Boston college announcing a
new psychology major in conjunction with the large Boston Medical
Center's Department of Child Psychiatry that would focus on preventive psychiatric intervention with at-risk families. Students would need to be accepted not only by the college but also by the Department of Child Psychiatry
at this teaching hospital. This was exactly what I wanted: something real,
something that helped families.

However, there were so many obstacles to overcome to get there. The
biggest one was that half of the program was at a Catholic women's college.
I still despised everything about the Catholic church. I totally believed that
this church was responsible for centuries of evil in the world, perpetrating
pain and suffering on millions with their greed and misuse of power and life
distortions in the name of their God. Could I even manage and balance what
I believed and felt so strongly, manage it enough to attend such a college? I
didn't have months or years to decide. I had weeks. And in those weeks I had
to gather all the materials needed to apply to the program.

The saddest hurdle was going to my former high school to pick up my
high school transcripts. They were nothing to be proud of. I did much, much
worse than I remembered. Fortunately, I had testing results and transcripts

from BU and the local community college. I had never taken the SATs, but BU had required I take a similar test before accepting me in 1965.

Despite being overwhelmed with pursuing such a big commitment and finding enough energy to complete the application processes, I managed to do it. I just focused on one step at a time, deflecting the "stinking thinking" of anxiety and depression. Everything was sent in before the end of March. Then I just waited. It was a short wait. The college tentatively accepted me in April, dependent on acceptance by the Medical Center's Department of Child Psychiatry. They would contact me. They did.

The first interview in May was a small group interview. I think I was too anxious to be intimidated by the other interviewees as my focus was only on the interviewers. Later, on the way home, I realized I was competing for a limited place on a team that would consist of nurses, doctoral students, social workers and first-year MD psychiatric residents.

The individual interview was far less intimidating as it ended up focusing on my experiences and on working with other SIDS parents in their homes and from church referrals. The interview also covered my subsequent realization during those sessions that many of these people needed more skill than I possessed. I was so familiar and passionate regarding the SIDS subject that I forgot to be nervous or intimidated. As it turned out, this program at the Medical Center was based on the research done in Boston where social workers and psychologists visited and followed families identified as at-risk.

The "letter" came before the end of May 1974. I was accepted. It totally blew me away. I was so excited that I signed up to take one of the courses I needed in the summer session and met the psychologist who eventually became my therapist for the next 12 years. Starting early actually proved far less stressful. It gave me time to adjust to driving in and out of Boston several times per week, sign up for courses, obtain the student ID and parking permit, figure out student loan applications, and arrange for babysitting for CW and Sally.

⁓ *54* ⁓
College and the Medical Center

M eeting with my student advisor, I decided that I would not be a continuing education student but a regular day student. I would not
transfer BU credits as I was planning on signing up for pre-med
science courses as well as the Medical Center's required courses. I signed up
for the minimum full-time, three courses, for the first semester to determine
if I could handle five courses per semester. My goal was to graduate in 1978.
And I did, cum laude.

In those four years, I never wandered from my goal. Disappointed over
the reality of not being able to make up missed science and math foundations
to pursue pre-med and psychiatry, I chose psychology.

The Medical Center's program was beyond anything I could have imagined. It was providential that I took only three courses each semester that
first year. I was with 13 men and women who had a minimum of a BSN, first
year of graduate school, or first year of psychiatric residency. I had never
heard of most of the authors of the assigned reading materials, all experts in
their fields of childhood developmental psychology or psychiatry. I was way
out of my comfort zone and playing in information overload.

That first year, besides the three full-time courses each semester, there
was the part-time, 25-hour-a-week job, a house, a husband and two children.
Every free minute was spent studying and reading assigned material from

the Medical Center and whatever else needed to be read to understand the assigned readings. The "whatever else" proved to be enormous.

Loving to read, I loved every minute of it. Understanding it, though, was a slow climb up a high mountain. Going to college and meeting the people at the Medical Center's Department of Child Psychiatry were like entering a totally new galaxy. Looking back, could I say that I was happy? No, I did not yet have much experience with that. But it was not painful. I believe the best description was excitement, or amazement, but it was on so many levels that describing it would be an exercise in contrast.

Classes, at first, were challenging academically. Being anxious, depressed and suicidal does not provide the best atmosphere in which to learn new things and take in new information. I had to learn to concentrate mentally on a level never previously mastered. I only knew how to focus on that level physically, as in exercise or physical labor, to complete a task, such as painting a room. Anything learned in the previous 12 years of schooling pretty much happened by osmosis. Other than English and history classes, I only remember social interactions and looking out the windows from where my grandmother's home once stood. But I had a passion for reading. I still believed that the TRUTH would be found in a book.

Despite all the personal and psychological operating deficits, I managed to take care of children, home chores, stupid market shopping, meal planning, a part-time job at a local hospital, studying and maintaining a 3.3 average, and seeing friends.

The most noticeable experiences at college were being taken seriously and being treated with respect. I don't think I trusted that or even registered this as a truth until the end of my junior year when I needed to sign up for next year's courses. A requirement for graduation and to receive a degree from this Catholic women's college was to take a 101 introductory course in Catholicism. I simply could not make myself even sign up for it.

My college advisor was now the Dean of Students. In his reaction to my (I'm sure) intense protestation of most of the reasons I could not be true to myself and take this course, he asked, "What happened to the quiet, humble, respectful, submissive young woman whom I first encountered three years ago?" After that meeting, he allowed me to waive that course and substitute Protestantism 101. In retrospect, without this course, it is doubtful when, and even if, I would have ever found even an intellectual God.

It may be hard to imagine, but the blossoming tolerance and interest in even considering a possible God entity was most likely birthed by my love of science fiction and the love of imagining anything out of the box and not necessarily human. I don't think I thought much was positive about the adult species I belonged to. I always loved children and always experienced a connection to them, but they grew to perpetuate the cruelty and indifference I still saw everywhere. The number of throwaway ragamuffin people continued to grow.

I had one of the most profound dreams during this two-semester course. It's significant as I rarely remember positive or negative dreams. In the dream I was in a 1950s-type classroom with a blackboard covering three of its four walls. I slowly became consciously cognizant that I was at the end of writing a math formula with chalk that covered all three boards that proved the existence of God. And in that moment, I understood the math and knew it to be truth. I may have dismissed it as just a dream, but I never forgot it. It was one of those dreams that seem more real than life.

∽ 55 ∽
New Friends

By the beginning of my sophomore year, I began working for the chairman of the Biology Department, Dr. G, and left the job at the hospital. This was a 30-hour per week job. How did this happen? Well, I propositioned Dr. G in the middle of my biology final exam essay question at the end of my freshman year. This proposition was probably more than just a joke. Was it impulsive? Oh, yes. But mostly it was funny and put him on the spot. Never, in a million years, did I think his response would be to offer me a job.

We joked around a lot. Thankfully, he was a super guy who liked the flattery but who liked our friendship and his wife and family more. I have little doubt how I would have responded to his taking me up on my offer. This job propelled me into a whole new life and a new world of friends who worked at the college. Most of the secular professors were close to my age and married with young children. I entered a totally different arena of friends who not only befriended me but also treated me as an equal intellectually and as someone fun to be around. The husband was welcomed as well, but I don't think he was ever comfortable. I had found my tribe.

I also began psychotherapy my sophomore year with a psychologist at the college, which turned out to be a 12-year relationship. Other than this psychologist and the husband, no one had any idea how depressed I was. The husband's understanding only covered the impact on his life. Even then, they never knew how close I was to suicide most of the time. It was a daily decision to live because of the Voice's pronouncements and of not being willing to do that to my children.

Working 30 hours per week and carrying four to five courses each semester literally meant that entire days, Monday to Friday, were spent on campus. For the first time in my life that I could remember, I felt like I belonged. I had found people more like me than not. No one acted or reacted to me as if I was less than. And there were so, so many perks. Because I was an employee, I could eat in the faculty dining room with my new friends and no longer had to pay for parking on the campus. I had an office and access to copiers. I only needed to be there when not in class and, if there was nothing to do, I could study. Because I was a full-time regular student, I ran for student council and got elected.

Through a new friend's faculty ID card, I had access to the Countway Library of Harvard Medical School. It is not much of a huge thing now with the internet, but back in 1975 it gave me access to journals, books, articles and published and unpublished PhD dissertations not available in a regular library. Without this access, it would have been much more difficult to obtain basic catch-up readings needed to participate fully in the Medical Center's program.

The fall of my sophomore year I tried medication from a local psychiatrist in an adjoining town. He started me on anti-depression medication that sent me into a zombie zone. Appointments were very strange. The poor man had been shot by a patient, and his office doors were like a bank vault. He had many twitches and twerks, and it was impossible to get comfortable and communicate. I stopped both the medication and the prescriber.

Every hour of my life was orchestrated. I still only needed four to six hours of sleep. I was carrying four to five courses at the college and the internship at the Medical Center plus working in the homes of two assigned families. First-year college grades' average was B+; Tufts' grades were a C+ average across all three semesters. The Medical Center's program continued through June and July. Work, school, Medical Center and home took on a rhythm. I was still depressed, but I didn't have time to give into it for long. The psychologist sent me to a psychiatrist he recommended for depression medication. This medication seemed to help and had no noticeable side effects.

Therapy went slowly and mostly dealt with current issues, Missy's death, DB or CW's illnesses. I found it impossible to talk about my childhood. And I found it equally impossible to talk about the parents or the brother. At the time I thought it was loyalty. It wasn't until I began writing this narrative that I discovered it was fear.

Even though I was aware that the father and the brother had threatened to kill me, I had totally dissociated the number of all these actual and implied threats over most of my life and reacted as if this was an acceptable regular interaction between family members. Processing this realization disrupted the writing of this narrative for more than two years.

∼ 56 ∼
Another Death, More Incidents and Another Move

One Sunday, early in November of 1976, I was teaching Sunday school after services. The minister, Rev. Z, came into the room and said, "Your husband called; you are needed at home." I got Sally and CW and went home. DB met me at the door and said, "You are needed at Kait's; she's dead and the kids are alone." I rushed to Kait's home, certain that the other neighborhood women were there before me, comforting her children. They weren't. It was just me and the children.

Jeff was out of the country. My task was to find him and take care of Kait's babies. They had found her. She was in the garage, with the car's motor running—my old backup plan of last resort.

I was totally unprepared for my reaction to her death. I was so angry... and so sad. She died maybe 80 steps from where I sat the night before. I flew through so, so many emotions all the rest of that day and that night, trying to find Jeff while comforting and feeding her children. It was their devastating loss, but they were much better prepared for it than I.

All that ran through my head, over the following days and weeks, was, "How could she do that to her babies? If she truly loved her children, how could she leave them?" Somehow through allIt noise the Voice turned my anger and sadness into "parents didn't have the right to kill themselves." A parent should not do such a thing until the parent had completed his/her

213

responsibility of raising the children. When the children all reached the age of 18, then, if I still wanted to off myself, I apparently could. Although the Voice never actually added that last part, it was what I held on to.

The months after Kait's death were full of surprises. During a Christmas Eve get-together with a friend and her family, the mother and the brother burst into my home in high drama. The father reportedly had gone into a rage and physically attempted to attack the mother. The brother had intervened and stopped him. That was the first time ever for the brother. They were terrified. Shortly thereafter, the father's car pulled up in front of my home. I called out to the children to go to the basement. However, everyone went down the basement, including my husband, the brother, the mother, my friend and her six-foot, five-inch, 240-pound husband, leaving my 100-pound self to deal with the father.

The father charged up my front stairs and grabbed open the screen door where I stood in the threshold. I was white-hot, ice angry. He went to push me out of the way, but I grabbed him by the neck and pushed him backwards down the steps, telling him that his rage was not allowed at my home or near my children and that he needed to leave. He did. My invited guests left, and the mother and the brother stayed the night.

The next day the mother and the brother were fearful of returning to the house. They wanted me to go check on the father to see if he had calmed down. I refused. Instead, I called the police to do a wellness check after explaining the previous night's incidents. They did. The brother and the mother returned to the parents' house while police were present. The police had arranged and talked the father into admitting himself for evaluation at a hospital's psychiatric unit about a half hour away. The mother and the brother refused to drive him or ride in a cab with him. They told the police I was the only one who could do this, and they would pay for the cab. I refused, but the police insisted. That half hour drive was shades of my childhood with the father hurling every past insult about me and a few new ones. Afterwards, I put the first boundary on both the mother and the brother.

Several weeks later, Jeff, Kait's husband, came over with a girlfriend, Allene, to introduce her, saying they wanted to have DB and I come over for dinner. I was once again totally without words. Unable to say anything, I accepted the invite. We went and discovered Jeff had been "dating" this woman for the past 12 years. She worked at the same hospital and could have been Kait's much younger sister. Jeff spoke as if he expected DB and I to pick up the relationship with him and Allene that we had with him and Kait. I had no words then and couldn't begin to describe the emotions I felt.

That September, the incident that was pivotal was CW's reaction to the first week of kindergarten with the same teacher Sally suffered through. He came home crying the second day and every school day for the next three school days. I met with the principal and asked to have him transferred. She refused. I pulled CW out of school. The cumulation of Kait's death, the incident with the father on Christmas Eve, Jeff's new Kait-look-alike girlfriend whom he moved into his home, and now CW, DB and I decided it was time to move. We picked a town 20 minutes north where DB now worked, found a house, got a mortgage, sold our house and moved all within three weeks' time. CW started in a private kindergarten. I held Sally back to repeat a grade.

After the move, everyday life at home changed incrementally as the children grew and became more independent. Contact and interaction with the mother became increasingly less. Geographically closer to the brother and his girlfriend, we saw them more. We had all gone to the same high school. The brother had always enjoyed the substances available when he lived in Cambridge. His college had been partially funded by a football and track scholarship. He avoided the draft because of an injury and subsequent surgery. After graduation he worked for a large Boston corporation, but soon after a regular physical it was discovered that he required more surgeries, resulting in several months of recuperation. After healing, he went and toured Europe and parts of the Middle East for a year. Upon his return from Europe in 1970, he started his own very lucrative businesses that resulted in the purchasing of many exotic cars and a rental house in a small exclusive town near Concord. He was living in a style that he enjoyed immensely.

~57~
Substances

I was never into substances other than caffeine, nicotine and, much later, alcohol. I did try a few that the brother offered since they were free, curious as to their appeal. The first try was at age 30. I got the munchy thing, but I apparently was not as much "fun" as everyone thought I would be. I fell asleep. The second try was at a party at the brother's home years later. This try required one to make an obnoxious noise while inhaling, which triggered my laughing and scattering the product in many directions. Despite everyone being quite annoyed, I was able to complete the process on the second try. For a whole 10 to 15 minutes, I just wanted to play chess. Cigarette smoking started at 14 on a dare. It wasn't pleasant at first, but I mastered the art of smoking in a matter of weeks. Coffee consumption began about 17 and alcohol not until much later in my late 20s. I didn't really like alcohol. I only used it when addressing severe toothache abscess pain.

People seemed uncomfortable when they were drinking alcoholic beverages and one wasn't. So, I pretended to drink in my early to mid-20s. I was disgusted by people who got drunk. I'm sure the father birthed that response. Before adulthood I was certain I would neither swear nor drink alcohol when I was older. Drinking happened by a very unusual route. The usage of four-letter words arrived with my third job as a therapist at an alternative mental health agency at the age of 37.

The drunk disgust discovery happened suddenly one evening in 1965 on my way home from Boston University at the end of a subway ride. As I was headed for the stairs after disembarking, an obviously excessively inebriated 50-ish male laid hands on me. My reaction was instantaneous: white-hot rage. I grabbed him and pushed him firmly towards the rail pit. The Voice screamed, "NO!" I stopped. The man looked terrified. I was shaking and ran out of the station. He was very drunk. But it so frightened me that approximately 110 pounds of me could push a five-foot, nine-inch, 180-ish pound man like he was nothing much. This was the first adult experience dealing with my own anger, and I had no idea I could react that violently.

I didn't drink until after my son was born. This is how it came about. After the problems Missy had with bottle formulas, I decided that I would nurse my son. He was premature at eight months, but he weighed nine and three-tenths pounds. I weighed 200 pounds from toxemia right before his birth. By his fourth week check-in with the pediatrician, CW weighed 14 pounds and wanted to be fed every two hours. I now weighed 115 pounds. The pediatrician wasn't sure that my milk was letting down, so he suggested I have a glass of beer to relax and stimulate milk production. (This was more than 50 years ago.) So I did. It did help for a while. But by my three-months subsequent appointment with my obstetrician, I weighed 96 pounds and had severe anemia, while CW weighed 19 pounds and looked like Buddha. He called CW's pediatrician, in front of me, and told him, "This kid is killing her," and to pick a formula. He did. CW was happier and I was too tired to miss nursing him every two hours. The OB said, "Keep the beer going. It has protein, vitamin B and calories. You're too thin." I did. But I still didn't like it.

Three years later, while in college, I was back under 100 pounds. I also was having some severe digestive issues, so I saw a gastroenterologist. He put me on stomach tranquilizers. I was still not digesting what I ate and had an overactive thyroid. When he heard my schedule, he explained that the thyroid medications were a trial-and-error, ongoing, adjusting course and that sometimes my thyroid might go underactive and I wouldn't have the energy to keep doing what I did every day. So, no medications. However, he did suggest that, along with the stomach tranquilizers, I continue having one or two glasses of beer an hour before dinner to see if that relaxed and slowed down the digestive process. It did help. Thus, I became a beer drinker and learned to like it.

Other than $500 given by the mother towards college, no one else ever contributed. My small income paid for school, books, gas, my clothing, my therapy, the children's clothing, CW's private kindergarten, Christmas, birthdays and car maintenance. College was expensive, and my money management was very tight. The brother proposed that I work for him. He offered to pay me thousands of dollars in 1977 to drive with both children to Florida and pick up shipments for him. The tricky part would be not getting stopped in Georgia. He was sure that the local law enforcement wouldn't stop a woman with two young children. I was dumbfounded. I told him no. However, I did know lots of people who used the products he sold and did consider being a seller for him. The Voice said, "NO."

The years between 1972 and 1980 were the time of the most interaction the brother and I had. We had the illusion of being close, but it was only one-sided. He would drop by with a girlfriend or alone, bringing his product. Since I was almost always involved with the children in some activity, he, his date and DB would party. Mostly he would talk about his exciting life and the semi-famous people he knew or supplied or sailed with or skied with and took trips with all over the world. There was intermittent pressure for me to participate in these activities, but I wasn't interested.

It was amazing to me that the parents never, ever questioned how the brother supported himself, especially the mother. They were so close. The father did question one thing, but it was not about how the brother made money. He was sure the brother was gay. The mother would go on about how much he was like her father, so smart and successful. This, for the first time, left me wondering if her father had been involved in illegal activity too. The brother never had legal employment after 1970 until his marriage in the 1980s.

58

New Skills
and Another Death

After the incident on Christmas Eve with the brother and the mother crashing into my family's life and the father's subsequent hospitalization, the father never spoke to me for eight months. That September in 1977 he was diagnosed with multiple organ cancers.

The fall of 1976, the previous year, I took on a second part-time job working for a group of local psychiatric and psychological professionals who met regularly and put on CEU training programs for other mental health professionals. For the first six months it only involved attending the meetings, taking the minutes and maintaining the financial books. However, in mid-winter, 1977, they decided to put on a conference. They would develop and handle the topics, while I was given the job of finding a printer for the brochure and setting up the entire logistics. Those were so beyond my known skills basket. However, not knowing how to do something had rarely deterred me from attempting something new. It was not because of having self-confidence. It was more of not knowing my limits. I never tried to do many new things as a child to avoid ridicule from the family. After the ridicule and derision I endured towards my writings at age seven, no one ever saw them again until college, and then not again until the 2000s. And those showed were few. Failure and mediocrity could be handled. Humiliation, mocking, ridicule and derision, not so much. There are so many who seem to delight in crushing emergent light and creativity.

I found a print business in my new town that took the brochure job on; I booked the conference at the college I attended, which came with dining facilities for lunch and multiple break rooms. The first nightmare was the sound systems needed. This was a very old college with very old equipment. The second nightmare was the typesetter at the print shop breaking her arm a few weeks before the brochures were to be printed and mailed. There was no time to find a new printer. Panicked, I talked her into teaching me how to use the typesetter machines.

I managed to complete and/or set in motion 95 percent of the preparations before the semester began in September 1977. The conference was scheduled for the weekend before Thanksgiving. The father was in the hospital in Rhode Island. His first set of operations scheduled for September were removal of an initial cancerous organ. He returned to the house to mend, and the second set of operations were scheduled for November. No one ever talked about it, but obviously cancer had metastasized and, other than removals, no post treatments were scheduled that I knew of.

I only remember visiting him once at their house. No one, other than the mother, visited him at the hospital. I do remember it was awkward and strained at first, but he never brought up the Christmas Eve incident. All he talked about was the brother and how he always thought he was gay. Of all the things we could have talked about, we discussed nothing real. No one mentioned "the father was dying" elephant.

I started the semester with four courses plus the Medical Center one day a week, plus following two families weekly, plus working 30 hours at the college and the 20 to 25 hours per week on the conference. I had added 40 minutes to the previous 30-minute commute to Boston five days per week, and CW's private kindergarten added an additional 20 minutes to an already 60-minute commute.

How did I cope with all this? Apparently, I coped the same way I did with the previous times I was overwhelmed and threatened with a loss. I found myself involved in a physical relationship. This time it was of my own choosing. Who did I choose as the father was dying? I chose a son of the mother's favorite relative. No psychological connections or acting out previous trauma or denial and dissociation going on here! And, oh, did I mention the migraine auras were back and that I was having so much difficulty concentrating that I had to drop a course, Experimental Psychology, which took me out of the Bachelor of Science program?

But I didn't feel depressed. I felt out of control maybe, but not depressed. I don't think I felt anything. I was very busy and back in La-la Land. But I persevered. I wish I could say I ended it, but I didn't; he did. I think I may have scared him, so nothing much happened. I don't know, for he never said one way or another. It was as if the opportunity never happened, which, at the time, was fine with me and the usual expected way the family dealt with anything real. He must have known the father was dying too, but neither of us ever mentioned it.

The day before the conference, the father was operated on.. The operation was a success, and he went to recovery. He never woke up. He slipped into a coma on that Saturday as I ran around checking all the lights, food, audio equipment and at least 100 other things. Sitting in the main auditorium listening to a panel discussion, I became aware that I couldn't see a small portion of the stage to the right with my right eye. Trying not to panic, it soon was my entire eye, then the corner of my left eye went, and I needed to find a dark quiet place to go blind.

I survived the day. The eyesight came back, but I was severely castigated for all the little failures and imperfections by the psychiatrist who had hired me. I didn't defend myself in any way. Although this bruised me, I didn't at all feel like that I or the conference failed in any significant way. I was amazed and proud of my accomplishment. I never told the psychiatrist that my father was in a coma. Although impressed that I completed this task, I was relieved as I knew I would never, ever do anything like that again.

The father's wake was where I learned so much about his family. I celebrated my relief with my friends in a room far away from all the relatives. I experienced a level of freedom unknown before, and the migraine auras rarely ever reoccurred.

~59~
Dr. H

My therapist, Dr. H, was a positive, kind, compassionate and social person. He was a professor at the college, and he was a priest. He triggered no warnings; in my partitioned mind he didn't even register as a male. I spent many sessions in the beginning sharing what I thought of the idea of a God and the many atrocities committed by the Catholic church, and he just listened.

I never elaborated on the specific details of my childhood abuse experiences other than that statement as a fact. I still did not have a feeling language at this point. It was only when alone. I didn't know then about trauma, narcissists, grooming, gaslighting and psychological abuse. The rare elicitation of any triggered emotion was always incredibly intense, leaving me frozen in time.

I am not sure even now that I will ever be able to find the true words to describe what this man gave me or maybe what I took from him. It had nothing to do with therapeutic technique or any amazing insights. He was a mirror where he consistently reflected to me, the me he saw, instead of the defective identity I had as projected by the parents and the brother. Basically, he re-parented me. Other than the attachment to DB's parents, and not counting one to DB himself (a relationship that ended up being built on sand), the attachment to Dr. H weathered 12 years of storms. And although he faltered at the end, I could not let a mistake destroy what was built. It may have been the first time I ever actually forgave someone after being wounded by someone I cared about.

Dr. H and I had a complicated relationship. There was never anything inappropriate, but because of my employment by the college, we could have almost daily contact. Sometimes the workplace even required crossover duties, assigned during vacation periods, where I was assigned to work for him. This sometimes put us both in closer proximity than is usual between a therapist and a client. By the 12th year, there was a strong friendship and therapeutic bond. Then I called him out on something and offended him. He ended the relationship.

It was a very conscious choice to let that matter go, long before I knew or understood the power of forgiveness. But it took many months of soul-wrenching pain and anger to get there. I seemingly magically came to a place in my mind where I knew I could erase him. But in doing so, the Voice said that I "would erase all the positive gains accumulated over the 12 years." I had to accept Dr. H as flawed, keep the gifts and move on. He did apologize a few years later.

During those 12 years in therapy with him, I birthed myself, becoming real in my own eyes. I made dozens of new friends; I found out that I was intelligent and that I had many gifts. I graduated college, began graduate school, earned a master's degree, was accepted into a doctoral program, discovered boundaries and totally changed my life and lifestyle. At 33 years old, I had birthed an existential libertarian agnostic bleeding heart liberal who cut off her afro hairstyle and entered the world.

~ 60 ~

1979 to 1980

I am more than the parts of a sum; more than a mind/body.
I am equal to, yet more and less than, you.
I am a gift, among many, slowly unfolding in time.

I am a circle within a circle, inside a concentric maze,
a constant convolution revolving day around a day.
A never-ending cycle, I am a wheel rolling out of itself.

I am the puzzle of an answer, a segment of the universe,
a fragment of all the universes.
I am my yesterdays and todays,
becoming my tomorrows. I am movement.

I cannot be contained in a jar of words,
described by marks on a piece of paper.
One cannot know my heart in an hour's meeting
or feel my warmth through a forced choice.

I cannot be measured, held in space, fed into a machine,
isolated and labelled in time.
One cannot analyze what I am, only glimpse at what I was,
and never know what I am becoming.
—jp, 1979

Most likely because of my three years of training at the Medical Center's Department of Child Psychiatry and my certificate as a therapy fellow from the Center (I had no idea what this even meant at the time), I was accepted into the master's degree graduate Counseling Psychology program at Boston University. This meant saying goodbye to my friends at college and my job there. It was a tremendously full program, basically nine to four, five days per week. Fortunately, because of the Medical Center's training, I also was given a paid practicum in a suburb of Boston.,

This small city had its own mental health system and medical clinic within the school department that provided outpatient as well in-school services to the city. I was supervised by the head of this outpatient mental health system as well as by a doctoral student at BU.

Outside of the pursuit of a graduate degree in Counseling Psychology, the graduate school experience itself was its own rite of passage. I watched fellow students far more intelligent than I self-destruct over the seemingly petty hoops required to be jumped through and tolerated without complaint. Only a few made it to the end.

That last April there, studying for finals, submitting research papers and their defense, and applying for spots in the doctoral program are a chaos of memories. Those memories are mostly overshadowed by the husband's declaration of "enough" on my pursuit of my doctorate. It was almost laughable. He paid for none of it. He didn't help. He woke up at 6:00 a.m., left a half hour later, was home by 4:00 p.m., and was in bed by 7:00 p.m. He never read to the kids, helped with Sally's homework, or played with the dog. He did what he wanted and bought what he wanted. His life was rarely disrupted.

Julie, our babysitter in the beginning of my journey, was still the babysitter after we moved. She was attending college in the town we moved to and was at the house for the children after school. After she transferred to another college, she found another local college girl to take over, and she was just as capable. Dinner was cooked, the house was cleaned, the laundry was done, the children were supervised, and the sitters had their own vehicles.

My life was almost completely scheduled and predictable, but there were still activities we did as a family. I just didn't realize then that I was the family. I had my own friends, the kids had theirs and DB and I had a few couple friends we saw on weekends. We went to the farm regularly in the summer. A few things stand out in my memory during the three years we lived in this little town.

I got salmonella poisoning in December of 1978, and the babysitter found me on the floor of one of the bathrooms three days later. DB and the kids must have either walked over me or used the other bathroom. She yelled at him, and I never saw his lack of a caring response until eight years later.

My beloved dog got caught in the electric frypan cord while I was frying chicken, pulling the pan and contents off the counter and hitting and splashing Sally and the dog with boiling oil. With that mother's speed and strength that one hears about, I literally tore the jeans off Sally seconds after the oil hit her backside. She never was even burned. The dog didn't fare so well. Half of the dog's entire back side and one leg were seriously burned. DB refused to get help for the dog and announced that he would not pay for her to be treated by a veterinarian. In what seemed like minutes I found an on-call vet, picked the dog up, and Sally and I took her for treatment.

On the weekends in the summer that we went to the farm, I was to have the VW bus packed and ready to go when DB got home from work on a Friday. That summer, I also bought my first horse.

I overlooked so much in my marriage with DB for so long. Never experiencing a real, interactive, participating father, I didn't recognize the non-participation, neglect and emotional abuse towards myself and our children. At this point, as far as I knew, DB never hurt them. I was positive they would tell me. I had raised them both to respond to "secret" alarms and stranger danger.

DB's "enough" statement included a proposal. He would be willing to move to a farm up north, and I could have all the horses, Angus cattle and animals I wanted, if I would not continue graduate school past the master's degree. It was tempting.

The last doctoral interview was scheduled for a Friday at 2:00 p.m. It was an overcast and muggy day. Traffic to my placement job was slow and bumper to bumper through Medford to the city. While driving, I experienced a popping sensation and a sharp pain in my right chest. The Voice said, "Your right lung has just collapsed." I never questioned this. My first thought was that I should probably go to the hospital. Talking to myself, I said, "Which hospital?" Then, "No, they'll keep you and you'll miss your doctoral interview." Then, "Just go to the placement and ask Dr. M what you should do." And that's what I did.

Dr. M said that if I wasn't in pain, it probably wasn't a pneumothorax. It was most likely a pulled muscle, he said. So off I went to my counseling appointments at the schools and to home visits. I started to get a little uncomfortable at the end of the school appointments, but I continued to the first home visit.

Discomfort morphed into pain, but now I had no time to go to the ER and still make my interview. I decided to go after the interview.

Boston University is a huge school spread out for miles along Commonwealth Avenue. The Counseling Psychology building was in an old multi-storied Victorian home refurbished into offices. My interview was on the third floor. By that time I was topping the pain off with anxiety. The only memory I have is of climbing those three flights of stairs, walking in and sitting down. I have no idea what the interviewer said or how I responded.

I drove home. I decided to go to the hospital in Concord. The sitter was staying. However, I forgot that DB and I were to pick up the brother and live-in girlfriend at Logan. They had been in the Caribbean sailing. So I would go to the ER when we got back. It was still suffocatingly muggy at Logan waiting for the brother's plane to land. It was boring and painful but got exciting when the Bruins disembarked and walked right by us. I got so excited that I passed out. No biggie. We drove the brother and girlfriend to his house near Concord. Still in pain, I questioned whether I was just being dramatic, so I went home and went to bed. I decided that I would go to ER in the morning. I didn't sleep much.

I walked into the ER the next morning and said to the intake lady at the desk, "I think my right lung has collapsed." She said, "This morning?" And I said, "No, yesterday morning." They saw me right away and sent me to X-ray, and yes, the lung was collapsed. After horrific attempts to get blood gases from an artery, the doctor wanted to admit me. I said no. He went on about the danger and the pain and talked about how the air in my chest was possibly disrupting my heart, and I still said no. It was exam week, and I had research papers due, or I wouldn't graduate. He got it. We worked out that I would stay in bed and reschedule my exams. I would write my papers in bed, which I did, and call him every afternoon at his office. I recovered. The doctor's warning that repeated collapses would occur, requiring an operation to fuse the lung to the rib cage, have never happened.

Although I had made huge gains in self-worth, my self-care instincts were still minimal. I was aware of the potential danger of the collapsed lung to my life on a surface level, but my life still did not have much value to me. I wasn't actively suicidal, but that choice was never far away. Work, interview, the brother, sleep—they all were more important than disrupting the normal flow. Disrupting the normal flow of things was looking for attention, still the unforgiveable sin.

A Wish

Somedays begin like this and I want only to lie in bed,
in the warmth that holds me, that asks nothing and
wants nothing from me. I lay there for hours, a lifetime
of peace, and each of them come in to look—to check
my breath. And the biggest, the one who has known
me more than half my life, says he loves me and wonders
out loud who will do the laundry as he needs clean socks
for work. And the other two parade back and forth,
sighing like the children they are. The middle one with
a look of disgust leaves the room with further proof of
my lack of love, and the smallest kisses me on the cheek,
saying he hopes I won't forget what he wants for
Christmas. The peace of my bed holds me tighter. I
loosen myself and think, just once, I wish someone
would simply touch me, softly saying my name.

—jp, 1979

DB's offer of a farm and animals was too tempting. It would be a fresh start, he said. We'll work on the marriage, he said. I checked with the BU doctoral program. Could I take a few years off and come back? I asked. Sure, they replied. So I applied for psychologist/therapist jobs in the White Mountains area. One responded, so interviewed for the school psychologist position in that area. I got it. We found a farm close to my new job.

I spent five days visiting and meeting the schools in the five towns I would be responsible for. The teachers and staff seemed terrific. The conditions in the schools and the poverty in this area in the early 1980s, not so much. There were lots of "tar paper shacks" in these towns with families and children greatly in need. On my last visit day, a teacher pulled me aside and informed me that the class my son would be in had two children who were deemed psychotic, and I would be the ONLY mental health professional for the five towns. It would be my job to manage these two children, their families and the class disruption.

Thankfully, the mortgage lender bank had worded the offer to purchase the house in a way that required the husband to find comparable employment locally. After a month of searching, he could find little employment available and nothing comparable. The offer died, and I refused the job.

We both were disappointed. We were both reluctant to give up our dream of a farm, but reality necessitated I find a job in Massachusetts.

Within a few weeks, while searching, I stumbled across a real estate ad for property on the New Hampshire border; it was for six acres. I called the broker. The property was temporarily off the market as it was being taken over by a holding company. The owners had been transferred, and the company was financing the property and going to relist it for sale. The broker said he would contact me when the property was relisted. However, he called me a few days later, saying he would "unofficially" show the outside, and we could walk the property.

The house was magnificent. It was a late 17th-century Federal colonial style with two Torey chimneys. It had 22 rooms, a carriage house, a three-level barn with a workroom, and a cedar tack room. Also, there was a separate stable, a three-season summer house, and about three acres of pasture and two acres of woods. The property was next to a 300-acre farm and backed up into the trails of the Hunt Club. I was totally smitten.

The first floor was enormous. The kitchen was at least 20 feet by 20 feet with a center island range and a chimney, along with a separate stove. There was a mudroom that was at least 8 feet by 12 feet with its own double sink and cabinets. The rest was a bit harder to peek through the windows and see. The front entrance had a double door with a hall and staircase right out of a movie. The husband was very skeptical that we could afford this property and wouldn't even go out to look or drive by.

Several weeks later the broker called and said it was relisted and that he could take me through the insides of all the buildings. Smitten turned into love. Also, the price had been dropped $40,000. Even without my having a job yet, it looked like we would be able to afford the property.

The husband agreed to see it that weekend, and we put an offer in and it was accepted. We put our home up for sale, and it sold in a few weeks for $20,000 more than we paid three and a half years previously. We moved by August of 1979, and I found employment about a half hour's drive away. The animals followed.

— 61 —
Going Downhill

I would like to be able to say that the marriage relationship improved. It didn't. However, our lives were much richer in our new rural environment. Possibly it was just mine and the children's lives that were richer. The horses, Angus cattle, chickens, pig, cats and dogs were wonderful. There were hundreds of specimen plants on the property and some wonderful tales of how they got there.

DB and I went to the registry of deeds and traced the history of the house and its many owners of three centuries. The house was the home to about 15 children from Britain during World War II. The British owner built the "summer house" on the property to be the schoolroom for these children. According to the locals, most of the specimen bushes, hedges and trees were stolen from other properties during his ownership. I never thought I would love a piece of property and the buildings on it, but it totally won my heart, and I worked hard to preserve and maintain its beauty.

DB and I didn't argue much; it was more that our lives slowly went in different directions. My time at home was focused on the children, restoring the buildings, landscaping and riding the horses. There were no more vacations or weekends at the farm as it was impossible to find anyone willing to commit to feeding and watering our animals several times daily.

DBs rages became more frequent, and he drank more. He eventually agreed to marital counseling, but he only went for a few sessions. My anger after the brother's disclosure that he had endangered my children did not lessen quickly. It increased after the discovery of DB's secret bank accounts, which indicated his lack of investment in our relationship. Did I handle the anger well? No. It grew exponentially after multiple incidents spread over four to five years. I cried a lot in the car and became increasingly depressed. Anxiety attacks followed that morphed into panic attacks.

My car was demolished one night while parked in front of the agency where I worked. DB refused to come and pick me up. He shot and buried my dog due to her being hit by a car when he was home alone. Because of the multiple incidents of disappearances and demises of multiple pets over the years on his watch, the children never believed this is how it happened. He called me at work and told me. I was devastated.

The biggest blow was delivered by my therapist of 12 years, Dr. H, who stated that I was too angry to be in therapy and that we needed to take a break. This was wildly ironic since one of his initial predictions, in the first year of therapy, was to the effect that I would someday become very angry. At the time, I thought he was so mistaken. This decision to stop therapy did not help my level of anger. I had no awareness that my life was spinning slowly out of control again, and what followed were a series of bad choices that birthed more bad choices. Dissociation and denial bounced back into my life.

The agency where I worked lost funding and I was laid off just as spring was changing into summer. It seemed like a dream of sorts. I was riding one horse in the morning and the other in the afternoon and playing with my children and my gardens in between. That mid-summer I came down with something flu-like that stubbornly hung on, requiring several antibiotics. They set off a yeast infection that did not respond to treatment, and I ended up with a pelvic infection that wouldn't respond to antibiotics. At the start of the flu, my weight was approximately 115 pounds, but over the course of the six-week prescription, it tumbled back into the 90s. The doctor tried a series of experimental antibiotics, and finally by that fall the infection cleared.

However, he discovered that I was about seven weeks pregnant. I was thrilled, then crashed. Three of the medications and treatments were experimental and were not recommended for anyone pregnant. The weighing of this choice was horrible. It was Missy and the teeth all over again, but weighed down by her subsequent dying anyway and my son's two-year illness and subsequent immune deficiencies. My marriage was a wreck, I was unemployed, still angry, depressed and anxious and had only just started gaining weight back. If the baby was handicapped, I didn't think I could emotionally or cognitively be able to handle it. DB barely handled our reality now, and Sally and CW would suffer the most. So I made the hardest decision of my life and terminated the pregnancy.

That decision cost a lot emotionally, and I became so ill immediately after, spiraling down into what ended up as a blood infection that most likely was a remnant of the recent pelvic infection. Dealing with it all played out for the next ten months, along with the resurgence of digestive and intestinal complications. All this did not help marital issues. Needing to contribute financially, I did find employment.

Handling loss and grief have never been a strength of mine, and the increasing health decline of DB's father, whom I loved, kicked off a variety of thoughts and emotions. His father slowly died over a two-week period in July that coincided with my two-week vacation from work. Attempting to deal with his impending death and making bedside visits while moving seven tons of crushed rock to build garden pathways, led to the realization that I loved DB's parents and that DB was just part of the package deal. Without his father, the illusion of family would be gone.

I was so torn. I was alone in a marriage. Ironically, I had still considered DB my best friend and never consciously intended or decided to end the marriage. I had attempted, over the 18 years of our marriage, to wait for the DB I dated for seven years, my trusted friend, to come back, but now I thought maybe it had never been real. Maybe I had wanted a family so badly, I had tricked myself.

Once again, I had no idea my life was slowly spinning into shards of distractions. Once again, loss set off the creation of my own reality. Distracted, I entered La-la Land and brought home an almost carbon copy of my first love, Margo.

Transition
There was one dream after you
empty of man symbols.
Only a ripe garden of women
harvesting each other.
Gathering melodies of knowledge,
unison in joy,
softly sharing intimacies
in moon timing with the seas.
—jp, 1984

DB announced that he was being transferred and didn't want to commute and that we would sell the farm. There was little discussion. He didn't want the expense and work of the animals and farm any longer. I did understand that part. We had no vacations. I drew up plans to convert the 22 rooms into an 11-room, two family house and the barn into a magnificent home for ourselves. He wanted no part of it. He was moving. I was so angry.

I had started a private practice in my house. This necessitated finding an office, which I did, in New Hampshire. I started selling my animals and my beloved horses and cried for days. We found what was probably the least expensive house in a very exclusive town with a great school system. The house had been on the market for over a year; no one wanted to buy it since the former owner had died in the house and wasn't discovered for weeks. It was small and was a mess. We got permission to start working on the inside of the house to make it livable. The farm sold quickly, and its closing date was set for the day before the closing date on the new house.

DB made all the logistical arrangements for the move. There were many discussions about our relationship and what was happening with La-la, but I was insistent that I was staying in the marriage.

About eight days before the closing on the farm, DB announced that the movers would be there in three days to load up everything. I asked him, "And then what?" He responded that we would sleep on the floor until the movers delivered everything after the closing on the new house. I told him that I wasn't sleeping on the floor for almost a week. I needed to have clothing and accessories for work and to get the kids ready to start school in 14 days. It was too late to reschedule the movers, he said, as the company was moving us, and they made the arrangements. Then I would stay at La-la's apartment, I announced.

Five days later, I realized that we had received no information for the time and place of the closing to the new house. I called the bank and was informed that there would not be a closing because the house was part of an estate that had never been filed in probate court. We had no home, no furniture. The kids had no clothes. The most fortunate thing was I would not be living with DB for these days before the new house. I was beyond angry. I thought I might hurt him.

DB worked out with the estate that we would rent the house until the probate court released it for sale, and the bank agreed to hold the mortgage commitment. DB and the kids moved in, and I resumed painting and purchasing furniture. As the work was messy with boxes everywhere, disorder prevailed, and I remained at La-la's apartment. In September, the kids started in their new school, and I purchased the new bedroom set. The plan was that I would begin moving back in when the set arrived. And I did.

But I began vomiting when at the house. Soon the nausea would strike me a mile before I reached the house and continued while I was there. It only stopped when I was a mile away from the house. I began to spend less and less time at the house. Both DB and I realized that I was not coming back. Since I had a place to stay, we agreed that he would stay at the house with the kids as I didn't want to disrupt their lives any further and I couldn't afford to carry house expenses on my salary.

I wasn't concerned about not living with the kids as I had always considered DB to be a passive but good dad. He had a temper and could be a rage-man, but other than the incident where he pushed Sally down the cellar stairs, there were no other abusive incidents that I knew of.

~ 62 ~
Back to Reality

I found a great but sad new job in the town next to our new home so that I would be only ten minutes away if the kids needed me. I stopped in often to check on them during the week, and I did things with CW every weekend. DB was dating a divorced friend of ours who was an alcoholic, and he intimated that she could get physically abusive. I inquired why he was "jumping out of the frying pan and into the fire" in this new relationship. He agreed that it wasn't a great idea. Sally would barely speak to me, and at 18, soon to be 19, I gave her space.

The sad job was at a locked, residential treatment facility for children aged 5 to 12 who were at risk to themselves and others and no longer needed an inpatient psychiatric facility. I was the social worker/therapist for the children and the family therapist for those children who had a family they might someday return to. The children were as well cared for as possible for a facility. It required travel to visit families all over the state. These children had terrible histories, and I would find myself deeply saddened and crying during long car rides.

I also started yelling at the God I didn't believe in as there wasn't anywhere or anyone else to release my anger to, and I had so much anger. It was most likely the same anger I had most of my life but did not know it. Why did people hurt children and how could they do the things they did to them? How could they throw children away? With every new intake I did, I thought, "This has to be the worst history." And it was, until the next one. So, I would yell and cry at the God who wasn't there and despair of a world where no one was able to fix or stop children from being hurt.

The relationship with La-la was not going well. She had a problem with alcohol, surprise, surprise. She also could become violent—a bigger surprise—and she could be a bully. She had a propensity to sleep around with others as well. But I didn't really care about that aspect. She could be with whomever she wished, whenever she wished, but not at the same time when she was with me.

Ironically, despite her violent side, I was never in fear of her hurting me. She only tried once. That's when I found out just how much rage I had and just how much energy I could access in self-defense and how strong I could be at such times. At the same time, I also discovered how much self-control I had.

I asked a neighbor to call the police. They did. It forever changed our relationship. It didn't end it; it just changed it.

But I did visit a church. It was a church that La-la's father had designed and built, and she wanted me to see it. We went on a Sunday to the service. I really thought she wanted me to see the architecture. I didn't realize at the time that this was the church she grew up in and that she knew most of the people who attended and they knew her. It was a Pentecostal church and totally over the top, but, ironically, I came away thinking that if there was a God, He was more at that church than at any other church I'd ever been in.

Around Thanksgiving, three months after the move, I became aware of CW not being his usual self and saying negative things about life. When I asked him about it, he responded that he just wanted to die. I was shocked. He wouldn't elaborate, so later I asked Sally what was going on and found out that DB wasn't even living at the house anymore. He was mostly at the girlfriend's house. He would come back twice a week and take CW to the supermarket, buy him frozen dinners, cereal, milk and a few staples, and leave some money for lunches. Sally bragged that she was partying at the house every weekend, and CW had been drinking alcohol. I was literally stunned. I thought DB was an okay husband and I was just a bad wife. But I thought he was a good dad and loved his kids.

Fortunately, I was now making enough money to rent a place of my own. I informed DB that I would be taking CW to live with me and Sally, if she would come. Or, I suggested, I could move into the new house. He refused that option. I found a townhouse in an adjacent town, literally on the town line, the rent was doable and it was close to where I worked.

I was amazed at what three short months could do to change our lives. The rental townhouse was simply terrific. The neighbors were great, and the unit itself was amazing. The space had three floors: a loft on top, two bedrooms and full bath on the second floor, and a kitchen/dining area, half-bath and living room on the first floor. CW met another teen, one year younger, who became his best friend.

Sally refused to come live with us, but she could be persuaded to spend a weekend a few times a month. CW's friend, DY, was at our condo most of the time. His mom worked long hours, and his dad had never been part of his life. He had no other family contacts. His mom was estranged from her family. DY and his mom were close and did well taking care of each other. He was an incredibly responsible child. DY was of mixed ethnicity and was having difficulty in school. As I tested children on a regular basis for work, his mom gave me permission to test him, and he tested out with an IQ over 150. DY was placed in the gifted program at school and soon was excelling. He still is.

Life was settling down. I liked my sad job and was making new friends. La-la was often around, but drama was kept to a minimum. Summer at the townhouse was great. The complex had a pool, and I would do my paperwork while sitting in a pool chair as often as possible. Sally graduated and went off to junior college that fall. We spoke frequently on the phone. She rarely heard from her dad.

That mid-winter the mother fell and managed to call me. It was determined that she couldn't remain in her home alone. The brother and she wanted me to move into the house so she wouldn't be alone. I agreed, under the stipulation that the kitchen and bathrooms be redone as well as a new bathroom be installed on the third floor for me. She would stay at the brother's until the work was done. The time frame was the end of June for it to be completed, and I gave notice at the condo. Moving time arrived but the house was not ready, necessitating a short-term rental for an additional six weeks. The furniture went into storage.

— 63 —

The Mother's House

The move went smoothly; CW enrolled in the new school and started making friends. I received a phone call from Sally that DB was selling the house and buying a one-bedroom condo. There was no place for her to go for summer break. Could she live with me at the mother's house? And would I come to her school since she had no money and very little useable underwear? She had basically no contact with her dad.

Living with the mother was difficult but manageable for the first three to four months. My new living space, the same space occupied by DB and I when I was pregnant with Sally, was totally remodeled with a huge bath and workout room. CW had new friends, and DY visited often. The commute to the sad job was more than an hour each way now, and I gave my notice. Sally obtained employment for the summer, and I began working as a contractor in a psychologist's office near the New Hampshire line. This worked out well as I still had my own office in New Hampshire.

During one of the general discussions with the mother, she let it drop that she was leaving her entire estate to the brother. When asked why "just the brother," she responded that I was married. Her logic failed me at that point as the brother also was married. . The mother reported redoing her will so that the estate would go equally to both the brother and me. But things were quickly deteriorating. Her relationship and interactions with Sally were okay. Her interactions with CW, however, were dismissive and borderline abusive. She treated him as if he was a servant working for her, which were shades of her treatment of DB years ago. CW had never been spoken to or treated the way she interacted with him, and at 15 he did not handle it well. She was verbally abusive to him and to me.

The mother also started making vague accusations that someone had taken the diamond out of her engagement ring and replaced it with a non-diamond substitute and that various items were missing. Initially not doubting these items might be missing since the mother had rented out rooms to a series of male friends of the brother's, I was surprised when the brother and MB#2 landed on me as the culprit. This totally reawakened the wounds of childhood. I was simply not engaging with the family on this level ever again. I gave notice that I was moving out. And I did.

I was able to rent a house in the same town, and life with CW and Sally became less tense. My priority was CW. He was doing well in school, and Sally had a job at a retail clothing store for the summer. The only concerning issue was that contact and conflict with the mother and the brother had kicked off my walking in my sleep. Since I was apparently leaving the house at night, CW rigged alarms on all the entrances and exits to the outside.

My private practice caseload was mostly women who were abuse survivors and children. I had lots of abuse referrals. I started a healing group for wounded women to explore all the new modalities in the area that focused on healing and recovery and differing ways to deal, heal or manage anxiety, depression and panic attacks instead of medications. Holistic methods, introduced as New Age, were popping up seemingly everywhere. The group explored herbal medicines, energy healing, yoga, massage, meditation, hypnotherapy and reiki, inviting practitioners in for demonstrations. We read *A Course in Miracles* and other spiritual healing books and explored various religious groups, even attending several healing services at local churches.

I had found a group of gay therapists who got together regularly for support and for fun and activities, many of whom loved to vacation, play golf and go to clubs together. This was a whole new world to explore; living close to Boston opened so many opportunities and adventures. I reconnected with some of my old college and graduate school friends. I was finally building a life.

At the last minute, I signed up for a four-day symposium on trauma held in Aruba. The hotel where it was being held was full, but I managed to find a small motel inland and rented a car. This was my first adventure alone, doing something I wanted to do. It was a huge step for me. I ran into psychologists and psychiatrists who had been my instructors at the Medical Center program and met Bessel van der Kolk and Judy Herman and a bunch of other soon-to-be pioneers in the treatment of PTSD and trauma. I was later asked to join the group. One meeting at Dr. van de Kolk's home was totally overwhelming. I followed from a distance.

Life was quiet and fun. CW got his license, and I bought a new car. We had a great Thanksgiving and Christmas, and even Sally was happy. So why did I move back to the mother's? I still ask myself that question. The only answer is because she apparently needed me and because they asked me to come back, apologized and promised me free range. I imagine some little wounded fragments in me still wanted a mother and a family. The house rental landlord let me out of the lease and back we all went thinking it would be different.

Surprise, it wasn't. It was worse. Once again, it was okay for a while until the little things started to happen again. The hostility towards CW by the mother was painfully visible. She denied doing so many petty little things to hurt him. Overlooking so many small woundings towards both him and me did not work either.

Then there were the bigger ones. We had separate refrigerators at her house. Ours was in the basement. It was much healthier for CW, Sally and me this way. The mother had never been particularly interested in being clean when I was younger. Now, with advancing age, it was far worse. Usually CW and I did food shopping for all of us. The mother had her preferences, which were very different from ours. She would often accuse us and especially CW of pilfering her food. We were all afraid of opening her refrigerator.

Her refrigerator died, and she asked me to get her a new one and said she would reimburse me. I went ahead and ordered a refrigerator to be delivered. It was. She denied that she said she would reimburse me. Not a big deal. I let it go.

About the same time frame, DB wished to remarry and wanted to go through with the divorce. Despite machinations from my lawyer to make it hostile, we completed the divorce amicably. We had split the proceeds of the last house, and I ended up buying a townhouse halfway between the mother's house and my office in New Hampshire. I planned on renting it first and moving there eventually. It was a great respite space, and I furnished it bit by bit exactly the way I wished.

That April around my birthday, she insisted on buying me an outfit at a local boutique in town. The clothing there was lovely but not my style.

Still, she insisted on picking one out for $600. This was 1988. It would be the equivalent of $1,450 now. I could not afford clothing that expensive then, nor would I have paid it even if I had that level of income. I like sales and bargains. I liked the challenge. While checking out, the mother declared that she had forgotten her charge card and could she reimburse me later. I didn't even see it coming.

Sally, CW and I maintained the mother's property inside and out, and I paid the electricity bill. CW was doing great in high school and had a bunch of friends there as well as staying in contact with DY. Sally was working full-time still, and I had my new therapist friends and activities. Sally had a young man interested in dating her that set off my every alarm. He was too charming and too smooth. Her last boyfriend had been abusive. I hired a friend to have a discussion with him, and he went away.

I decided to take the entire month of August off for vacation and rented a house with a pool in Provincetown. I packed up Sally, CW and DY, and off we went for the first week. It was a great week; the weather was perfect, and the pool was ten steps away from the slider. It was an entire week of beach, board games, the boys skateboarding, shopping, food, pool and laughter. Just fun.

Immersion into the gay community at 40 years old was my first and only socially inclusive experience. This was a level of acceptance previously unknown. I met so many kind and wonderful, quirky people. Undoubtedly it was a tribe I was seriously trying on. But like all tribes, one-on-one, intimate relationships had their pluses and minuses I had never even considered.

One week alone there, then two more spent with friends, were hilarious. It was the best vacation yet. I ended the month with signing a purchase and sales agreement to buy an almost completed condo right outside of the downtown and closer to the beach.

I came home relaxed and happy. The sense of well-being was short-lived. The mother had apparently been discussing and urging Sally to go on for a bachelor's degree in college. At the time it was unclear if this was even something Sally was interested in doing, but the mother would not let it go and offered to pay for the two years if Sally would agree. I pointed out that colleges would be starting in two weeks, and it was too late for Sally to be accepted anywhere. The mother insisted the deal was now or never if she was going to cover the costs of tuition. There was only one college where there could be a fighting chance of this happening. It took many visits and multiple favors and phone calls, but Sally was accepted into my alma mater.

Sally and I ran around getting her ready for this next adventure, and the time came for the first tuition to be paid. The mother reneged. Now, the mother had done nasty to me for so long it was just a given. The nasty to DB was laughable in its time. The nasty to CW, I watched very closely and spoke to her as that behavior not like a grandmother's. The nasty to Sally, the girl whom she said she loved and considered hers, was a knife in my heart and a wound to Sally. I told the mother and the brother that I had had enough. I was done and out. Their response was that the mother was selling the house and moving into a condo. Then the mother, MB#2 and the brother accused me of using her charge cards, running up thousands of dollars in debt, and not paying the electricity bills. I was ceremoniously handed all my baby pictures and taken out of the will.

~ 64 ~
Transition Again

The move to the condo went smoothly. CW would be finishing up his senior year and would commute back and forth. Sally would stay at the mother's until the mother moved so she could keep her job and would move to the condo with us later. I hired some carpenters to convert half of the garage into a bedroom for CW and put in a folding stair access to the attic space. As CW and Sally spent most weekends elsewhere, I acclimated to my new home and city life.

The trauma group continued to meet weekly and periodically scheduled outings to healing gatherings in a 30-mile radius. My private practice and the psychologist I worked for part-time became swamped with new referrals from women who described being in cults or involved in satanic rituals and clients who seemed to have dissociative identity disorder. The years 1988 to 1993 were peak years for this type of referral.

My gay friends' therapist support group continued to meet regularly for fun, growth and encouragement. I dated intermittently but was a bit wary and cautious after the experience with La-la. I met an amazing woman who became serious much too quickly for me. My children really liked her, but I was not only not ready for a serious relationship, I also wasn't sure of how involved I wanted to be. I wasn't really a sexual person. People seemed to hook up too quickly. And wrapping an identity in a lifestyle seemed to narrow an experience.

I was depressed and anxious when I wasn't working, so I worked a lot of hours. My own practice was thriving. I had contracts with a few New Hampshire schools and courts. The word had gotten out that I liked doing groups, so there were lots of referrals from a local psychiatric hospital. I was still wounded from the situation with the mother and the brother. There was no contact with them. I was considering going back into therapy again, so I began the search for someone with expertise in dealing with trauma.

Reading a lot of metaphysical and spiritual books had grown into reading philosophy and theological-type books. I read books ranging from *The Celestine Prophecy* and *A Course in Miracles* to Paul Tillich's books *The Courage to Be* and *Systemic Theology*, to the works of Jose Ortega y Gasset in a background of Nietzsche, Jaynes' *Origin of Consciousness*, and books on quantum mechanics and science fiction.

This was the background setting in which I experienced the encounter I described at the beginning of this book. Change didn't happen suddenly. It was very slow. I decided to revisit the little church I had gone to with La-la. The experience that God was there was much stronger than before, so I kept going every Sunday. But I didn't want to be seen; I didn't want anyone to notice or talk to me. I still had PTSD, and this entire God experience was overwhelming. I needed time to process without having to deflect any energy into self-conscious social interactions that would unnecessarily be colored by the barriers of internal safety measures and might negatively stain the processing. I braided my hair and wore teen clothes and sat with the adolescents, and no one spoke to me for six months. When I was approached, they turned out to be the couple who were the youth pastors.

But I did start reading the Bible. It was the only significant spiritual book I had never read. I had skimmed it as a child and dismissed it as not logical and not even fun fiction. This time I read it in the first six months. Since by that time I was a participant in my trauma healing group, I shared my God experience as best I could. I didn't share what I called "the Encounter" as I still didn't have any words to adequately describe the experience. It was incredibly private. Nor did I want them to think I had gone totally over the edge or that I was making myself out to be special. I did eventually share pieces of it with the youth pastor couple, Bill and Carol, as we became close friends. They were sure that the fragrance was Jesus, and since I had no reference point, I didn't agree or disagree. They did a great deal of counseling in their church and were involved in their own small deliverance ministry. We worked closely together in mine and their ministry for several years.

You might wonder what happened to my gay lifestyle. I had shared a small amount of information with my therapist friends' group, and they were very alarmed and spent hours attempting to reprogram me back to my senses. They wanted to take me away for a weekend intervention, which I declined, and we ended up parting company. I was able to explain to the woman I was dating what I was experiencing and how I wanted to take the time and energy to focus and explore. She shared that she had been raised with the Bible and understood. So it wasn't as if I had a sudden turn of mind; it was more that I slowly lost what little interest I had. It was never really my lifestyle. I liked the acceptance and camaraderie. I found more intelligent women with similar interests and activities. But I now had an interest that I liked so much better than any before.

It wasn't that I immediately accepted the written contents of the Bible as being the absolute, authoritative, unadulterated, inerrant, infallible word of God. I don't accept anything new quickly. It was more like a process where the more I read and meditated, the closer my relationship became with Jesus, and it seemed to just happen. I chose to believe it, choice by choice, as it grounded me in a stability that I had never experienced before. I still dealt with depression, anxiety and panic attacks. They didn't magically go away. God isn't magic. But they did gradually lessen as I used God tools. I grabbed hold of the concept of capturing every thought and bringing it into obedience to Christ.

The 27th psalm grabbed hold of me. I memorized it. Every time a stinking thought would start or a panic attack began, I would keep saying this psalm until the attack passed. Fairly soon, I didn't even get farther than the third or fourth stanza, and eventually it became automatic. No stinking-thinking, negative thought lasted more than a second before it was captured. And I did and do seek God's face.

For me the process was more like a journey up a mountain. As I climbed, my life realties changed and my own self-made obstacles fell away through my growing relationship with God as His new reality of life enfolded me. . This resurfacing did not happen quickly. At first, it was like being high on a drug. I had rarely experienced any type of momentary happiness for any length of time except through my children, sports, focused exercise or intellectual pursuits. Joy was just a three-letter word. Now I flew. I think it was a lot like being three years old again. I seemingly went from cautious, closed, suspicious, hesitant and careful to exuberant, hopeful and open. I felt alive. Protective boundaries came down. Before, I had only an intellectual understanding of what healthy boundaries looked like in real life with other people. Who knew joy had wings?

Did I just make good choices? I made a few, but some were not so good. That whole notion of "not leaning on one's own understanding" caused a wealth of choice problems for me for a while. I went from trusting no one to trusting everyone who said that he or she was a Christian. I didn't realize at the time that the protective boundaries I had relied on were the only ones I had. This change played out okay for a while. My new guides, Bill and Carol, were terrific and knowledgeable in the guiding, but there were many bumps. They, and several others in the church, introduced me to Don, who attended the same church. He came with rave reviews as a seasoned believer and a leader in the church. The story went that his wife of 18 years ran off with another man, and they were divorced. His three children lived with him in a nearby town. My alarm system disarmed, there were no red flags thrown.

～65～
Don, In and Out
and Another Again

The first missed flag was that my children did not like him. Everyone involved with me dismissed my children's dislike as a reaction to my becoming a Christian and my having "rules" now. CW was angry and was not quiet about it. Sally spent as much time away as possible and had reconnected with the young man I had paid someone to chase away more than a year earlier. The second missed flag was that Don's oldest daughter moved to California to live with an aunt and his two children at home had no contact with their mother. Don repeatedly assured me that he was in agreement with my profession and with my new ministry to wounded women and hoped to become a part of it as well.

I had found a new therapist highly recommended by someone I respected in the trauma informed treatment field and began seeing him weekly. He was very expensive and did not take insurance. He had a questionable procedure of allowing the sessions to go more than 50 to 55 minutes and would bill me extra for those minutes. These sessions were not productive and, when confronted with what direction he thought treatment should go in, he responded that I needed to become "enthralled" with him. I responded that that would never happen as the only being I intended to be enthralled with was God. That was our last session.

After eight months, Don asked me to marry him, and I said yes. Three months later we were married and off to Florida for our honeymoon. The third flag I saw was three days after our marriage. Mr. Wonderful became critical, judgmental, controlling and a shade threatening. I gave him the benefit of doubt. In the next six weeks I learned more than I wanted to know about the man I had just married and his previous marriage. The short version was that he had physically and emotionally abused his wife and children for 18 years. He was a rage-man. He literally would try to terrorize his kids and myself by trying to run over animals with his car on our way back from church. The more upset the children became, the harder he would laugh. Later they told me that he had always played this game and would actually run animals over. He had managed to completely alienate my children who no longer would go to church with me or participate in any activities with me or with my new friends.

Bill and Carol were supportive but skeptical at first. After all, they had known Don for ten years and me barely two. But within a few short weeks they witnessed Don go into a rage and become threatening towards me. Bill wouldn't let me go home with him. Apparently, our church was aware that he had been abusive to his wife and children and had still supported him. They had never mentioned any of this before our marriage. What unfolded next was his youngest daughter wishing to live with her mother and her mother's new husband. That cemented it. I moved in with a friend since my condo was rented. Divorce followed shortly thereafter. Don was engaged again within a few months. Bill, Carol and I went to another church. I wrestled with sorting out being tricked again. But it was not by God. I had been tricked by someone I trusted. Again. I was too naïve and vulnerable.

Sally had moved into an apartment with her new bad boyfriend, Red, near her job, and CW went with her. Even though Don was out of my life, there was very little contact with them. They were still angry. My reaction and dealing with the emotions of grief and loss had not improved significantly enough for me to not make some poor choices. Living with my friend Angel was a gift as I couldn't move back to the condo until the renters left, and I was an emotional mess and clueless how to make amends with my children. The only respite was work, which continued uninterrupted despite all my personal emotional upheavals outside of it. Bill and Carol left our current church to start a new church with a pastor they'd met. It was too much change too quick, and though I saw them several times a week, I did not follow. I went to another church in New Hampshire.

I had had no contact with the mother or the brother since the move and the marriage and the next move. I had forgiven them all way back and adjusted as necessary as my relationship with Jesus and God played out. I was comfortable with this boundary and knew that God would let me know when it was time to see her, and He did about ten days before she died. Angel went with me, and the mother either did not know who I was or pretended to not know who I was. It was not traumatic. My children and I attended the wake and funeral.

In my grieving over my children, I failed to listen to what probably was the Voice. Because the delivery was different, I rationalized it away. It came in a dream when I was sleeping and made a warning statement. I was rarely aware of dreaming, but when I did, it always followed a pattern. This was just a matter-of-fact sort of statement like in the dreams where you're getting dressed or making dinner. It basically said that my friend Angel was going to hit on me. I would have bet a great deal of money that it would never happen. No one who knew Angel would have believed it either. It was so strange. I told her about this dream, and we both laughed.

CW eventually called and came for a visit. I cried the entire time. He told me that Sally was marrying bad boyfriend Red and that I wasn't invited. Slowly I was feeling less fragile emotionally and more grounded, but dealing with Sally's rejection was difficult even though I understood. I had hired someone previously to make bad boyfriend Red go away. I'm sure he didn't want me to have any influence over her.

Once my condo was free, Angel and I moved there with her two children. It seemed that Angel did want an intimate relationship. She was my best friend and had seen me through an emotional and disillusioned upheaval, repeatedly putting me back together. I loved her. I wasn't "in love" with her. I don't think I knew what that even meant. There wasn't any physical attraction. I had only experienced that once in my life, and that was with La-la. I never, ever wanted another experience like it. It was addictive. It set off a series of poor choices and more drama and chaos than a soap opera. I'd only watched soap operas the year Sally was born. They were depressing, so I stopped. I didn't watch television or movies that were sad. I've never understood why anyone would subject themselves to "fake sad" in order to experience an emotion. The experience wasn't real. It was all drama and emotional masturbation, emotion for the sake of emotion.

People needed to have emotional controls and a firm foundation to stand on. I wasn't aware yet that I experienced my emotions and others' emotions as overwhelming. I didn't enjoy movies or television shows that triggered any emotional reactions. I was totally traumatized as a child by

255

the movie *Bambi. Alice in Wonderland*, both physically and cognitively, terrified me. Disney's *Fantasia* was literally repulsive, and the music from it still can trigger a powerful negative reaction. The movie *2001: A Space Odyssey* launched my first migraine. Unless a movie is science fiction, comedy or cartoon-like, I don't go to movies. I don't really watch television; I mostly listen to it while playing a simple game like solitaire on the computer. I like medical and action series, but I have an acute physical reaction to portrayed violence and the sight of blood, real or as a prop. My gastrointestinal tract jumps, and it is painful physically and overwhelming emotionally. I didn't know that there was a term for these experiences until I learned of mirror and mirror pain synesthesia. It is what contributed to ending my pursuit of medical school.

Intellectually, I still didn't have a view on physical intimacy as anything special. As an adolescent and young adult, I put it in the same category as sleeping, eating and elimination. These were necessary and annoying bodily functions that I couldn't completely control. I had rarely instituted sexual activity; there was always something better to do. I never thought about it, and I was still totally surprised when someone was attracted to me in that way. I didn't label any of those other bodily functions as okay or not okay. I thought they just were, like the sun or a rock. I couldn't wrap my head around why anyone would try to label a bodily function as bad or restrict it to only one context. Nevertheless, I was getting closer to understanding some of God's rules, however slowly.

Cognitively as a therapist, I knew that grief and mourning were necessary for healing. I rarely ever looked at experiencing loss and grief as necessary for healing for myself. I apparently attempted to get rid of these emotions and most other emotions as quickly as possible. I apparently got rid of them regularly. I didn't realize yet that my reexperiencing loss and grief seemed to trigger new physical relationships as a response. That chaos most often resulted in changing the focus to resolving the chaos rather than dealing with what choices had let the chaos enter was slow to enter my awareness.

These relationships seemingly just happened when I was emotionally overwhelmed and my guard was down. My new relationship with God, though, was taking me on a step-by-step dismantling of an internal world of my own making and of my own rules that were not only out of alignment with His views on things, but that also took me down the same road repeatedly.

It's difficult to convey in words the experience of a being and mindset that never experienced itself as a part of or belonging to anything other than itself. Even as a child I knew rationally that I wasn't really invisible or a Nothing or No Thing. But there was still an emotional upside-down reality operating alongside the rational. I was thrown away. And this internal, upside-down reality built its own world with rules, values and morals and interacted and defined its own life.

Every neurodiverse entity has created to some degree something similar in order to be and survive, even if that person must mask and pretend for a time when in the defining neurotypical world. Most neurodiverse have some things they do to self soothe, whether it be some form of stimming, eating the same thing every day for breakfast, counting objects, rocking or braiding threads.

~ 66 ~
More Changes

A pearl is a wound that has healed. ... When a grain of sand penetrates the shell, the nacre cells begin to work and cover the grain of sand with layers and more layers, to protect the helpless body of the oyster. As a result, a beautiful pearl begins to form. There is no way for an oyster that has never been wounded to produce pearls, because a pearl is a wound that has healed (Macedo, 2013).

Life went smoothly for a while; there was a minimum of bumps until I was injured at work when catching a very angry five-year-old who had propelled himself headfirst towards a door in my office. Sitting on the floor, I had reached up and grabbed him, injuring nerves surrounding my scapula and causing the loss of the use of my right arm and more pain than I had ever experienced. I was knocked out on oxycontin 24/7 as well as muscle relaxants for three weeks, plus in physical therapy for four weeks to regain minimal use of my right arm. I was able to go back to work by the fourth week, but since my car had a manual transmission, I had to be driven back and forth for three months. I was almost totally dependent on Angel.

Did this now-intimate relationship work out well in the long run? No. It was eventually a disaster. But we did buy a house together, which enabled me to take in Sally and my new grandson to live with us after the bad boyfriend husband left her in her eighth month of pregnancy when he finally realized there was no family money. He moved in with a woman ten years younger than me who did have money. They began a lengthy and expensive custody battle that ended with custody being split.

Sally and I worked out an agreement that she would be a stay-at-home mom until my grandson was five and, in lieu of rent, would do the house care, shopping and cooking chores while we worked. We all were stable for a while until Angel had a car accident and got a concussion and started using illegal substances in the middle of the custody battle for my grandson. This ended our relationship, and she and her children moved out.

These were the years where managed care took over private mental health and medical practices. The message was join and be assimilated or take on fee for service. Since my practice was by now almost exclusively trauma-based and morphing towards biblical counseling, there were not any similar local practices to be absorbed by. Fee for service drastically cut down the size of my referral base, which led to a smaller shared office space. Eventually financial survival necessitated a full-time job, and I found one working for a mental health managed care company and seeing clients on nights and Saturdays.

Bill and Carol's new church had collapsed when the pastor reportedly took off with all the money, and they were forming another new church with another pastor, Roger. Still close to and working with Bill and Carol in our trauma healing groups, I slowly became more involved in this church with them. Along with the Christian school, they also were interested in exploring a Christian counseling program. Roger was a charismatic deliverer of sermons, and he and his wife and family soon became close friends. Bill, Carol and Dan were supportive and encouraging, sponsoring my attending seminary for my master's in divinity.

CW had moved in with Sally, my grandson and myself, and he contributed to some of the household expenses. My employment with the managed care company ended abruptly when they were bought out by a larger managed care company. Finances were tight, but I still had a small private trauma practice and the church counseling center. This allowed me to go full-time at the seminary and complete the first year.

I was still in almost constant pain from the scapula nerve injury and had minimal use of my right arm, which also affected my neck and right arm and shoulder. I was unable to lift anything higher than my waist, and the motion required to remove a hanger in a closet off its pole was impossible. And the worst was, I couldn't play golf. Since I didn't want to be on pain and/or muscle relaxants indefinitely, the neurosurgeon recommend-ed an operation that would sever a nerve. This would remove the pain but reduce my ability to turn my head. I wrestled with this decision for several weeks. One day, on my two-to-three-mile walk listening to praise and worship music and talking to God, it occurred to me to ask God to take the pain. He did.

By this point I'd been a Christian for approximately ten years. I'd been part of a praying deliverance team and healing ministry. I had prayed for hundreds of people. I realized that it had never occurred to me to ask God for anything for myself alone. It had never occurred to me to ask anyone for help. I was "the used postage stamp" of my childhood. I would just be seeking attention or be like the boy in *Oliver Twist* asking for more. I also considered it might be pride, and that was a definite possibility as far as asking a person for help. But that turned out to have more to do with some-one sending pity my way, which would have shamed me. Avoiding shame triggers was always a goal.

I realized I still had an aversion to referencing God as God the Father. My go-to choice was Jesus and the Holy Spirit. It wasn't an aversion to the essence or reality of God as a father; rather, it was the old childhood aversion to the term and the human concept. This was a huge obstacle. I discussed this issue with Bill, Carol and Roger, and we went after this wound successfully along with a few others.

I was slowly regaining joy and peace. Depression, anxiety and panic attacks had slowly faded away. I had reached the conclusion that I needed to choose to stay in the circle of God's love, protection and blessing of His will, that I could simply choose to believe His rules. I also could take on boundaries based on scripture and on my having worth and value as His creation. After all, I had become a temple of the Holy Spirit. I chose to believe all of it.

I loved my year of full-time study at seminary. Studying the Bible, herme-neutics and exegesis and trying to learn Hebrew were like playing. For the second time in my life, I had found a tribe plus a church, and joy became a daily experience. Even the reality that Sally and CW wished to go out on their own wasn't alarming. The fact that I wasn't earning six figures any longer to carry the expenses of our beautiful home was sad. But I didn't want to work like that any longer. The loss of the managed care job and my children mov-ing out meant I would have to sell the house.

I tried contacting Angel. She wouldn't respond. I asked my lawyer to try to contact her since she was on the deed. After many weeks my lawyer called.

Prefacing his statement that Angel seemed like a very interesting person, he reported that she had stated she would "rather burn in hell than see me getting a dime out of that house." There was no other choice, the lawyer explained, but to declare bankruptcy. This didn't sit well with me, but it would allow me to keep my car, furniture and personal items. Sitting back and watching my home go into foreclosure was painful, but God held me through it.

Bill and Carol offered me the use of the basement apartment in their home, which I accepted and moved into in March of 1999. They had a lovely home and a beautiful, landscaped yard that was, because of plantings, totally private. The basement apartment was ground level in the back with its own entrance and looked out on the gardens.

To supplement my very limited income I had accepted a few landscaping jobs in the area, which kept me busy doing an activity I loved. One job was redesigning the brother's yard and plantings. Contact had slowly increased after the mother's death eight years previously. That spring and summer were peaceful and productive.

At the end of July, the head pastor, Roger, pulled me aside to say that he thought the young woman who had been Bill and Carol's foster child for several years was trying to tell him something he thought was best for her to tell me. Red flags flew like a flock of birds. Despite those sinking feelings of oncoming doom, I spoke with this young woman and encouraged her to talk to Carol directly to address whatever situation or situations that were causing her pain and discomfort. She did.

The phone call came early that evening from Carol. The former foster girl had shared with Carol that Bill and she had been involved physically while she had been in foster care at their home. Bill had admitted it, and they wished to have me help them work out a plan to address this in a responsible Christian manner for all concerned.

The four of us met. As the girl was still living there part of the time, we worked out an arrangement for her to move into her own apartment near where she was going to college as soon as possible. As she was an adult, the girl stated that she did not want to report the abuse to any authorities or pursue charges against Bill.

That being done, Bill, Carol and I came up with a tentative plan as to how this was going to be addressed as far as their roles in the church and other considerations. Bill would step down as principal of the school and seek counseling and accountability, and any reconciliation would be determined by Roger and the church elders. Both Bill and Carol would agree never to take a foster child into their home again and would sign a contract to that effect, with the understanding that personally and as a mandated reporter I would report them. They agreed to all terms and signed the contract. Roger was informed and agreed, and I stepped out of that role.

What did I think and how did I feel? There were so many other things I was trying to deal with at the same time, such as the loss of my home and the bankruptcy that took the condo. Angel was suing me, and I still cared for her. Did I mention that I don't deal well with loss? Bill, Carol and Roger were the major supports in my life. I loved them. There were a few other friends, but we did not share the same type of connection. These three were all my family. I was so sad that this had happened and was very sad for Bill, but my relationship with him and Carol didn't change. I didn't judge either of them.

We all went on. Angel's lawsuit was dismissed by the court. The house was auctioned off. I went for a visit to the brother and his wife's summer place, got nostalgic by the sailboats and called a friend in Maine I'd met while working for the managed care company. We caught up on news; he told me that his daughter was getting married in August, and we agreed that we'd get together soon. I babysat my grandson for a week while my daughter went to Nova Scotia with her boyfriend, and everything was settling down.

One afternoon I came home from landscaping in late August to see Carol talking to a woman in her backyard. Later Carol knocked at the apartment door. She informed me that the woman was from social services and wanted her and Bill to take a 14-year-old girl into foster care. It was surreal. I responded that she and Bill had signed a contract that they would not do that ever again. Carol responded that she had talked to God and that He told her to take this girl. She knew I would understand. I responded that God was not in her pocket, this just happened less than an hour ago, and if she went through with taking in this girl, I would have to report the abuse to social services. She responded that she knew I would not do that. I responded that yes, I would. She again responded that she knew I wouldn't because I loved them. I responded that yes, I did love them, but she did not know me very well if she believed I wouldn't. She responded with, "We'll see, won't we."

I was in shock. I called Roger and went over to his house. I was visibly shaken. I explained what Carol had said she was doing and what I answered in response. This was not good, but I had no idea what, if anything, could be done next. Roger listened and agreed that it was not good. I now know that I was expecting more from Roger—a plan to speak with Carol and Bill, at least. Something other than nothing. All those red flags that had taken flight initially were circling back.

— 67 —

Roger, Carol and Bill

There were no additional talks with either Roger or Carol. For a week we all were pleasant. I was praying for God to speak to Carol or Bill since what she was planning was wrong on so many levels. As an intermittent member of regular La-La Land, I couldn't even imagine in what reality she thought this decision would end well. There were so many ways all four of us could have handled this situation better so as to not allow this error to spread to so many other people. The fallout from this incident in this small little church spilled onto 50-plus adults, possibly more, and close relationships were permanently severed. I just heard from one longtime friend from this incident who mentioned that her daughter, in 2023, is just finding her way back to God and church attendance some 24 years later.

Coming home early that day, the new foster girl and her social worker were already at the house. Carol introduced me to the new girl. She looked just like a replica of their former foster daughter. The new girl would move in the following day. I told Carol again what I had to do. She had broken the contract. Poor Bill. Poor me. I called Roger and told him what had happened and what I was now going to do. He thanked me for informing him and hung up. No, "I'm here for you" or "I'll pray for you." Nothing. What was I feeling? I felt abandoned, once again, by people who said they loved me. But not by God. I did feel that I was back reaping the red-flag harvest, hanging onto the limb of relationships and community by a finger, knowing that I was going to let go on purpose. And I did let go. Did I consider how this might impact me? Not really.

I called an old friend at social services who was a supervisor. This was too important, too sadly intimate, to be done over the phone. We met the next morning, and I shared the entire story. She was sad too. Carol and Bill were well thought of in the agency. They had taken many girls. The new foster girl was removed within an hour. I called their former foster daughter and told her what happened and what I had done, and I said that she would most likely be hearing from social services soon. She wasn't thrilled but said she understood. I let Roger know.

Carol was furious. And I was living in their house. She threatened to sue me for breach of confidentiality. I informed her that she breached, nulled and voided the contract covenant she had made with me that spelled out exactly what I would to do in the event they chose to take in another foster girl. We were nose to nose, and her pupils were large and all black, rage-man eyes. I really was so surprised by her actions. I had trusted her. I was aware that they had faults. I didn't expect them to be perfect, but I did expect Carol to be true to her word. They knew and were part of their own and my ministry to abused and wounded women. They were aware of the damage that sexual molestation caused. They were instrumental in the last legs of my healing. They were my family.

And Roger…. I felt so set up, so betrayed. From the first moment he suggested I be the one to talk to the girl, I wanted to not believe that my world would go upside down again. But I also understood that he had a wife and children to support and a church to protect. I despise feeling thrown away.

So there I was, alone again and devastated. But it was different. I had felt all the feelings of loss from Angel, her suing me, the house foreclosure and the bankruptcy. Those feelings were all there then, but that was different too. I felt held from the inside out. It wasn't like an emotional feeling; It was more like an actual experience of being touched, except not from the outside in but from the inside out. That feeling just got stronger. So, I was devastated but okay. I did not feel alone or abandoned. God was close. I needed Him to be. Most of the people in that world avoided or stopped speaking to me. Very few from the church would meet my gaze. Awkwardness prevailed. Roger was formal and distant.

By the end of that week, Carol announced that she was putting their home on the market, they would be moving to Florida, and I needed to find another place to live as soon as possible. She and Bill had pulled their financial support from the church. Roger wouldn't take my calls. I did track him down, but the relationship was distant. He continued to be polite but cool. My choice to report affected his life and that of his family, as well as the church that soon would be no more. Roger would have to get another job, and I had to move with hardly any money and no credit after just filing bankruptcy. No one in this tribe was coming to rescue me.

Carol and Bill's home sold within a week. The closing date would be in three weeks, and I needed to be out before then. My children had no space. The brother might have let me stay at his home for maybe a month, but I was so wounded that that would have been putting myself in danger. Other friends were sympathetic, but no offers were coming. Time was running out.

Ari, my psychologist friend from Maine and former managed care days, had been staying in touch by phone. We had tried dating about 18 months before, but the distance became a factor. He surprised me by driving down from mid-Maine in a U-Haul truck and took as many smaller items as he could back to his own home. He offered me a place to stay until I found a job and decided where I wanted to live. Reality had narrowed my choices down to homelessness or Maine.

Moving day arrived quickly, and I said goodbye to Bill and Carol. Ironically, the warmest goodbye was from Bill. The small moving van followed me to the rural town in Maine that I would be calling home for a while.

Arriving in late September 1999, I was met with the visual of big yellow ribbons tied around two maple trees at the entrance of the driveway and greetings from Ari and his daughter. Later, when the movers and Ari's daughter had left, Ari poured two glasses of wine to toast my new venture, saying, "To whatever future happens, welcome to Maine. Whether you stay for a month, a year, or never leave. Whether we stay just friends, or the relationship grows into something more, just know this: I will never marry again." And we both laughed very hard for probably very different reasons. I knew then that, some day in the future, Ari would ask me to marry him.

I found a job in October as a case manager to children and their families involved with the department of social services. I made lots of new friends in just a few months. The new job entailed lots of travel to surrounding towns and involvement with the schools, courts and mental health agencies. I still had several clients in Massachusetts and New Hampshire and would drive down every other Thursday night to see them over the weekend and then come home on Sunday. I would stay at the home of a close friend. I did this roughly for about seven years, until 2006.

My life in Maine was full. I had researched in the first year several churches and picked the one I would attend when I was ready. But "ready" got complicated. Healing had happened slowly, but so much sadness remained. I had forgiven all three—Bill, Carol and Roger —and had even visited Roger and his family in their new home, but the effort to retain any relationship was all one-sided.

I used the excuse of living in sin with Ari, but I wasn't sure I wanted to get involved in another church. I didn't blame God. He didn't let me down. People did. I wasn't sure I even wanted any real-time, active church-going, Christian friends again—especially any "God in their pocket" Christians. I wasn't sure I could trust that level of relationship. I still talked to God, read my Bible and listened to praise and worship music and several ministers on the radio. I took theology courses at a not-so-local small seminary and found Dave Ramsey on the radio. I used his skill in financial management to reset my credit, build up my emergency fund and savings, and set up retirement goals. I just couldn't make myself go to a church. Some wounds cut deep.

～ 68 ～
Ari

I loved Ari's home, especially his land. The house was across the street from a lake to which he had the right of way to but rarely used. There were few plantings around the house and no gardens. He had some beautiful old maples and fir trees, and his lawn was shameful. Starting slow that first spring, his acreage slowly grew many gardens and plantings.

He had a sailboat, and we sailed all around Penobscot Bay, anchoring at many untouched islands for weekend getaways and vacations in the summer. He did ask me to marry him three times, and three times I said no. Right before the fourth time, on a Valentine's Day, he gave me the deed to his property with my name on it. I cried. Then he asked me again, and I said yes. We were married six weeks later in the British Virgin Islands.

Ari isn't perfect, but we are comfortably compatible. He is as quirky and peculiar as I am. He is intelligent and has some amazing skills. We love to debate just about everything, especially the Tanakh, Midrash and Talmud commentaries, religions and history. I am forever grateful to him for being him and to God for sending him. His biggest complaint was that I was too self-contained and self-sufficient and didn't need him. Mine was that he was too dramatic. He discovered early that I preferred tools over flowers or jewelry, and I have a plethora of them. He's totally spoiled me, and I've grown to like it. Ari doesn't understand my relationship with God and views all religions as superstition and ignorance, including the one he was born into, but he does seem to enjoy our endless discussions about my belief and my Jesus that he initiates.

He is as tolerant of my foibles as I am of his, and we both have many. His strengths so far outweigh his foibles that I let most go by. I feel loved by him. It's not a romantic kind of love; neither of us are romantic. He doesn't need to say "I love you." His is a steady, undemanding love. Ari simply takes care of me in so many little ways no one has ever done before. In 23 years, we have never run out of toilet paper or paper towels. I can count on him. I feel secure and mostly safe. And for those times when I may not, it gets resolved. We laugh a lot, mostly at ourselves. I remember to be careful about mentioning anything I might want, as it can suddenly appear. I'm basically frugal, except for sneakers on sale, books and plants. He never had a savings account until we were together. We've travelled, and he's taken me to some amazing places I would never have even thought of to go on my own or with anyone.

After many failed attempts over several years, I did eventually go to the church I'd picked when I came to Maine. I literally had to fight through months of anxiety and panic attacks. It was and is a good church with many terrific people. It sometimes seems like one had to continually prove one's faith by walking and talking in the same trails, as if anything spoken in a different voice or parallel trail looked dangerous. But then, I had two backup churches I frequented that did two services on Sunday in the winter. Each of these filled the space of the need to express joy.

It took several years before I felt comfortable enough to get involved with this church and for them to get comfortable with me and start a ministry to women who had been or were being abused.

— 69 —
Becoming Who God Created Me to Be

I am an out-of-the-box Christian. I'm probably an out-of-the-box person. I am ADHD with some "on the spectrum"-like peculiarities, and I am intense. I don't know how not to be. I am neurodivergent. I can mask, but it's exhausting. I don't like to go out, except in my yard. I love being home, and I'm rarely ever bored. I am not comfortable in groups, with loud noise, drama, sudden change, other people's food or any high stimulus.

I was most comfortable in academia, but I didn't finish a doctorate. I've had many friendships; a few have lasted more than 25 years. Most friends died way too young, and a few friendships ended without any discernable explanation those friends wished to share. I don't enjoy surface interactions or talking about other people. I'm not a people pleaser or peacekeeper.

I comfort eat the same thing for months. I'm a high taster; food textures, consistency and flavors are intense. Smells, hearing and all my senses are intense. Eyes, not so much anymore. I can't eat spicy foods, some for allergic reasons. I have many allergies and lots of tactile sensitivity issues. I don't wear clothing, belts and jewelry that are restrictive or not soft for any length of time. I rarely enjoy being touched or hugged by anyone I don't know well and have a relationship with. Socializing with people exhausts me, and I need alone time to refuel. Being with more than three people formally for

271

an extended length of time can cause me to break out in a cold sweat and my core body temperature to drop.

I cannot watch people or animals be hurt. The sight of blood or damaged body parts on others, myself or animals still causes an immediate painful gastrointestinal lurch and lightheadedness, and I feel totally overwhelmed. I have fainted. I still don't watch many television shows. Mostly I listen while doing other activities that don't need a high focus. I rarely go to movies. I do watch some movies on television, mostly children's movies or animated ones like *Despicable Me*, *PAW Patrol* and *The Secret Life of Pets*.

I am comfortable when I know the rules and the parameters of other people's expectations of me. Others' emotional or physical suffering upsets me. I care about people, but in groups their energy often overwhelms me. One-on-one interaction is best. I can be arrogant around stupidity and cruelty. I despise surprises. I've spent a lifetime studying human behavior and 40-plus years working as a psychotherapist. If I can understand people's basic motives and what is behind their behaviors, then I am most comfortable. I'm addicted to learning. I've always just wanted to help people be real and heal. And true healing comes with God.

I work on trusting God totally; others measure more in percentages. I have a multifaceted relationship with Jesus, God and the Holy Spirit. I'm enthralled with all of Them. My mind loves theology and all the different aspects where one can immerse oneself—all the commentaries, all the scriptural variations, the critiques and interpretations of the different denominations, and the depths of play in researching minutia. Any minutia about Jesus, the era He lived and the religion He was born, raised into and studied, can produce musings and meditations for hours.

My love and interaction with Jesus and the Holy Spirit bathes my mind and heart in joy and energy. Experiencing the spark and humility of being loved and held by Them is my addiction of choice; it transports me on flights of countless journeys and reliving of my Encounter experience and of imagining possible variations, future elaborations and extrapolations beyond accepted grids.

For the past ten years I have been able to live my dream of offering trauma-informed therapy and counseling to wounded women individually and in groups as a love offering ministry. During the pandemic it grew to include adolescents, married couples and a few men. My vision has been to train women who have experienced or are experiencing comfort and healing through God's mercy and grace to comfort and support other wounded women in their churches and communities who are experiencing distress, shame and crippling symptoms of trauma abuse so they, in turn, may comfort and support others in healing.

God is real. Go "boldly to the throne of grace" and seek His face, the Bible says in Hebrews 4:16. Intimacy with God is a relationship. It is more than knowing. It is an experience of being, of quantum entanglement with one's Creator. You will know when you get there that there is no questioning, no doubt and no turning back.

When you can get to this exquisite, ineffable place where you no longer just know God is in charge and He's got you, but this fact has become the center of your being…then all the drama, rejections, pain, conspiracy theories and evil entanglements require only momentary attention and are not personally upsetting or destructive to identity. Because God wins.

— Epilogue —
Just a Dream

12/16/2020

I am in a safe house with some other people; they are guarding me. I seem to be in Israel, in Jerusalem, at the old city. I have a suitcase, so I have everything I need. I am not afraid or anxious. I go out into the market area. It's a sunny day. My sister-in-law walks by and gives me a look or expression of disdain but does not speak. I go back to the safe house and walk up some stairs. The inside is like an old style, 1900s narrow house with many floors, and the walls are covered in rich wood paneling. It is expensively but tastefully furnished.

At the top of the safe house are a group of older women having a tea party with little finger sandwiches and cakes. I have some, interact a bit and go over to a desk with a landline phone to check for messages. There is one message for me. I call and I'm to go meet my real Father (not bio) at another house. My real Father is talking to another man who sounds like a real estate person. They show me the house. It is small but lovely. My real Father buys it for me. The real estate person asks me how many children I have. I say two. I say to both, "I have no furnishings; I have nothing." My real Father looks at me like, "duh, you will have everything you need," and hands me something. I'm making a list of who needs what in my head. But it's the feeling and my reaction that are so new that I must try it on, turning like I'm looking in a mirror at a new outfit. I'm not excited that I've been given a new home and everything I need; I'm basking in a sense of having value, of worth, for just being. I am valuable to this Father.

References

Bianco, Margery W. 1983. *The Velveteen Rabbit*. New York: Henry Holt Books for Young Readers. Page 12.

Burgmeester, Alexander. n.d. Quotation. America's best pics & videos. Accessed July 12, 2023. https://americasbestpics.com/picture/many-narcissists-are-obsessed-with-money-they-think-about-how-mx7M0Cg79.

Macedo, Bishop Edir, in collaboration with Gabriela Coimbra. 2013. "An oyster that has never been wounded will not produce pearls." Universal. December 4. https://www.universal.org/en/bispo-macedo/an-oyster-that-has-never-been-wounded-will-not-produce-pearls/#:~:text=When%20a%20grain%20of%20sand,beautiful%20pearl%20begins%20to%20form.

McKay, Sarah. 2015.[MORE INFORMATION NEEDED.]

Moon, Tom, M.F.T. 2009. Blog. "Are We Hardwired for Unhappiness? – 1. The Brain's Negative Bias." Accessed July 12, 2023. http://www.tommoon.net/2009/01/01/are-we-hardwired-for-unhappiness-1-the-brains-negative-bias/.